GIANT DAYS

VOLUME THIRTEEN

BOOM! BOX™

ROSS RICHIE	CEO & FOUNDER		GWEN WALLER	ASSISTANT EDITOR
JOY HUFFMAN	CFO		ALLYSON GRONOWITZ	ASSISTANT EDITOR
MATT GAGNON	EDITOR-IN-CHIEF		SHELBY NETSCHKE	EDITORIAL ASSISTANT
FILIP SABLIK	PRESIDENT, PUBLISHING & MARKETING		JILLIAN CRAB	DESIGN COORDINATOR
STEPHEN CHRISTY	PRESIDENT, DEVELOPMENT		MICHELLE ANKLEY	DESIGN COORDINATOR
LANCE KREITER	VICE PRESIDENT, LICENSING & MERCHANDISING		MARIE KRUPINA	PRODUCTION DESIGNER
ARUNE SINGH	VICE PRESIDENT, MARKETING		GRACE PARK	PRODUCTION DESIGNER
BRYCE CARLSON	VICE PRESIDENT, EDITORIAL & CREATIVE STRATEGY		CHELSEA ROBERTS	PRODUCTION DESIGNER
KATE HENNING	DIRECTOR, OPERATIONS		SAMANTHA KNAPP	PRODUCTION DESIGN ASSISTANT
SPENCER SIMPSON	DIRECTOR, SALES		JOSÉ MEZA	LIVE EVENTS LEAD
SCOTT NEWMAN	MANAGER, PRODUCTION DESIGN		STEPHANIE HOCUTT	DIGITAL MARKETING LEAD
ELYSE STRANDBERG	MANAGER, FINANCE		ESTHER KIM	MARKETING COORDINATOR
SIERRA HAHN	EXECUTIVE EDITOR		CAT O'GRADY	DIGITAL MARKETING COORDINATOR
JEANINE SCHAEFER	EXECUTIVE EDITOR		AMANDA LAWSON	MARKETING ASSISTANT
DAFNA PLEBAN	SENIOR EDITOR		HOLLY AITCHISON	DIGITAL SALES COORDINATOR
SHANNON WATTERS	SENIOR EDITOR		MORGAN PERRY	RETAIL SALES COORDINATOR
ERIC HARBURN	SENIOR EDITOR		MEGAN CHRISTOPHER	OPERATIONS COORDINATOR
MATTHEW LEVINE	EDITOR		RODRIGO HERNANDEZ	MAILROOM COORDINATOR
SOPHIE PHILIPS-ROBERTS	ASSOCIATE EDITOR		ZIPPORAH SMITH	OPERATIONS ASSISTANT
AMANDA LaFRANCO	ASSOCIATE EDITOR		JASON LEE	SENIOR ACCOUNTANT
JONATHAN MANNING	ASSOCIATE EDITOR		SABRINA LESIN	ACCOUNTING ASSISTANT
GAVIN GRONENTHAL	ASSISTANT EDITOR		BREANNA SARPY	EXECUTIVE ASSISTANT

BOOM! BOX™

GIANT DAYS Volume Thirteen, June 2020. Published by BOOM! Box, a division of Boom Entertainment, Inc. Giant Days is ™ & © 2020 John Allison. Originally published in single magazine form as GIANT DAYS No. 49-52. ™ & © 2019 John Allison. All rights reserved. BOOM! Box™ and the BOOM! Box logo are trademarks of Boom Entertainment, Inc., registered in various countries and categories. All characters, events, and institutions depicted herein are fictional. Any similarity between any of the names, characters, persons, events, and/or institutions in this publication to actual names, characters, and persons, whether living or dead, events, and/or institutions is unintended and purely coincidental. BOOM! Box does not read or accept unsolicited submissions of ideas, stories, or artwork.

BOOM! Studios, 5670 Wilshire Boulevard, Suite 400, Los Angeles, CA 90036-5679. Printed in China. First Printing.

ISBN: 978-1-68415-542-2, eISBN: 978-1-64144-708-9

GIANT DAYS™

CREATED + WRITTEN BY
JOHN ALLISON

ART BY
MAX SARIN
WITH JOHN ALLISON (CHAPTER 49)

COLORS BY
WHITNEY COGAR

LETTERS BY
JIM CAMPBELL

COVER BY
MAX SARIN

SERIES DESIGNER
GRACE PARK

COLLECTION DESIGNER
MARIE KRUPINA

EDITOR
SOPHIE PHILIPS-ROBERTS

SENIOR EDITOR
SHANNON WATTERS

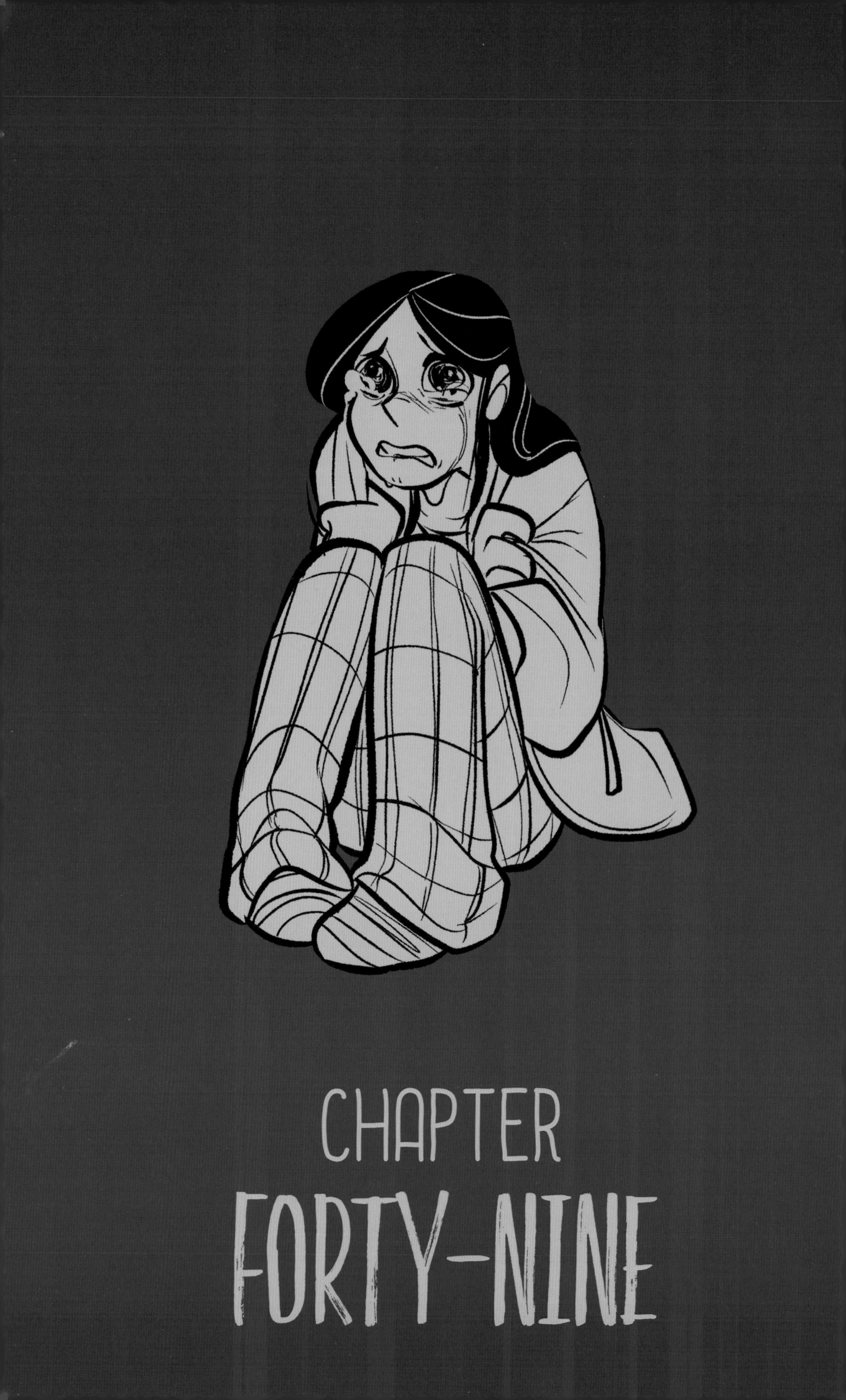

CHAPTER FORTY-NINE

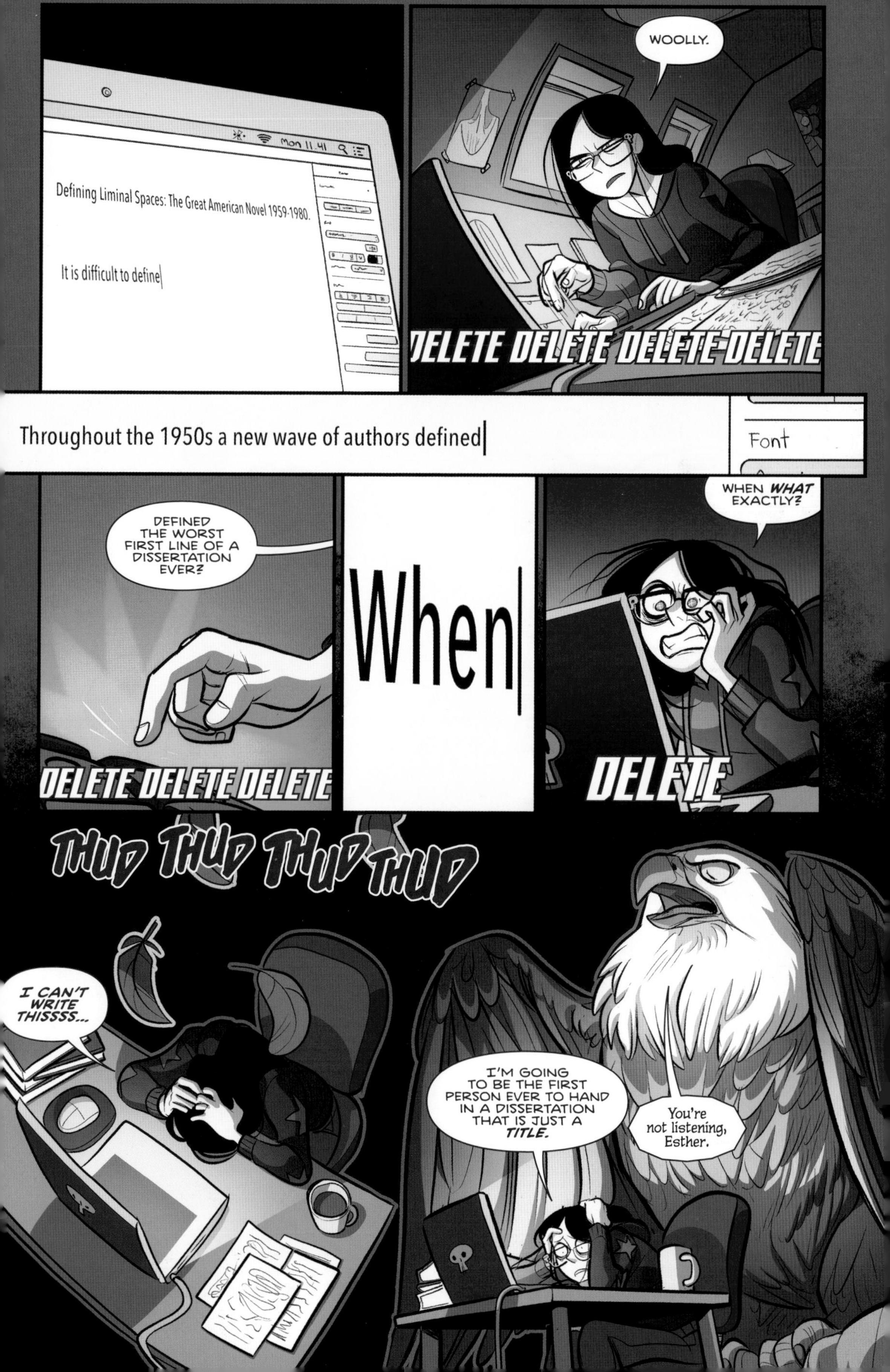
Mon 11.41
Defining Liminal Spaces: The Great American Novel 1959-1980.
It is difficult to define
WOOLLY.
DELETE DELETE DELETE DELETE
Throughout the 1950s a new wave of authors defined
Font
DEFINED THE WORST FIRST LINE OF A DISSERTATION EVER?
DELETE DELETE DELETE
When
WHEN WHAT EXACTLY?
DELETE
THUD THUD THUD THUD
I CAN'T WRITE THISSSS...
I'M GOING TO BE THE FIRST PERSON EVER TO HAND IN A DISSERTATION THAT IS JUST A TITLE.
You're not listening, Esther.

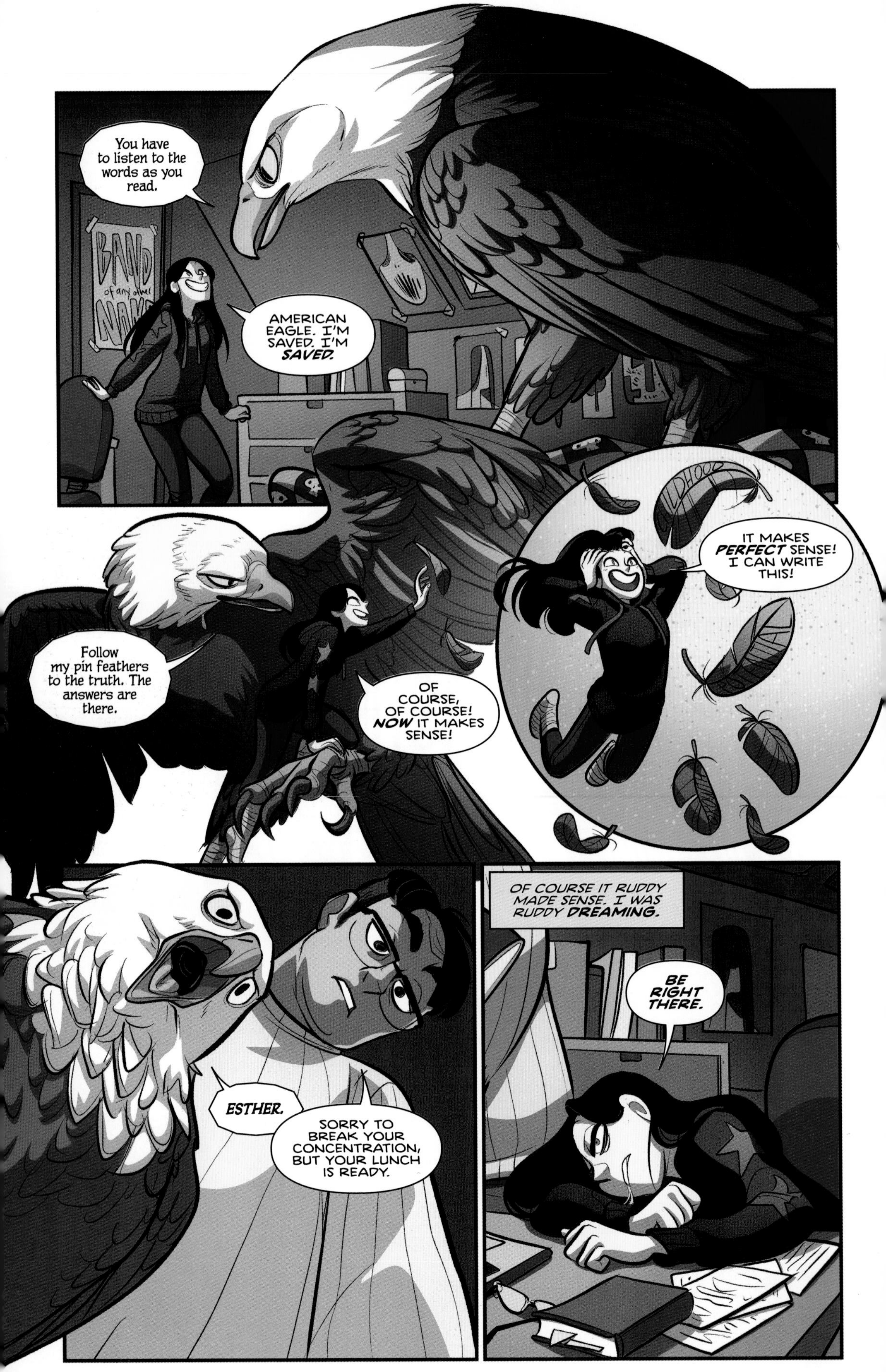
You have to listen to the words as you read.
BAND of any other NAME
AMERICAN EAGLE. I'M SAVED. I'M *SAVED.*
Follow my pin feathers to the truth. The answers are there.
OF COURSE, OF COURSE! *NOW* IT MAKES SENSE!
IT MAKES *PERFECT* SENSE! I CAN WRITE THIS!
ESTHER.
SORRY TO BREAK YOUR CONCENTRATION, BUT YOUR LUNCH IS READY.
OF COURSE IT RUDDY MADE SENSE. I WAS RUDDY *DREAMING.*
BE RIGHT THERE.

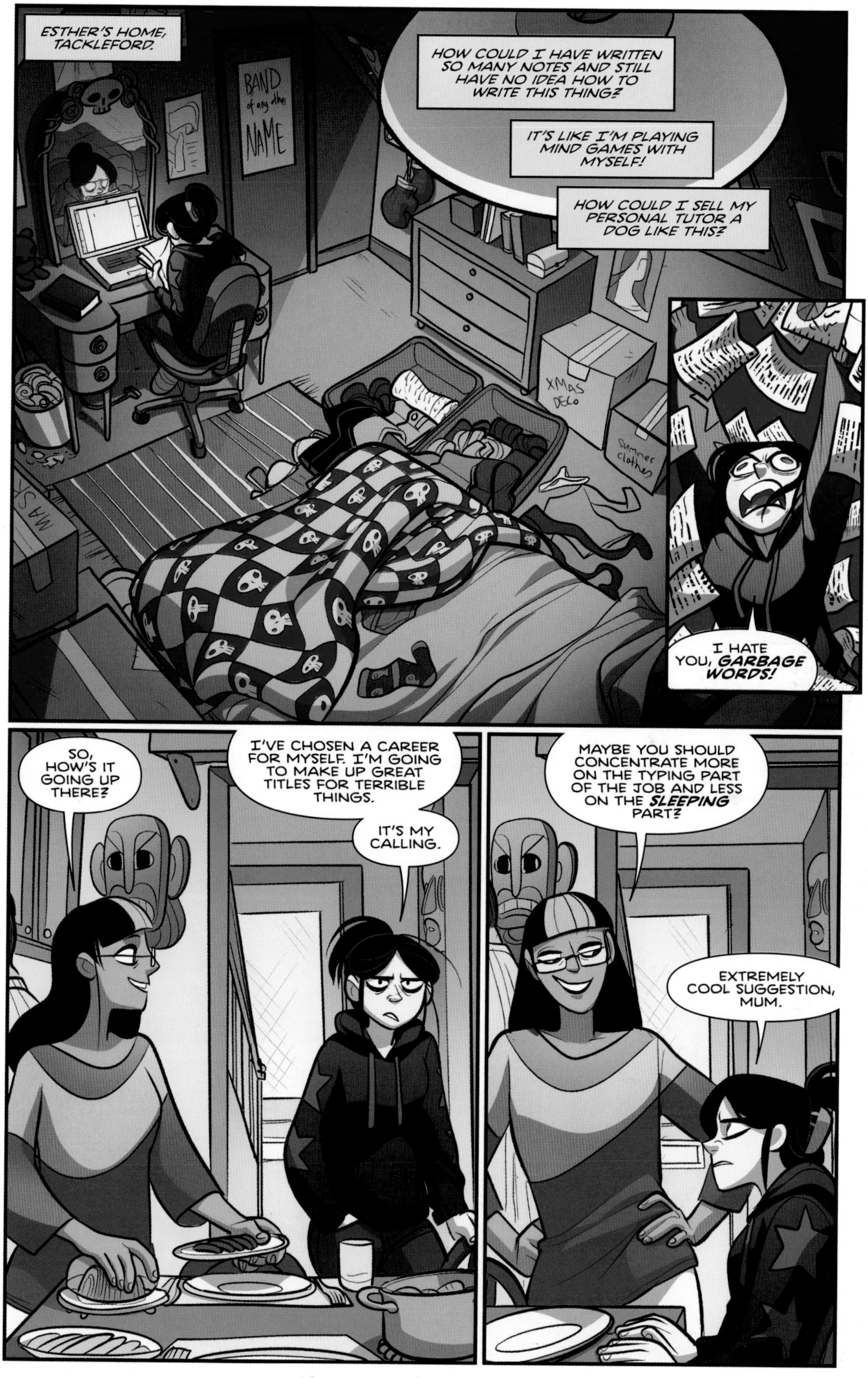
ESTHER'S HOME, TACKLEFORD.
BAND of any other NAME
HOW COULD I HAVE WRITTEN SO MANY NOTES AND STILL HAVE NO IDEA HOW TO WRITE THIS THING?
IT'S LIKE I'M PLAYING MIND GAMES WITH MYSELF!
HOW COULD I SELL MY PERSONAL TUTOR A DOG LIKE THIS?
XMAS DECO
summer clothes
I HATE YOU, GARBAGE WORDS!
SO, HOW'S IT GOING UP THERE?
I'VE CHOSEN A CAREER FOR MYSELF. I'M GOING TO MAKE UP GREAT TITLES FOR TERRIBLE THINGS.
IT'S MY CALLING.
MAYBE YOU SHOULD CONCENTRATE MORE ON THE TYPING PART OF THE JOB AND LESS ON THE SLEEPING PART?
EXTREMELY COOL SUGGESTION, MUM.

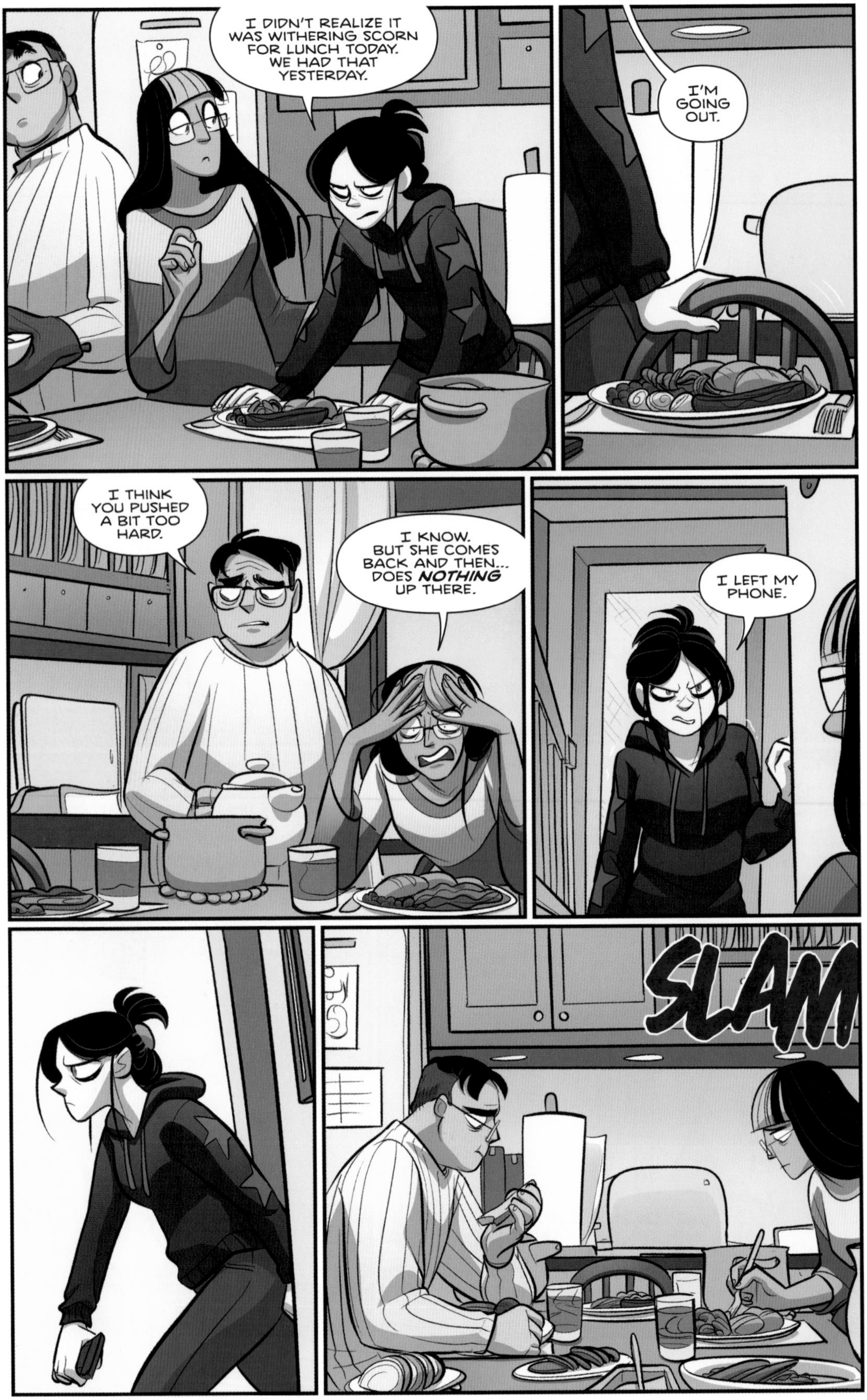
I DIDN'T REALIZE IT WAS WITHERING SCORN FOR LUNCH TODAY. WE HAD THAT YESTERDAY.
I'M GOING OUT.
I THINK YOU PUSHED A BIT TOO HARD.
I KNOW. BUT SHE COMES BACK AND THEN... DOES NOTHING UP THERE.
I LEFT MY PHONE.
SLAM

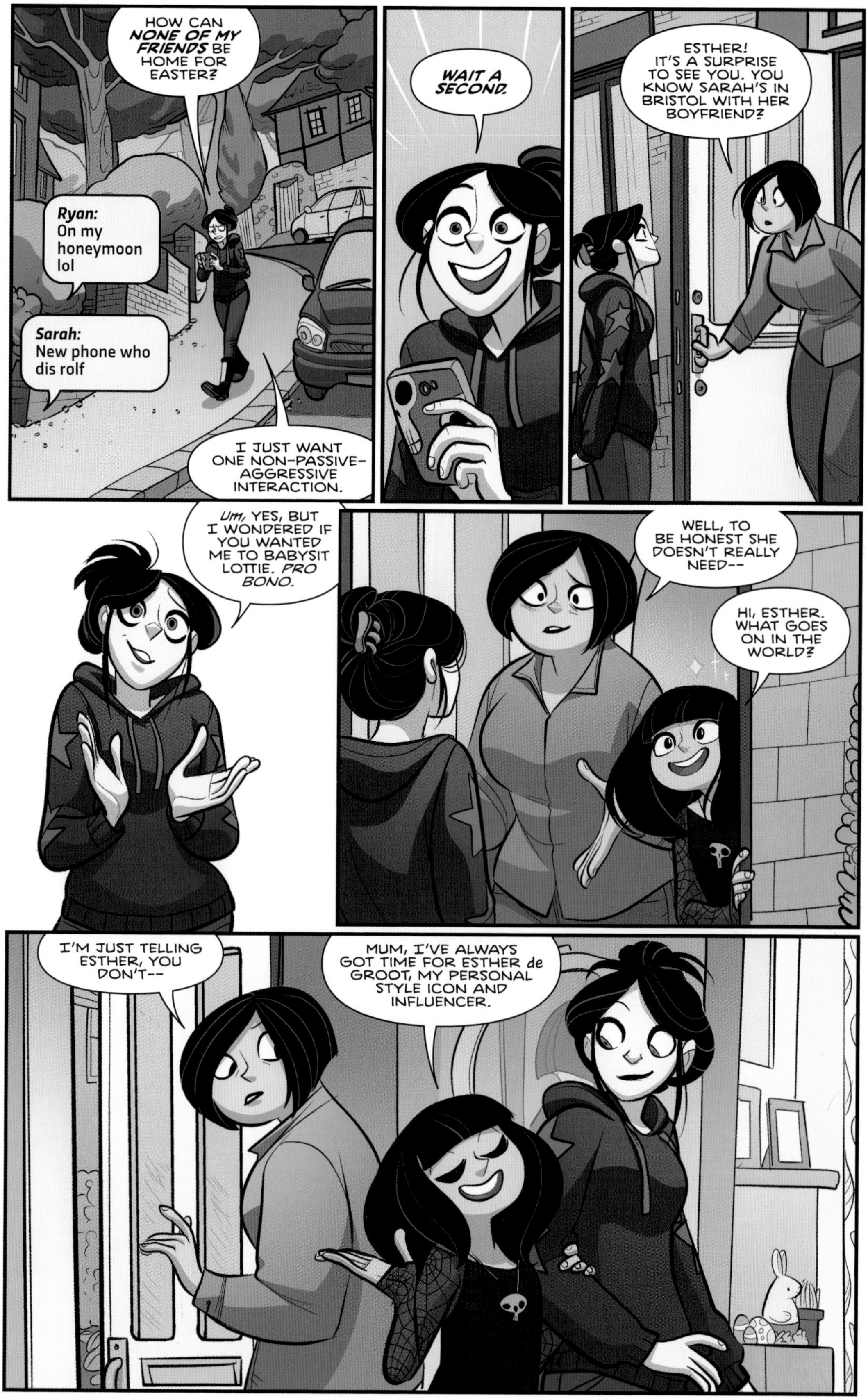

HOW CAN NONE OF MY FRIENDS BE HOME FOR EASTER?
Ryan: On my honeymoon lol
Sarah: New phone who dis rolf
I JUST WANT ONE NON-PASSIVE-AGGRESSIVE INTERACTION.
WAIT A SECOND.
ESTHER! IT'S A SURPRISE TO SEE YOU. YOU KNOW SARAH'S IN BRISTOL WITH HER BOYFRIEND?
UM, YES, BUT I WONDERED IF YOU WANTED ME TO BABYSIT LOTTIE. PRO BONO.
WELL, TO BE HONEST SHE DOESN'T REALLY NEED--
HI, ESTHER. WHAT GOES ON IN THE WORLD?
I'M JUST TELLING ESTHER, YOU DON'T--
MUM, I'VE ALWAYS GOT TIME FOR ESTHER de GROOT, MY PERSONAL STYLE ICON AND INFLUENCER.

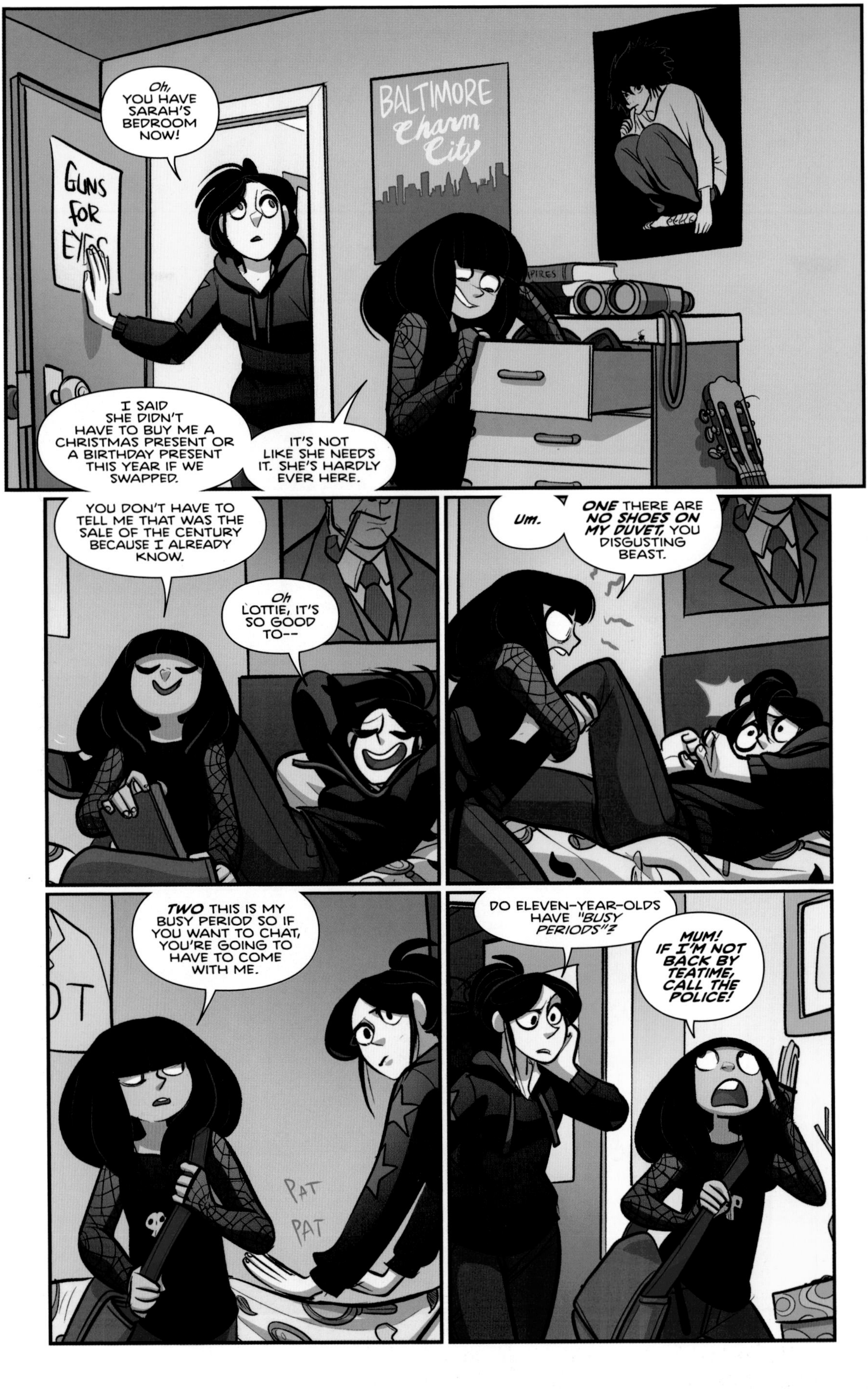

GUNS FOR EYES
BALTIMORE Charm City
VAMPIRES
Oh, YOU HAVE SARAH'S BEDROOM NOW!
I SAID SHE DIDN'T HAVE TO BUY ME A CHRISTMAS PRESENT OR A BIRTHDAY PRESENT THIS YEAR IF WE SWAPPED.
IT'S NOT LIKE SHE NEEDS IT. SHE'S HARDLY EVER HERE.
YOU DON'T HAVE TO TELL ME THAT WAS THE SALE OF THE CENTURY BECAUSE I ALREADY KNOW.
Oh LOTTIE, IT'S SO GOOD TO--
Um.
ONE THERE ARE NO SHOES ON MY DUVET, YOU DISGUSTING BEAST.
TWO THIS IS MY BUSY PERIOD SO IF YOU WANT TO CHAT, YOU'RE GOING TO HAVE TO COME WITH ME.
PAT
PAT
DO ELEVEN-YEAR-OLDS HAVE "BUSY PERIODS"?
MUM! IF I'M NOT BACK BY TEATIME, CALL THE POLICE!

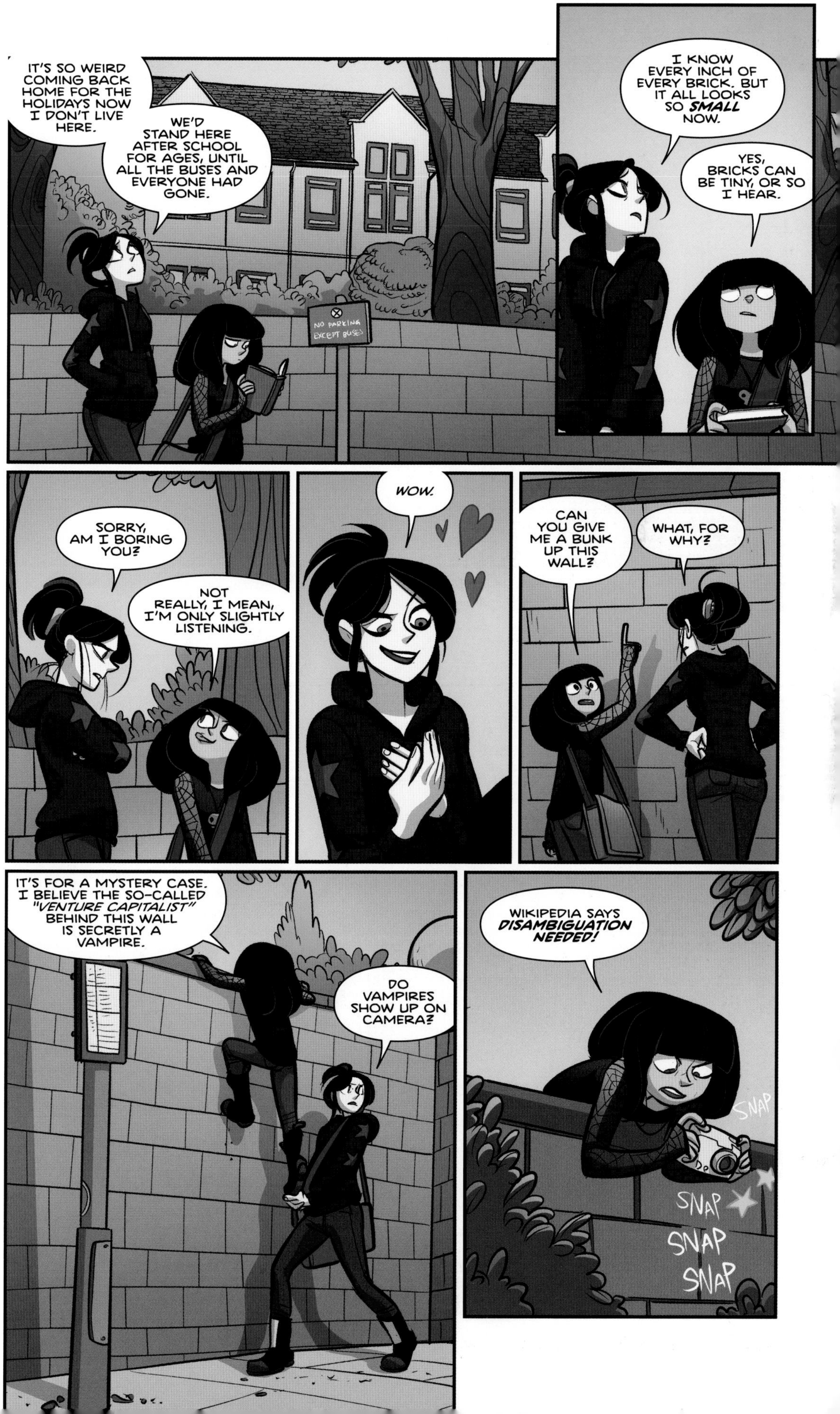
IT'S SO WEIRD COMING BACK HOME FOR THE HOLIDAYS NOW I DON'T LIVE HERE.
WE'D STAND HERE AFTER SCHOOL FOR AGES, UNTIL ALL THE BUSES AND EVERYONE HAD GONE.
NO PARKING EXCEPT BUSES
I KNOW EVERY INCH OF EVERY BRICK. BUT IT ALL LOOKS SO *SMALL* NOW.
YES, BRICKS CAN BE TINY, OR SO I HEAR.
SORRY, AM I BORING YOU?
NOT REALLY, I MEAN, I'M ONLY SLIGHTLY LISTENING.
WOW.
CAN YOU GIVE ME A BUNK UP THIS WALL?
WHAT, FOR WHY?
IT'S FOR A MYSTERY CASE. I BELIEVE THE SO-CALLED *"VENTURE CAPITALIST"* BEHIND THIS WALL IS SECRETLY A VAMPIRE.
DO VAMPIRES SHOW UP ON CAMERA?
WIKIPEDIA SAYS ***DISAMBIGUATION NEEDED!***
SNAP
SNAP
SNAP
SNAP

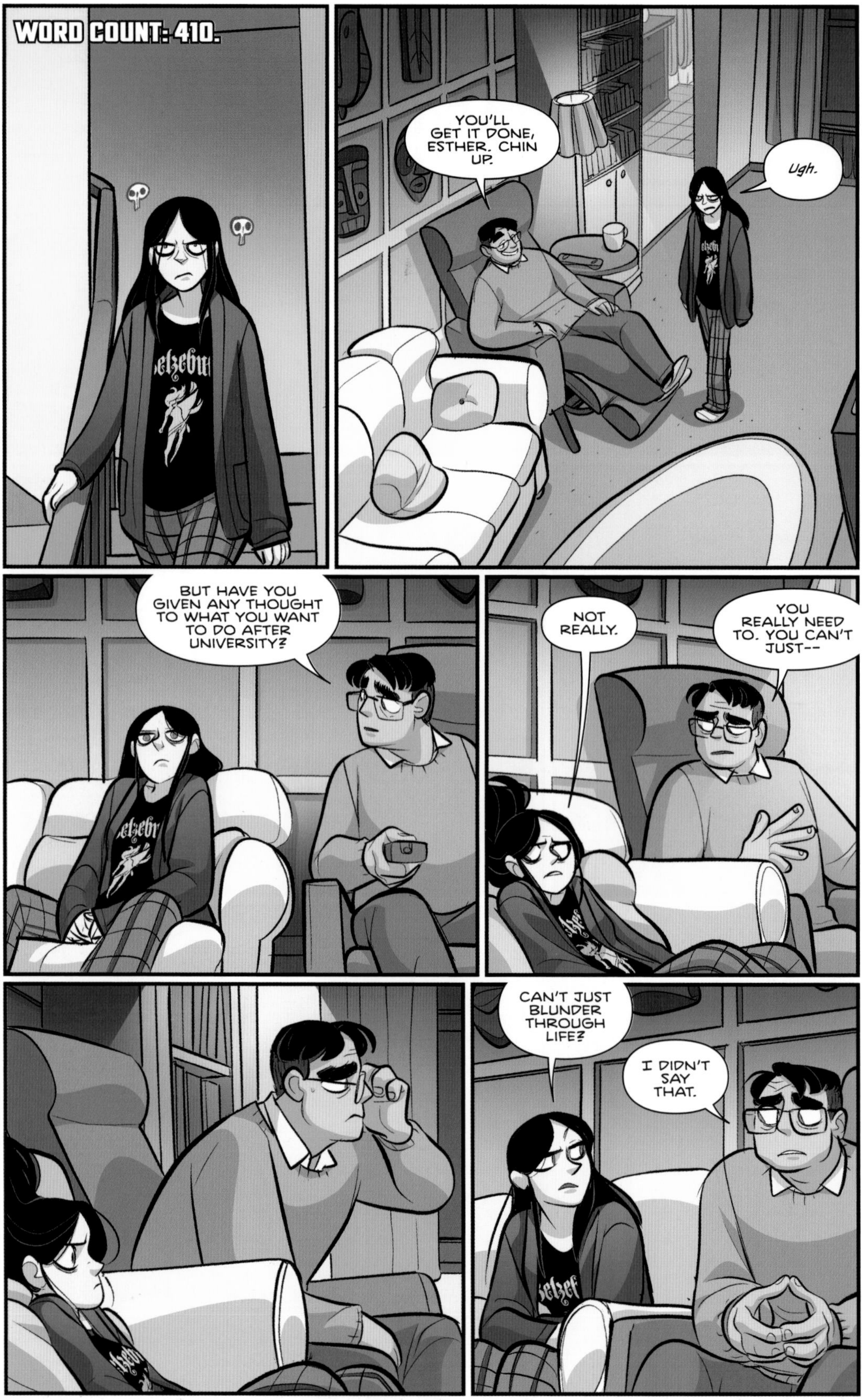
WORD COUNT: 410.
YOU'LL GET IT DONE, ESTHER. CHIN UP.
Ugh.
BUT HAVE YOU GIVEN ANY THOUGHT TO WHAT YOU WANT TO DO AFTER UNIVERSITY?
NOT REALLY.
YOU REALLY NEED TO. YOU CAN'T JUST--
CAN'T JUST BLUNDER THROUGH LIFE?
I DIDN'T SAY THAT.

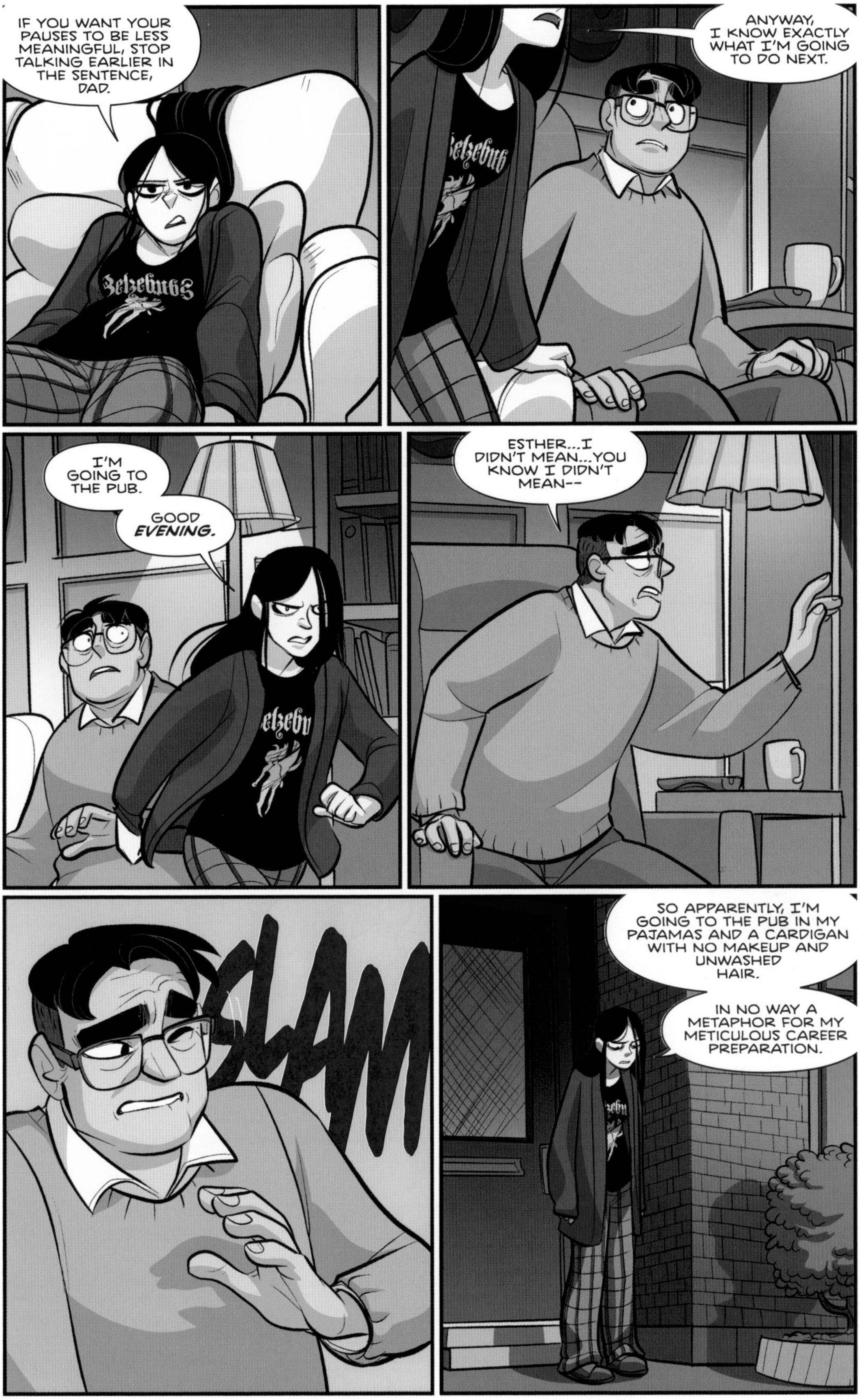
IF YOU WANT YOUR PAUSES TO BE LESS MEANINGFUL, STOP TALKING EARLIER IN THE SENTENCE, DAD.
Belzebubs
ANYWAY, I KNOW EXACTLY WHAT I'M GOING TO DO NEXT.
I'M GOING TO THE PUB.
GOOD *EVENING.*
ESTHER...I DIDN'T MEAN...YOU KNOW I DIDN'T MEAN--
SLAM
SO APPARENTLY, I'M GOING TO THE PUB IN MY PAJAMAS AND A CARDIGAN WITH NO MAKEUP AND UNWASHED HAIR.
IN NO WAY A METAPHOR FOR MY METICULOUS CAREER PREPARATION.

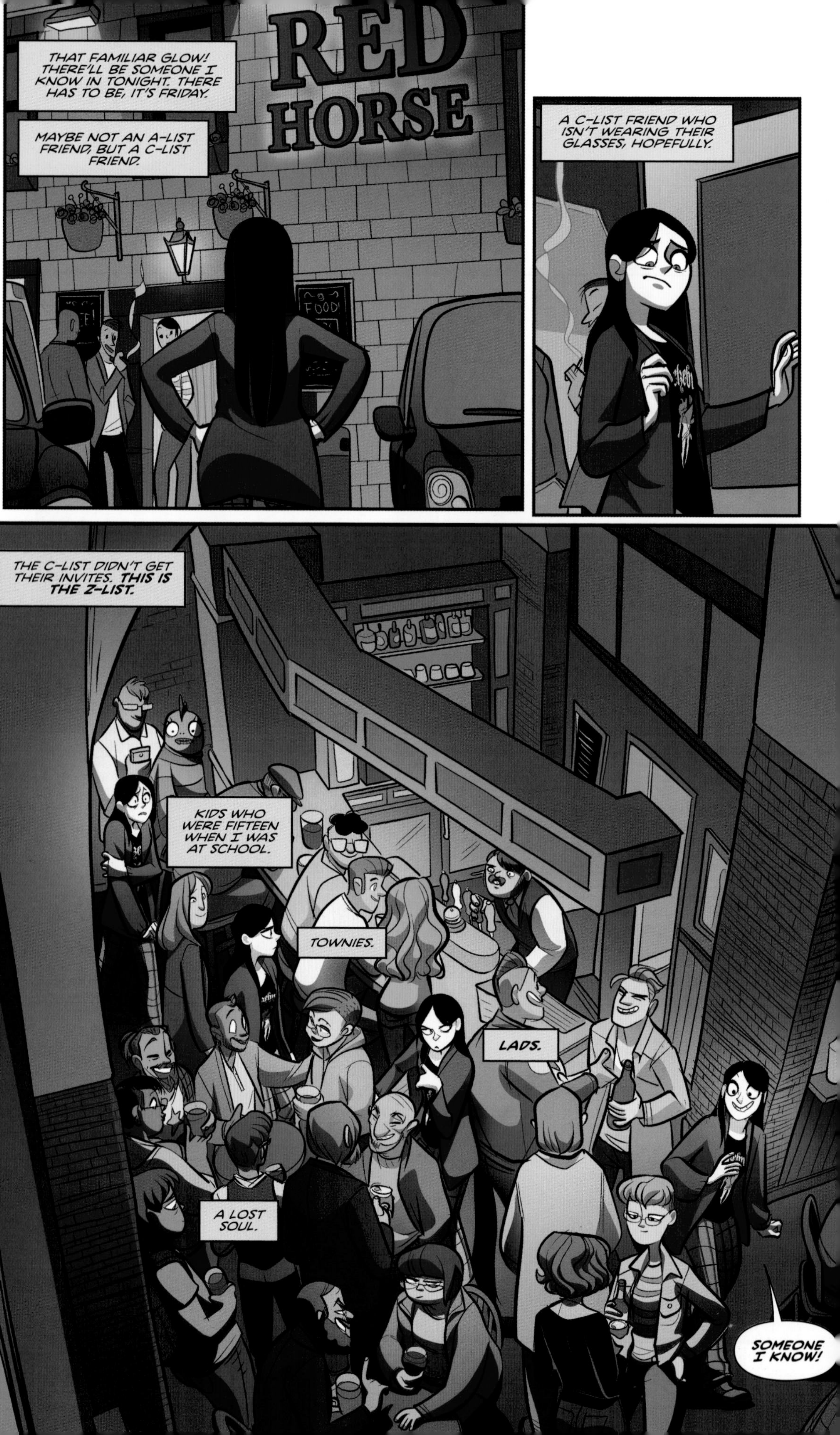

RED HORSE
THAT FAMILIAR GLOW! THERE'LL BE SOMEONE I KNOW IN TONIGHT. THERE HAS TO BE, IT'S FRIDAY.
MAYBE NOT AN A-LIST FRIEND, BUT A C-LIST FRIEND.
FOOD!
A C-LIST FRIEND WHO ISN'T WEARING THEIR GLASSES, HOPEFULLY.
THE C-LIST DIDN'T GET THEIR INVITES. **THIS IS THE Z-LIST.**
KIDS WHO WERE FIFTEEN WHEN I WAS AT SCHOOL.
TOWNIES.
LADS.
A LOST SOUL.
SOMEONE I KNOW!

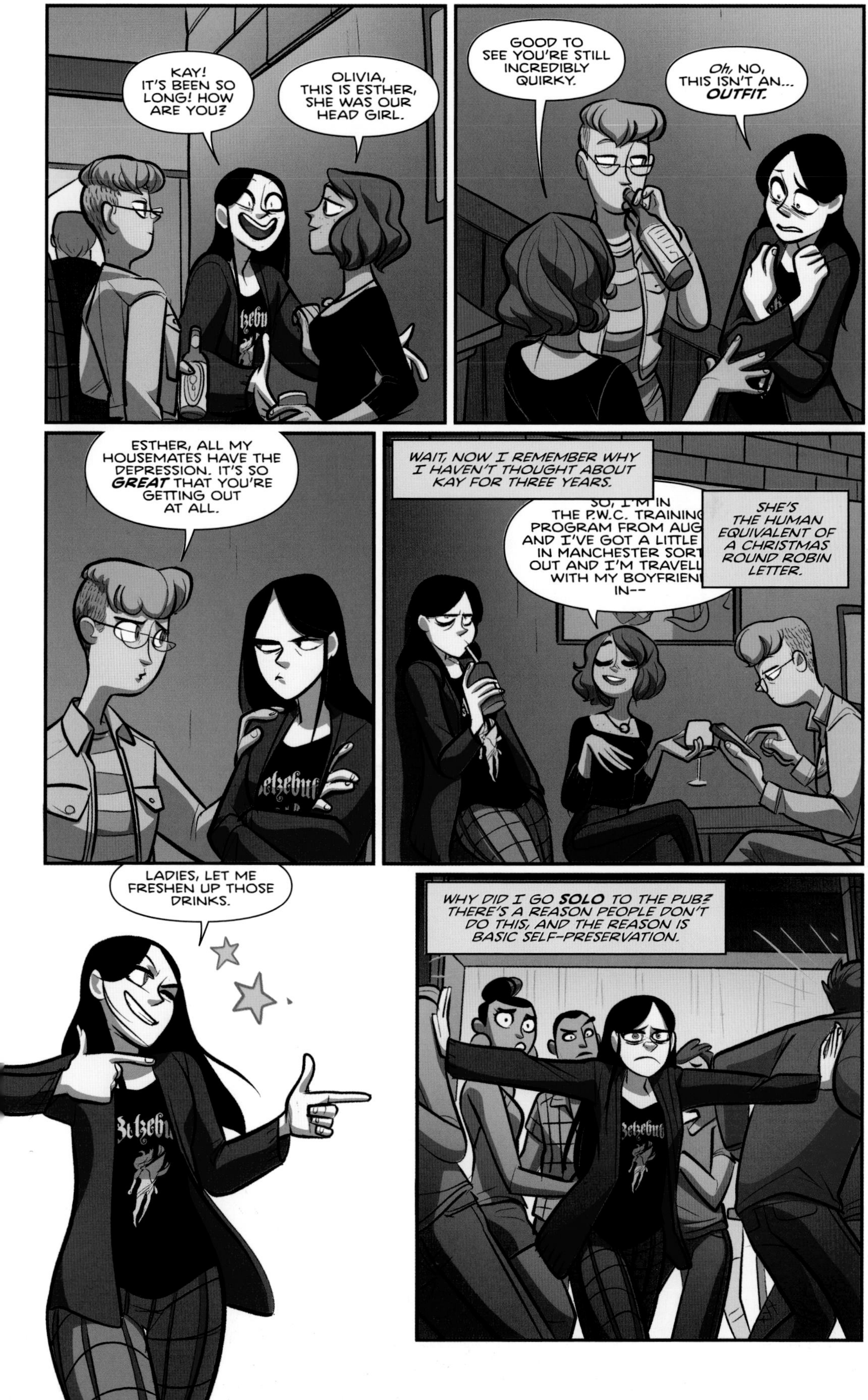
KAY! IT'S BEEN SO LONG! HOW ARE YOU?
OLIVIA, THIS IS ESTHER, SHE WAS OUR HEAD GIRL.
GOOD TO SEE YOU'RE STILL INCREDIBLY QUIRKY.
Oh, NO, THIS ISN'T AN... ***OUTFIT.***
ESTHER, ALL MY HOUSEMATES HAVE THE DEPRESSION. IT'S SO **GREAT** THAT YOU'RE GETTING OUT AT ALL.
WAIT, NOW I REMEMBER WHY I HAVEN'T THOUGHT ABOUT KAY FOR THREE YEARS.
SO, I'M IN THE P.W.C. TRAINING PROGRAM FROM AUG AND I'VE GOT A LITTLE IN MANCHESTER SORT OUT AND I'M TRAVELL WITH MY BOYFRIEN IN--
SHE'S THE HUMAN EQUIVALENT OF A CHRISTMAS ROUND ROBIN LETTER.
LADIES, LET ME FRESHEN UP THOSE DRINKS.
WHY DID I GO **SOLO** TO THE PUB? THERE'S A REASON PEOPLE DON'T DO THIS, AND THE REASON IS BASIC SELF-PRESERVATION.

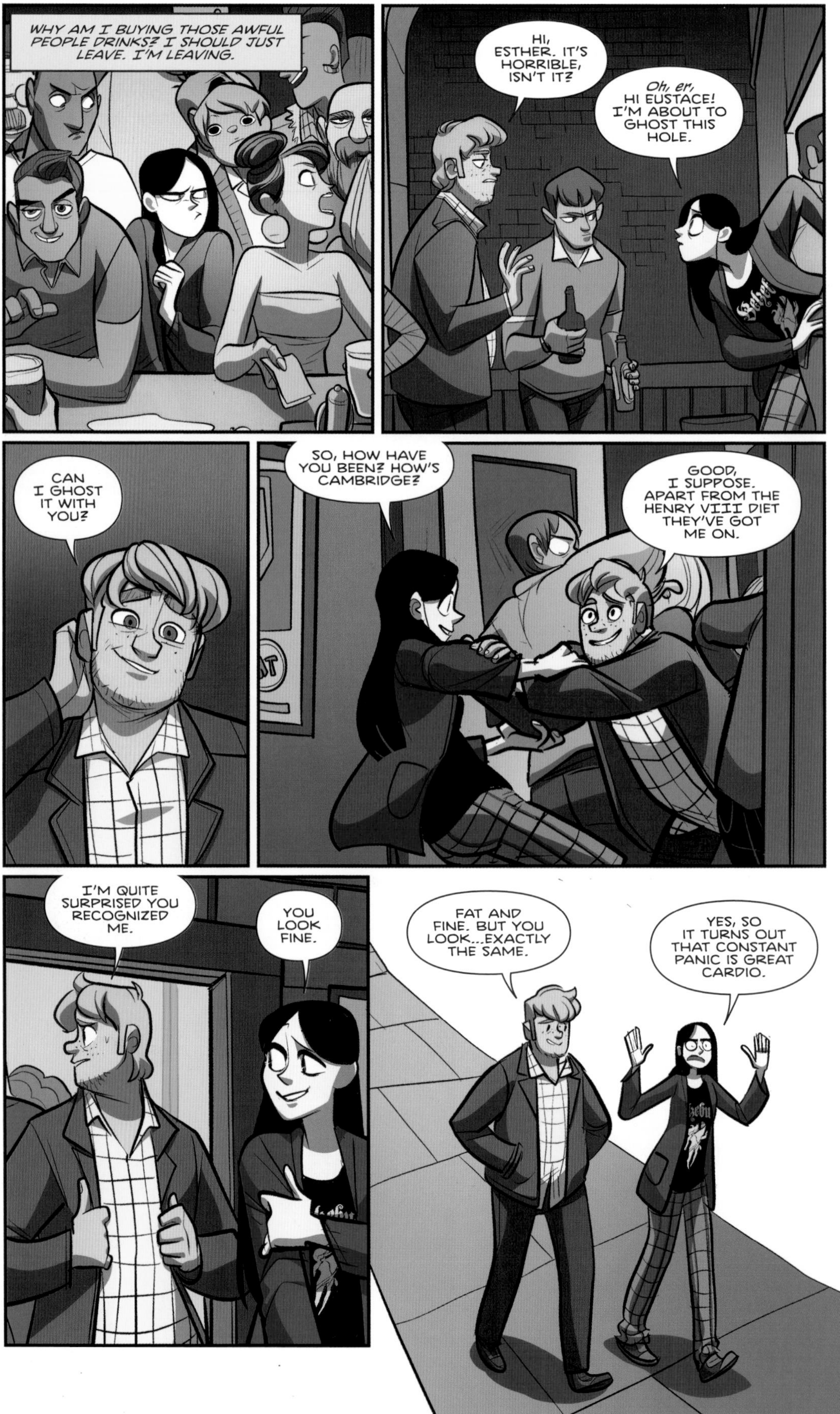
WHY AM I BUYING THOSE AWFUL PEOPLE DRINKS? I SHOULD JUST LEAVE. I'M LEAVING.
HI, ESTHER. IT'S HORRIBLE, ISN'T IT?
Oh, er, HI EUSTACE! I'M ABOUT TO GHOST THIS HOLE.
CAN I GHOST IT WITH YOU?
SO, HOW HAVE YOU BEEN? HOW'S CAMBRIDGE?
GOOD, I SUPPOSE. APART FROM THE HENRY VIII DIET THEY'VE GOT ME ON.
I'M QUITE SURPRISED YOU RECOGNIZED ME.
YOU LOOK FINE.
FAT AND FINE. BUT YOU LOOK...EXACTLY THE SAME.
YES, SO IT TURNS OUT THAT CONSTANT PANIC IS GREAT CARDIO.

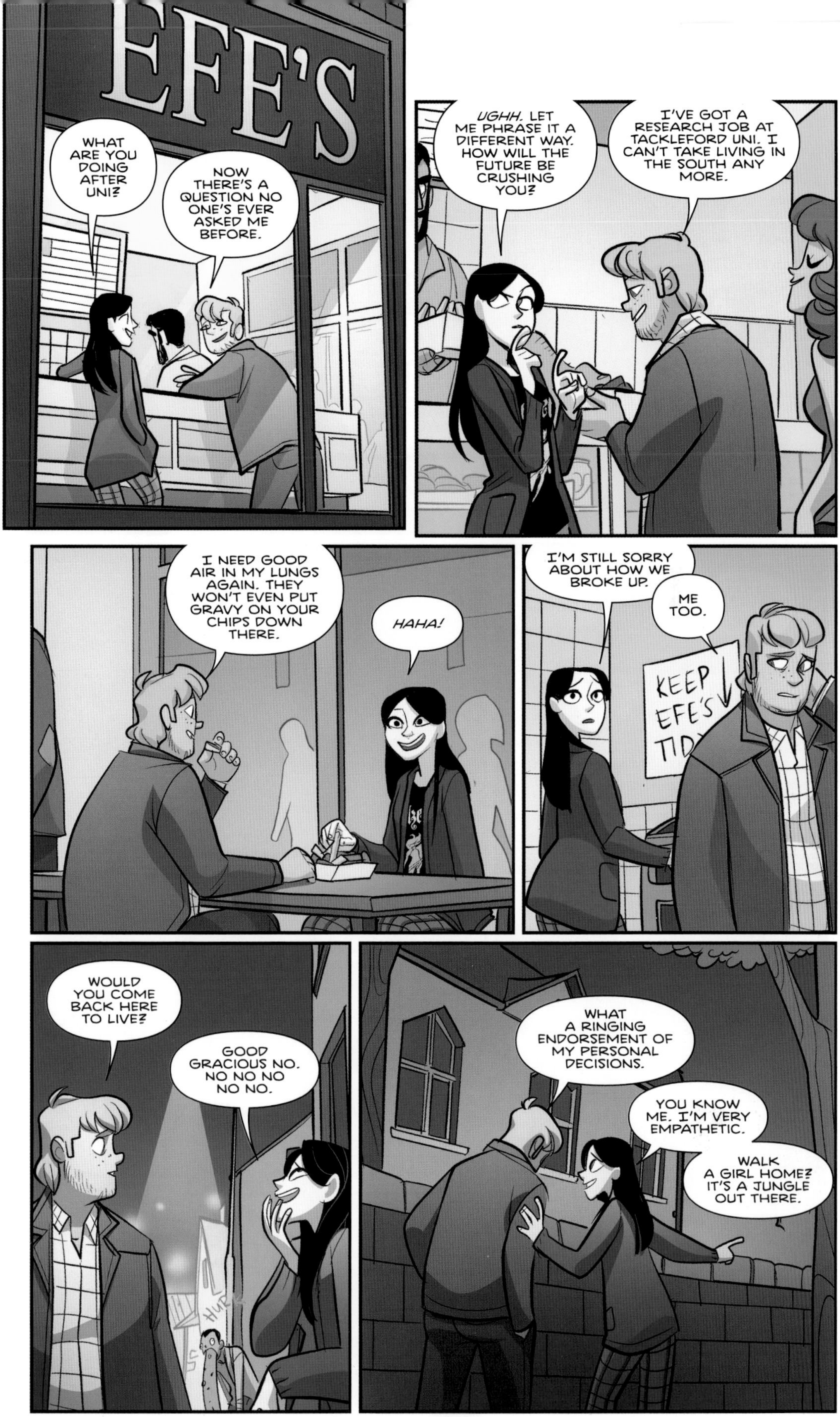
EFE'S
WHAT ARE YOU DOING AFTER UNI?
NOW THERE'S A QUESTION NO ONE'S EVER ASKED ME BEFORE.
UGHH. LET ME PHRASE IT A DIFFERENT WAY. HOW WILL THE FUTURE BE CRUSHING YOU?
I'VE GOT A RESEARCH JOB AT TACKLEFORD UNI. I CAN'T TAKE LIVING IN THE SOUTH ANY MORE.
I NEED GOOD AIR IN MY LUNGS AGAIN. THEY WON'T EVEN PUT GRAVY ON YOUR CHIPS DOWN THERE.
HAHA!
I'M STILL SORRY ABOUT HOW WE BROKE UP.
ME TOO.
KEEP EFE'S
WOULD YOU COME BACK HERE TO LIVE?
GOOD GRACIOUS NO. NO NO NO NO NO.
WHAT A RINGING ENDORSEMENT OF MY PERSONAL DECISIONS.
YOU KNOW ME. I'M VERY EMPATHETIC.
WALK A GIRL HOME? IT'S A JUNGLE OUT THERE.

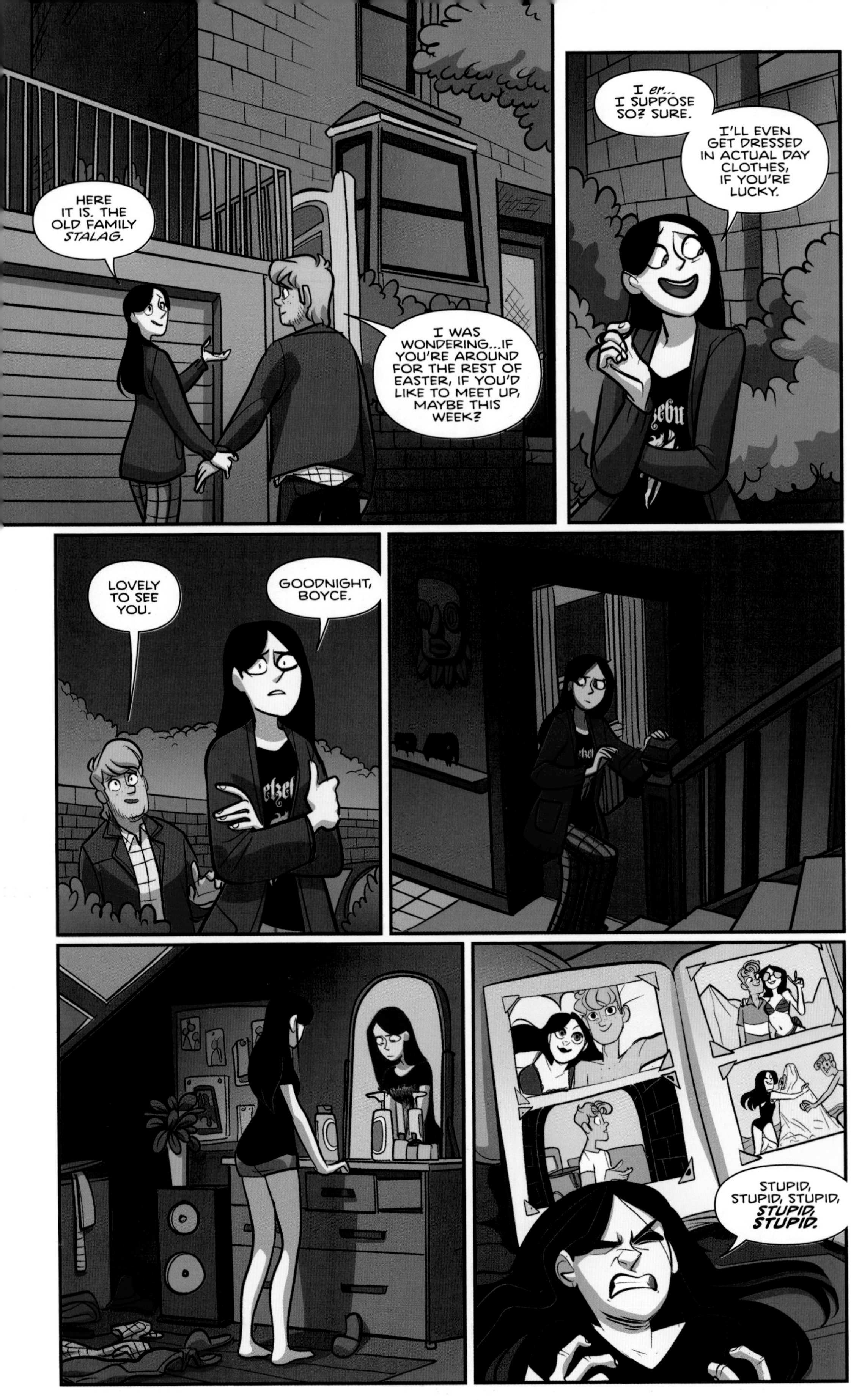
HERE IT IS. THE OLD FAMILY *STALAG.*
I WAS WONDERING...IF YOU'RE AROUND FOR THE REST OF EASTER, IF YOU'D LIKE TO MEET UP, MAYBE THIS WEEK?
I *er*... I SUPPOSE SO? SURE.
I'LL EVEN GET DRESSED IN ACTUAL DAY CLOTHES, IF YOU'RE LUCKY.
LOVELY TO SEE YOU.
GOODNIGHT, BOYCE.
STUPID, STUPID, STUPID, ***STUPID, STUPID.***

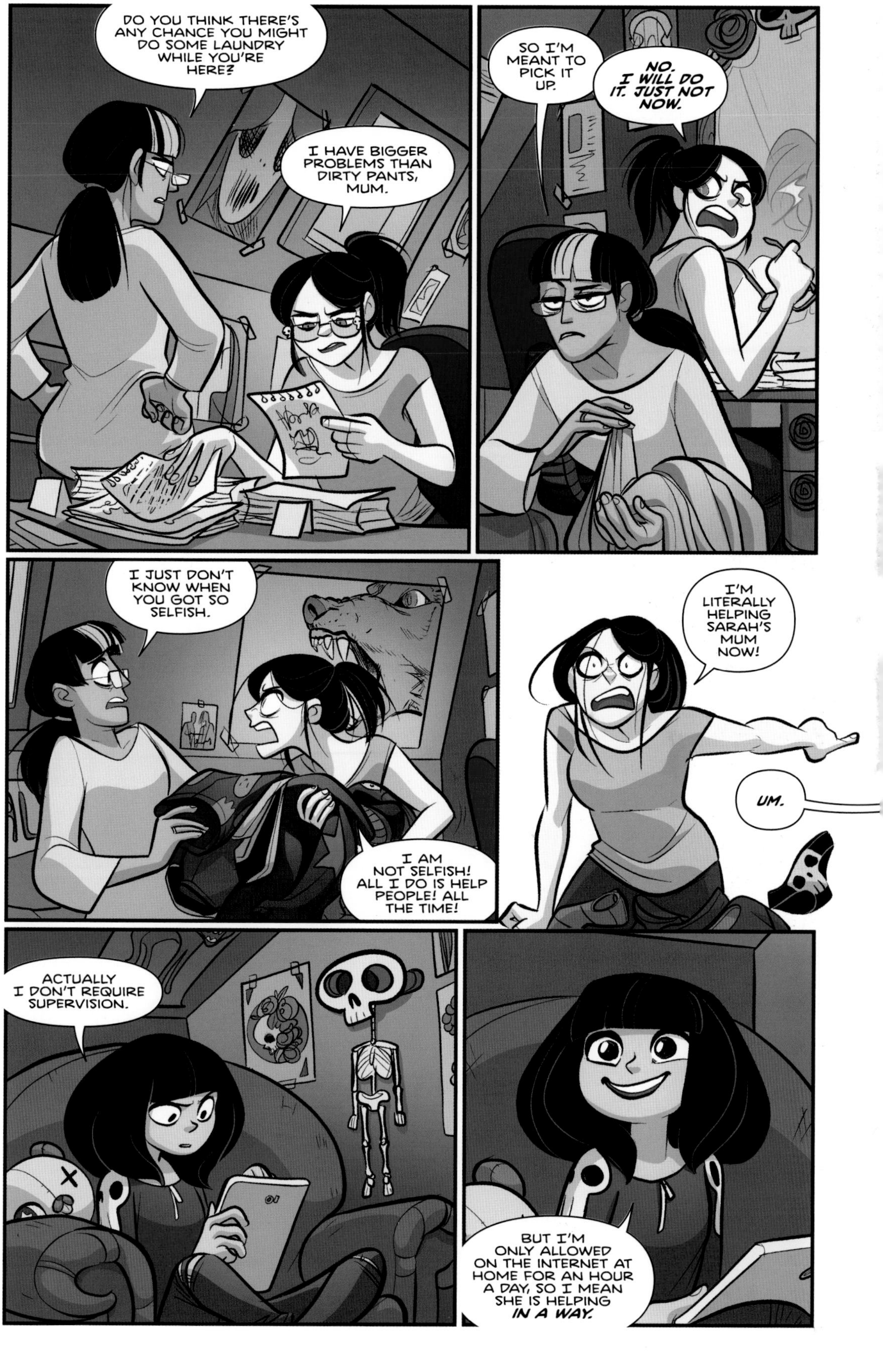
DO YOU THINK THERE'S ANY CHANCE YOU MIGHT DO SOME LAUNDRY WHILE YOU'RE HERE?
I HAVE BIGGER PROBLEMS THAN DIRTY PANTS, MUM.
SO I'M MEANT TO PICK IT UP.
NO. I WILL DO IT. JUST NOT NOW.
I JUST DON'T KNOW WHEN YOU GOT SO SELFISH.
I AM NOT SELFISH! ALL I DO IS HELP PEOPLE! ALL THE TIME!
I'M LITERALLY HELPING SARAH'S MUM NOW!
UM.
ACTUALLY I DON'T REQUIRE SUPERVISION.
BUT I'M ONLY ALLOWED ON THE INTERNET AT HOME FOR AN HOUR A DAY, SO I MEAN SHE IS HELPING *IN A WAY.*

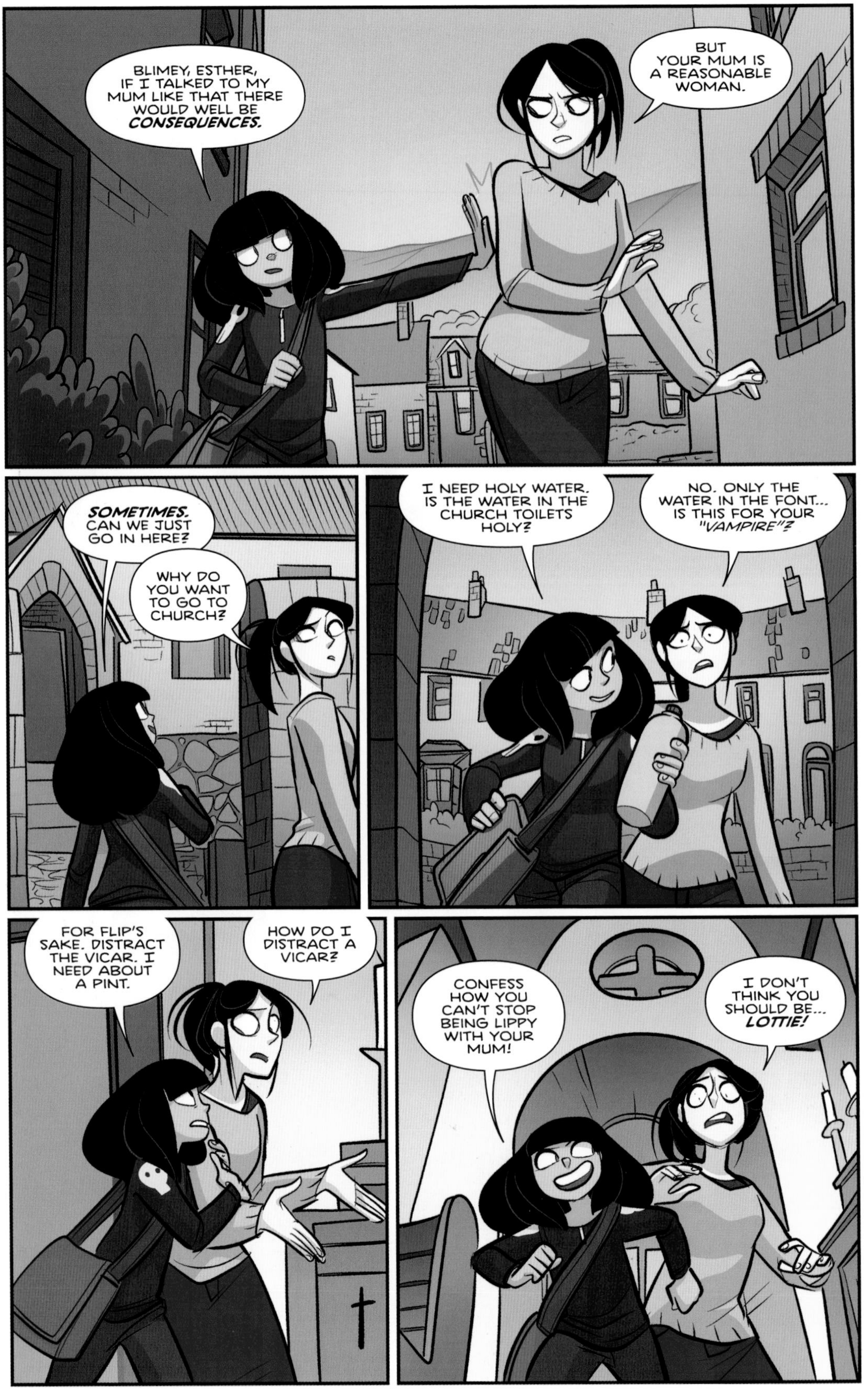
BLIMEY, ESTHER, IF I TALKED TO MY MUM LIKE THAT THERE WOULD WELL BE *CONSEQUENCES.*
BUT YOUR MUM IS A REASONABLE WOMAN.
SOMETIMES. CAN WE JUST GO IN HERE?
WHY DO YOU WANT TO GO TO CHURCH?
I NEED HOLY WATER. IS THE WATER IN THE CHURCH TOILETS HOLY?
NO. ONLY THE WATER IN THE FONT... IS THIS FOR YOUR *"VAMPIRE"*?
FOR FLIP'S SAKE. DISTRACT THE VICAR. I NEED ABOUT A PINT.
HOW DO I DISTRACT A VICAR?
CONFESS HOW YOU CAN'T STOP BEING LIPPY WITH YOUR MUM!
I DON'T THINK YOU SHOULD BE... *LOTTIE!*

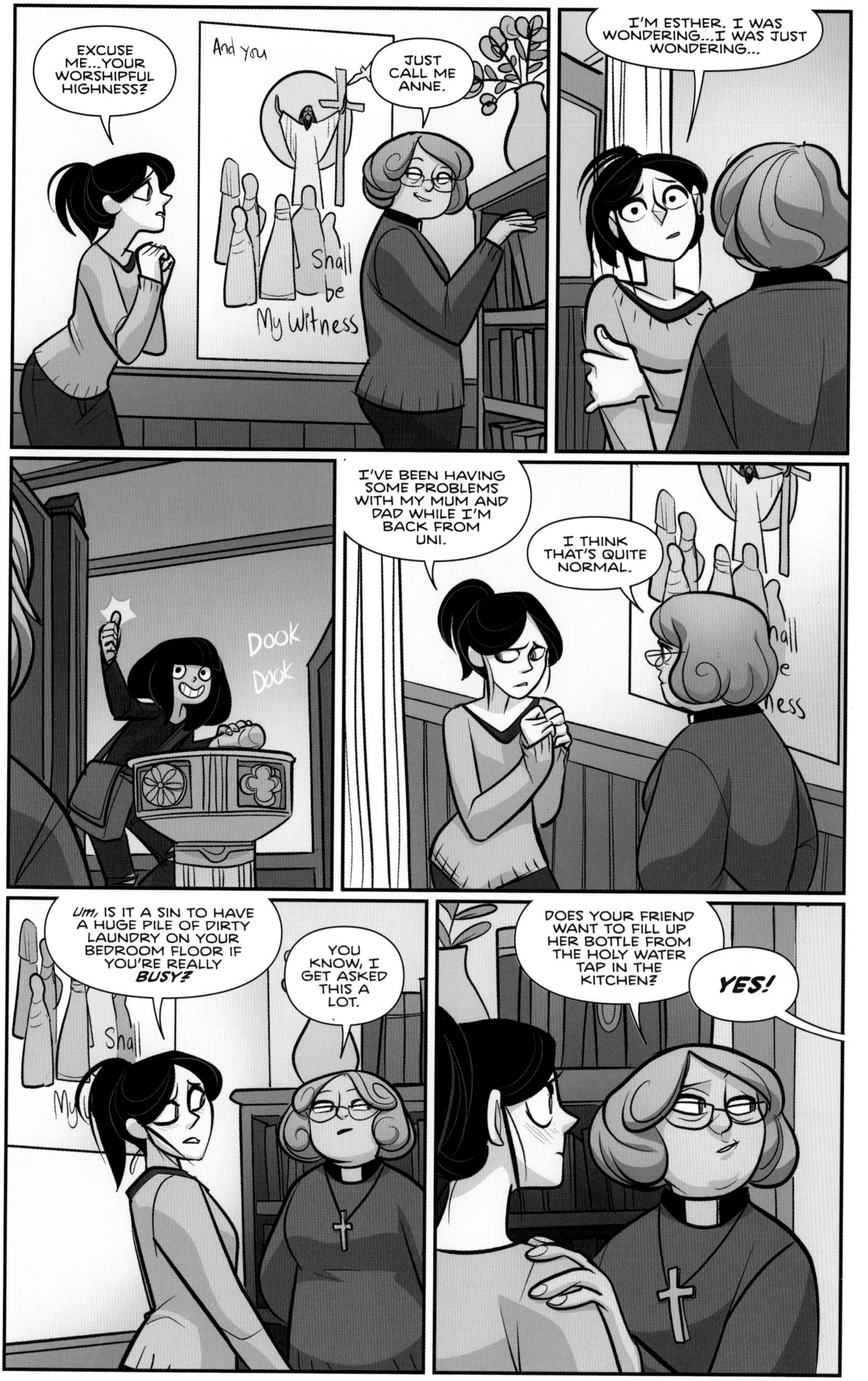

EXCUSE ME...YOUR WORSHIPFUL HIGHNESS?
And you
Shall be My Witness
JUST CALL ME ANNE.
I'M ESTHER. I WAS WONDERING...I WAS JUST WONDERING...
DOOK DOOK
I'VE BEEN HAVING SOME PROBLEMS WITH MY MUM AND DAD WHILE I'M BACK FROM UNI.
I THINK THAT'S QUITE NORMAL.
UM, IS IT A SIN TO HAVE A HUGE PILE OF DIRTY LAUNDRY ON YOUR BEDROOM FLOOR IF YOU'RE REALLY BUSY?
YOU KNOW, I GET ASKED THIS A LOT.
DOES YOUR FRIEND WANT TO FILL UP HER BOTTLE FROM THE HOLY WATER TAP IN THE KITCHEN?
YES!

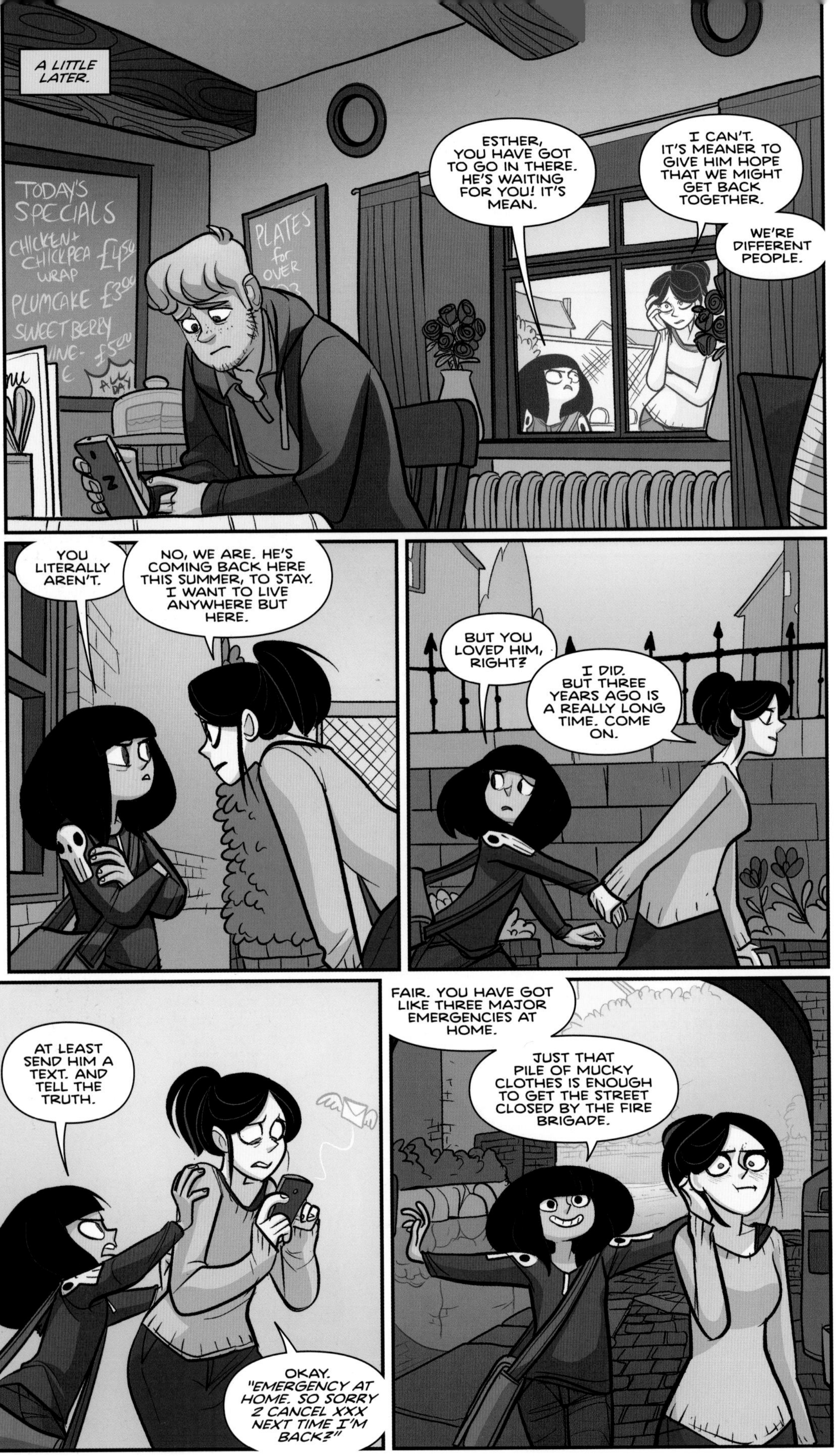

A LITTLE LATER.
TODAY'S SPECIALS CHICKEN + CHICKPEA WRAP £4.50 PLUMCAKE £3.00 SWEET BERRY WINE- £5.00
PLATES for OVER
ESTHER, YOU HAVE GOT TO GO IN THERE. HE'S WAITING FOR YOU! IT'S MEAN.
I CAN'T. IT'S MEANER TO GIVE HIM HOPE THAT WE MIGHT GET BACK TOGETHER.
WE'RE DIFFERENT PEOPLE.
YOU LITERALLY AREN'T.
NO, WE ARE. HE'S COMING BACK HERE THIS SUMMER, TO STAY. I WANT TO LIVE ANYWHERE BUT HERE.
BUT YOU LOVED HIM, RIGHT?
I DID. BUT THREE YEARS AGO IS A REALLY LONG TIME. COME ON.
AT LEAST SEND HIM A TEXT. AND TELL THE TRUTH.
OKAY. "EMERGENCY AT HOME. SO SORRY 2 CANCEL XXX NEXT TIME I'M BACK?"
FAIR. YOU HAVE GOT LIKE THREE MAJOR EMERGENCIES AT HOME.
JUST THAT PILE OF MUCKY CLOTHES IS ENOUGH TO GET THE STREET CLOSED BY THE FIRE BRIGADE.

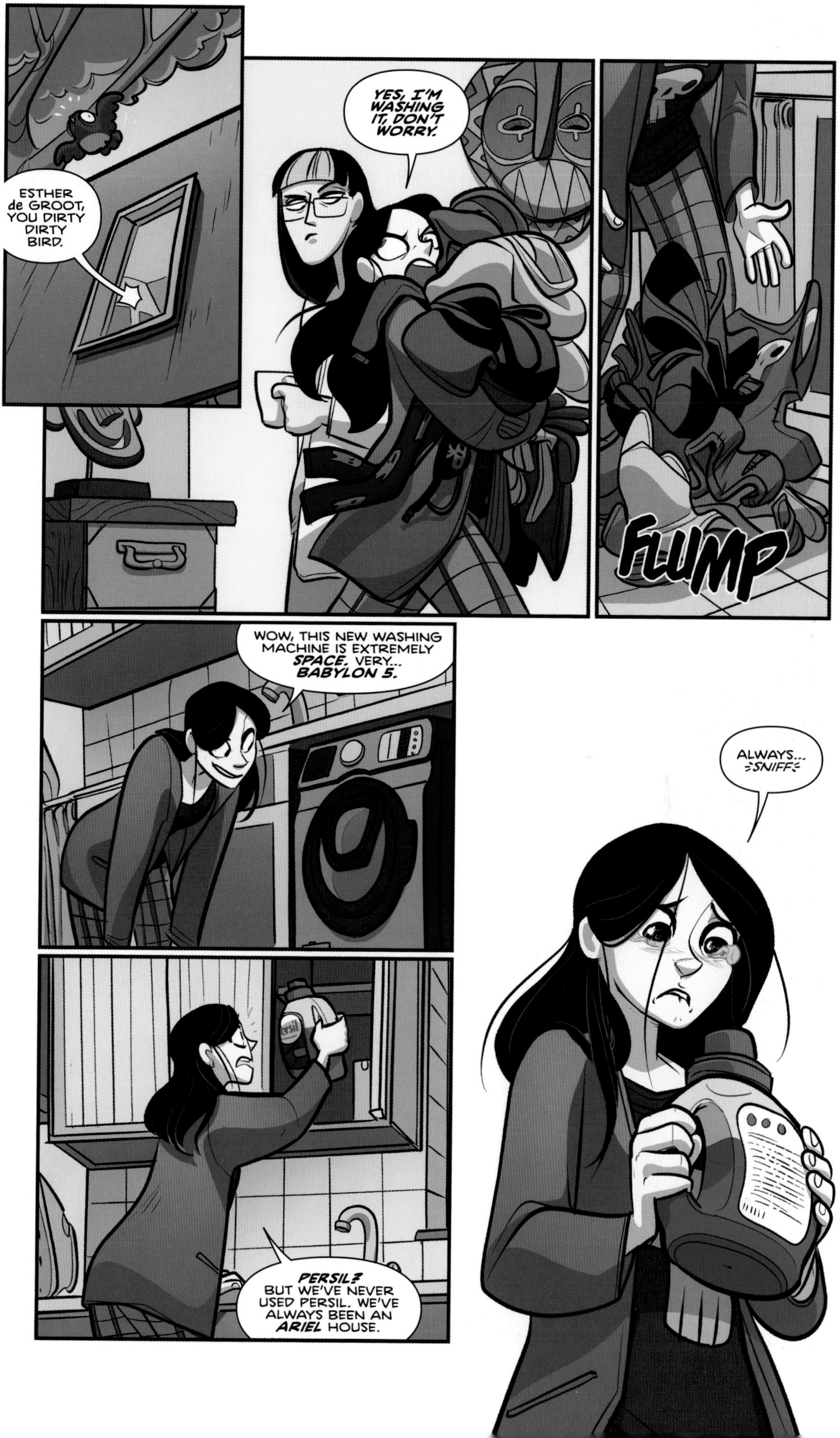
ESTHER de GROOT, YOU DIRTY DIRTY BIRD.
YES, I'M WASHING IT, DON'T WORRY.
FLUMP
WOW, THIS NEW WASHING MACHINE IS EXTREMELY SPACE. VERY... BABYLON 5.
persil
PERSIL? BUT WE'VE NEVER USED PERSIL. WE'VE ALWAYS BEEN AN ARIEL HOUSE.
ALWAYS... SNIFF

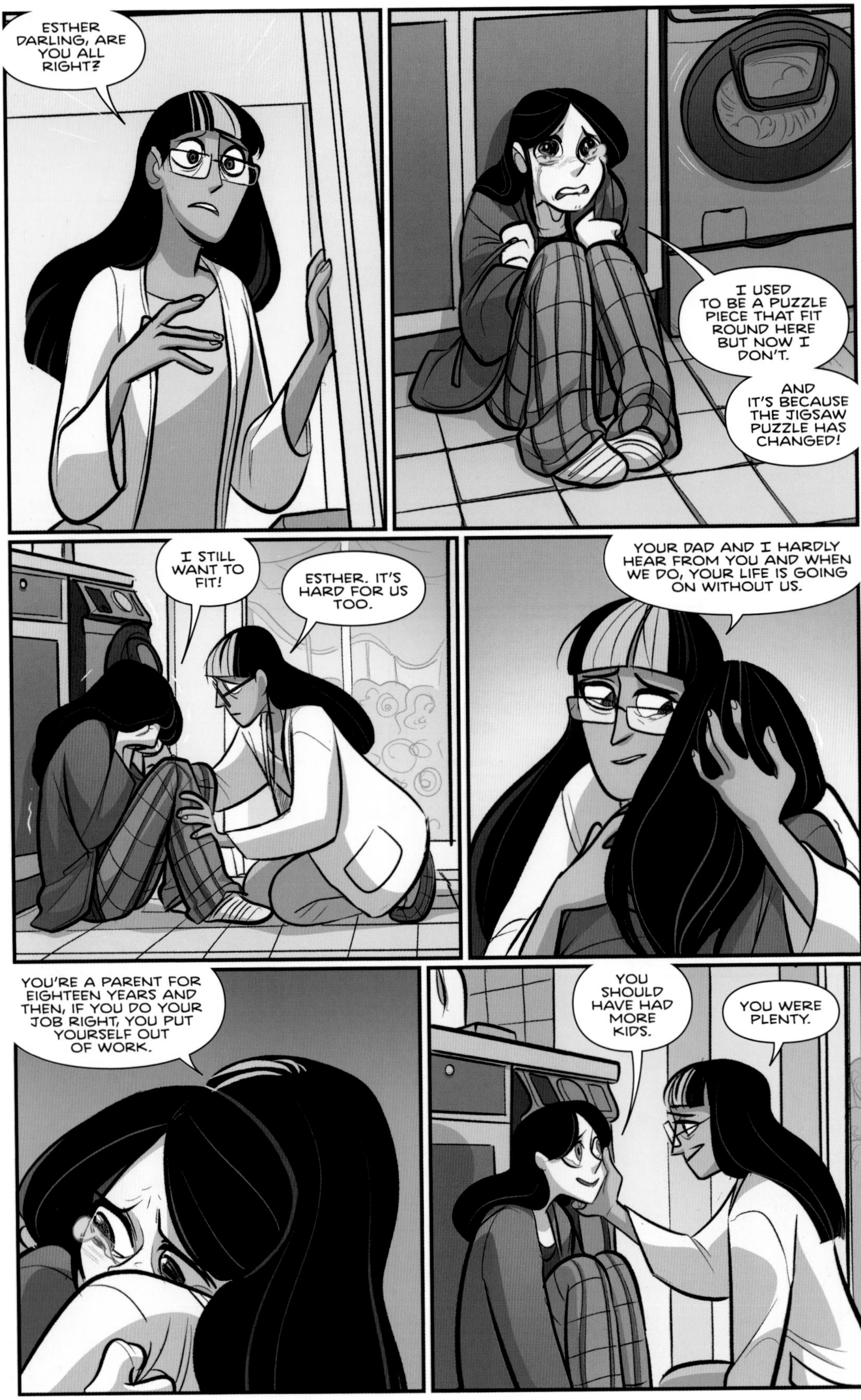
ESTHER DARLING, ARE YOU ALL RIGHT?
I USED TO BE A PUZZLE PIECE THAT FIT ROUND HERE BUT NOW I DON'T.
AND IT'S BECAUSE THE JIGSAW PUZZLE HAS CHANGED!
I STILL WANT TO FIT!
ESTHER. IT'S HARD FOR US TOO.
YOUR DAD AND I HARDLY HEAR FROM YOU AND WHEN WE DO, YOUR LIFE IS GOING ON WITHOUT US.
YOU'RE A PARENT FOR EIGHTEEN YEARS AND THEN, IF YOU DO YOUR JOB RIGHT, YOU PUT YOURSELF OUT OF WORK.
YOU SHOULD HAVE HAD MORE KIDS.
YOU WERE PLENTY.

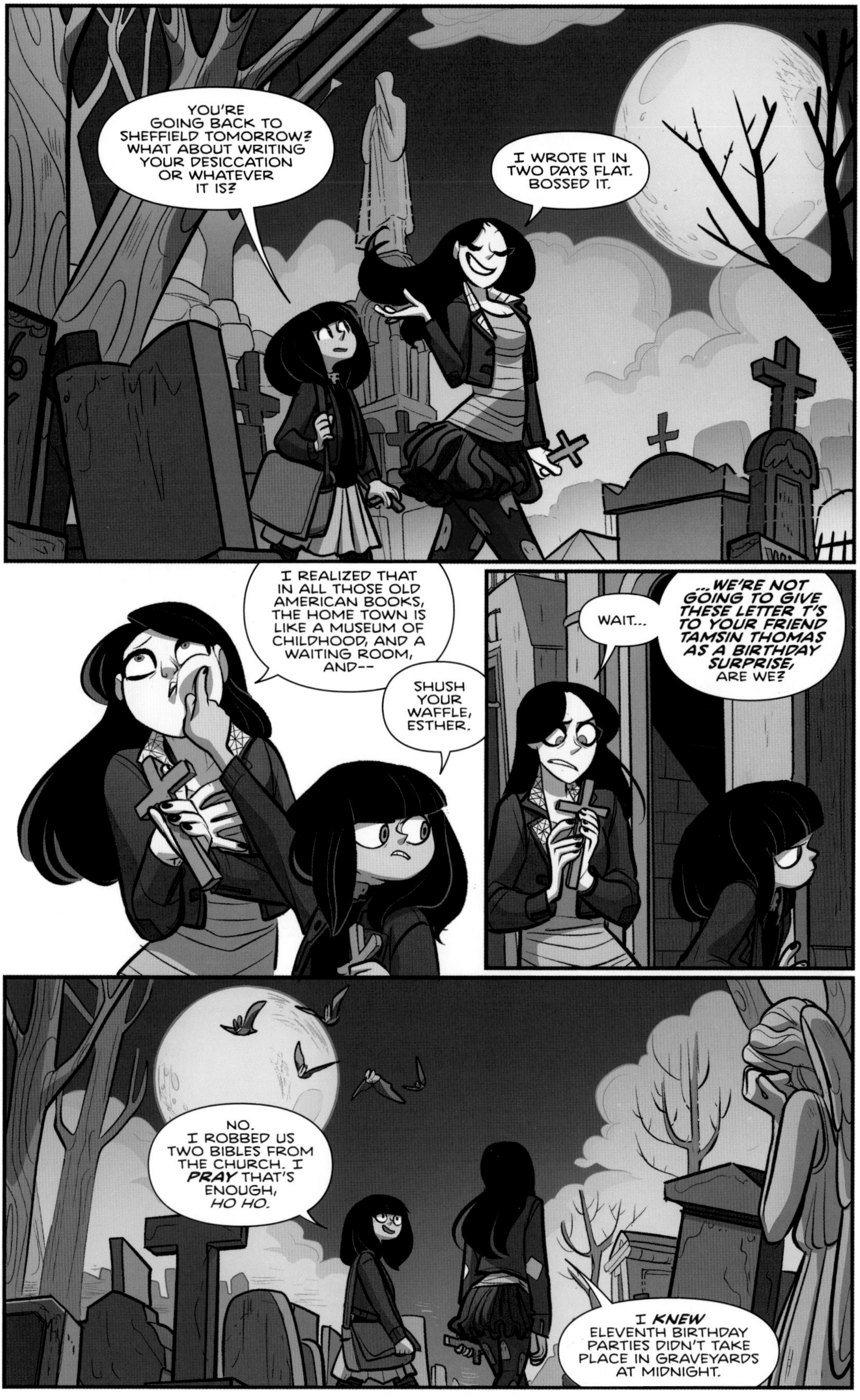
YOU'RE GOING BACK TO SHEFFIELD TOMORROW? WHAT ABOUT WRITING YOUR DESICCATION OR WHATEVER IT IS?
I WROTE IT IN TWO DAYS FLAT. BOSSED IT.
I REALIZED THAT IN ALL THOSE OLD AMERICAN BOOKS, THE HOME TOWN IS LIKE A MUSEUM OF CHILDHOOD, AND A WAITING ROOM, AND--
SHUSH YOUR WAFFLE, ESTHER.
WAIT...
...WE'RE NOT GOING TO GIVE THESE LETTER T'S TO YOUR FRIEND TAMSIN THOMAS AS A BIRTHDAY SURPRISE, ARE WE?
NO. I ROBBED US TWO BIBLES FROM THE CHURCH. I PRAY THAT'S ENOUGH, HO HO.
I KNEW ELEVENTH BIRTHDAY PARTIES DIDN'T TAKE PLACE IN GRAVEYARDS AT MIDNIGHT.

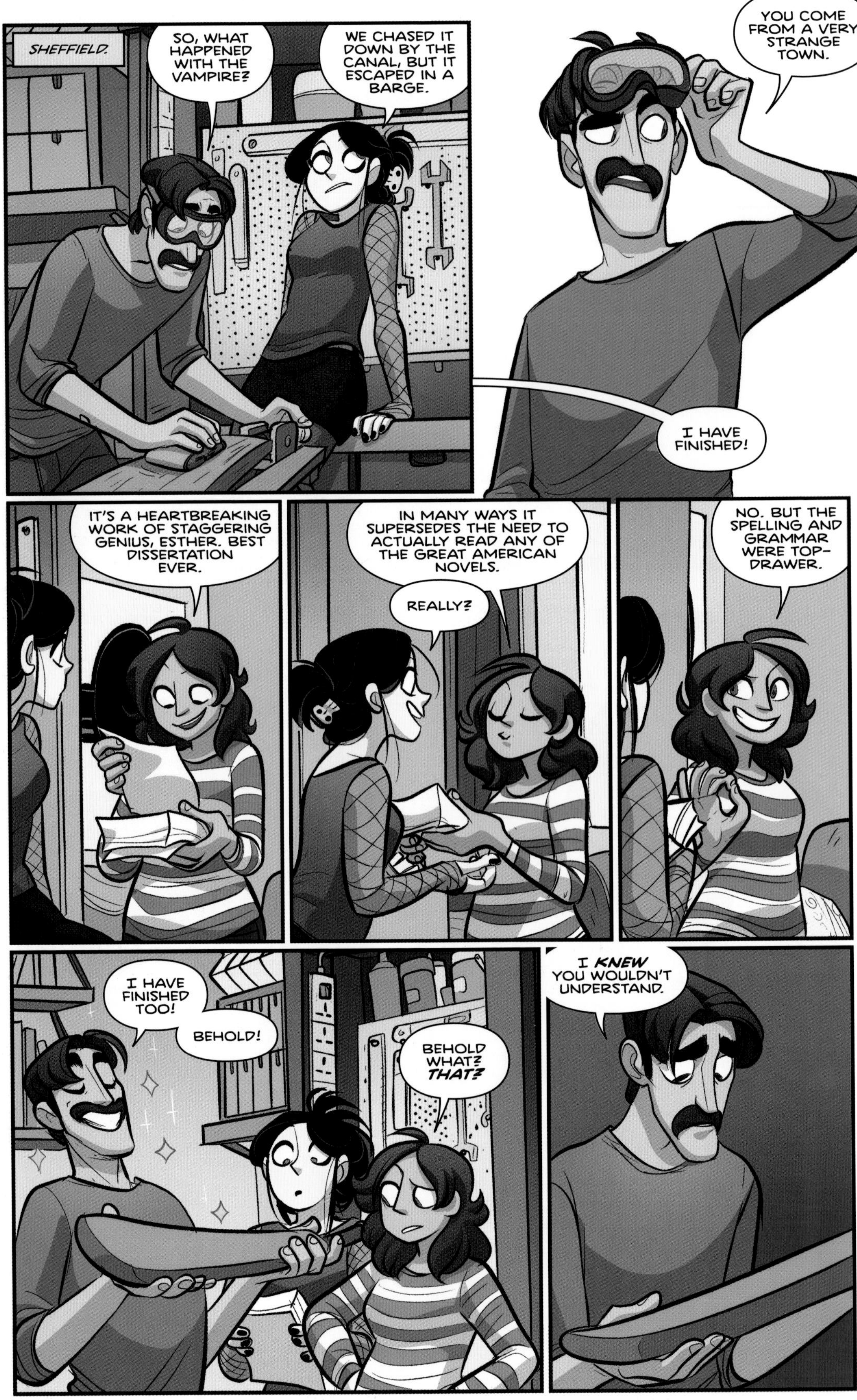
SHEFFIELD.
SO, WHAT HAPPENED WITH THE VAMPIRE?
WE CHASED IT DOWN BY THE CANAL, BUT IT ESCAPED IN A BARGE.
YOU COME FROM A VERY STRANGE TOWN.
I HAVE FINISHED!
IT'S A HEARTBREAKING WORK OF STAGGERING GENIUS, ESTHER. BEST DISSERTATION EVER.
IN MANY WAYS IT SUPERSEDES THE NEED TO ACTUALLY READ ANY OF THE GREAT AMERICAN NOVELS.
REALLY?
NO. BUT THE SPELLING AND GRAMMAR WERE TOP-DRAWER.
I HAVE FINISHED TOO!
BEHOLD!
BEHOLD WHAT? *THAT?*
I *KNEW* YOU WOULDN'T UNDERSTAND.

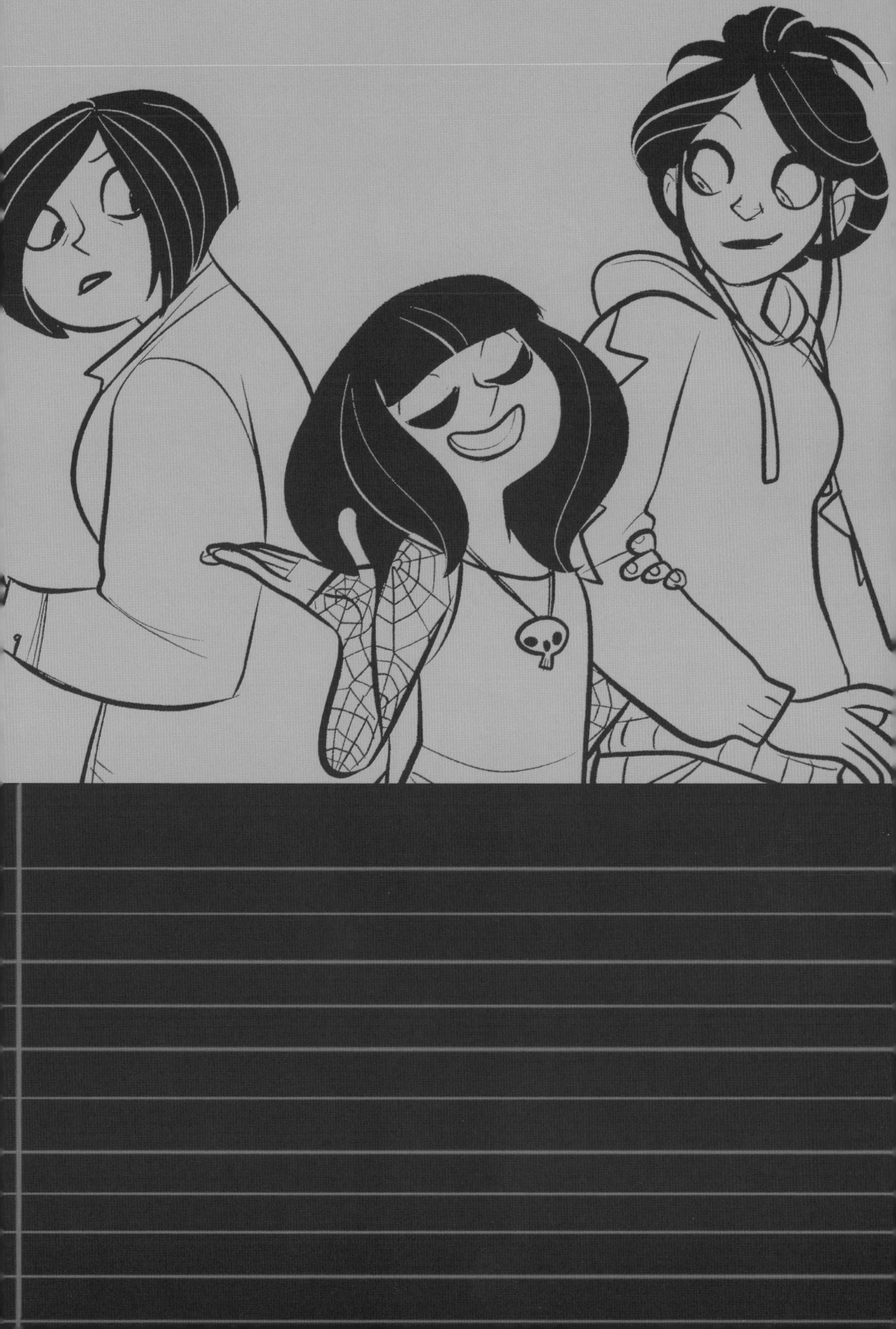

CHAPTER
FIFTY

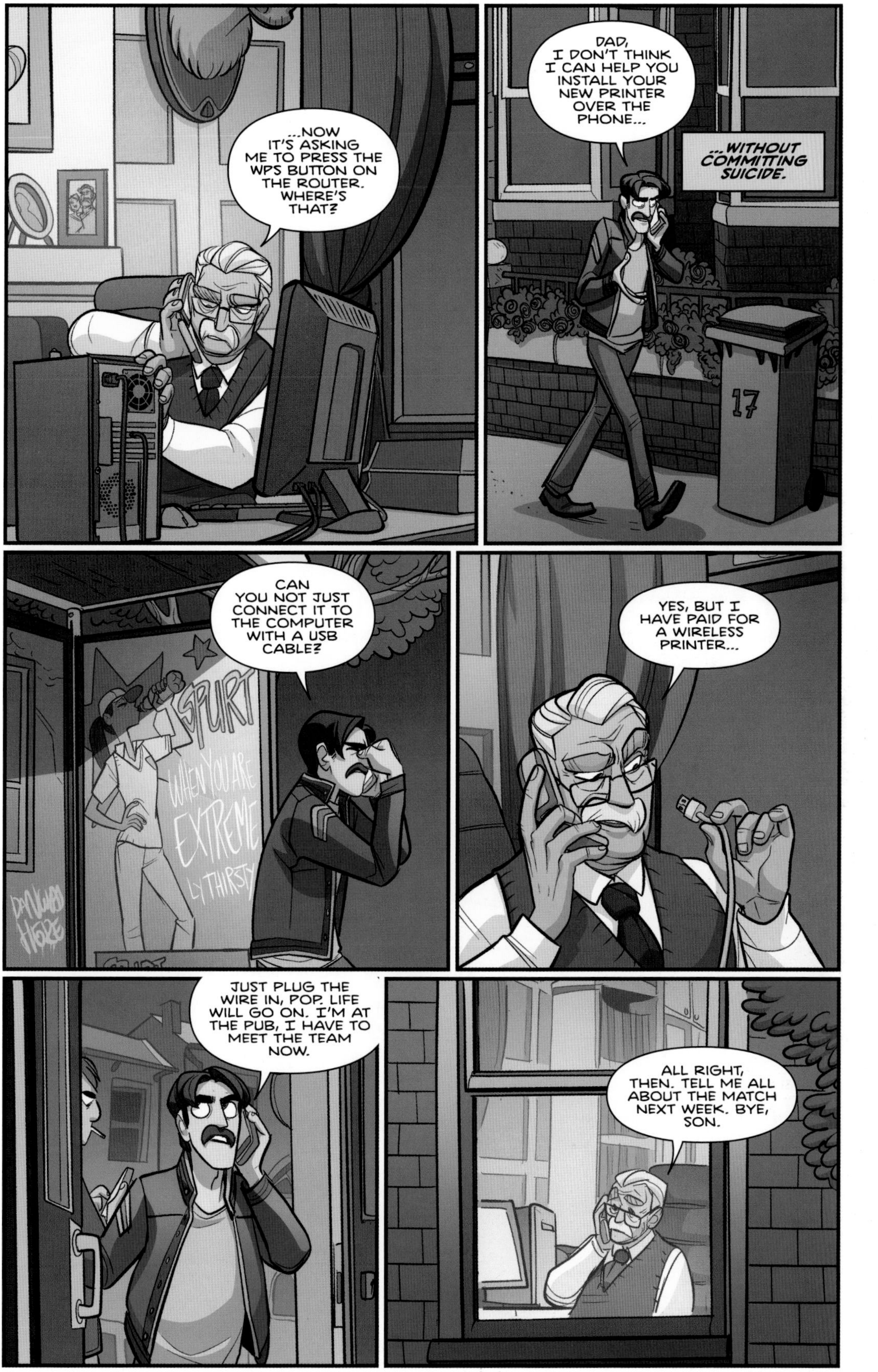
...NOW IT'S ASKING ME TO PRESS THE WPS BUTTON ON THE ROUTER. WHERE'S THAT?
DAD, I DON'T THINK I CAN HELP YOU INSTALL YOUR NEW PRINTER OVER THE PHONE...
...WITHOUT COMMITTING SUICIDE.
17
CAN YOU NOT JUST CONNECT IT TO THE COMPUTER WITH A USB CABLE?
SPURT
WHEN YOU ARE
EXTREME
LY THIRSTY
YES, BUT I HAVE PAID FOR A WIRELESS PRINTER...
JUST PLUG THE WIRE IN, POP. LIFE WILL GO ON. I'M AT THE PUB, I HAVE TO MEET THE TEAM NOW.
ALL RIGHT, THEN. TELL ME ALL ABOUT THE MATCH NEXT WEEK. BYE, SON.

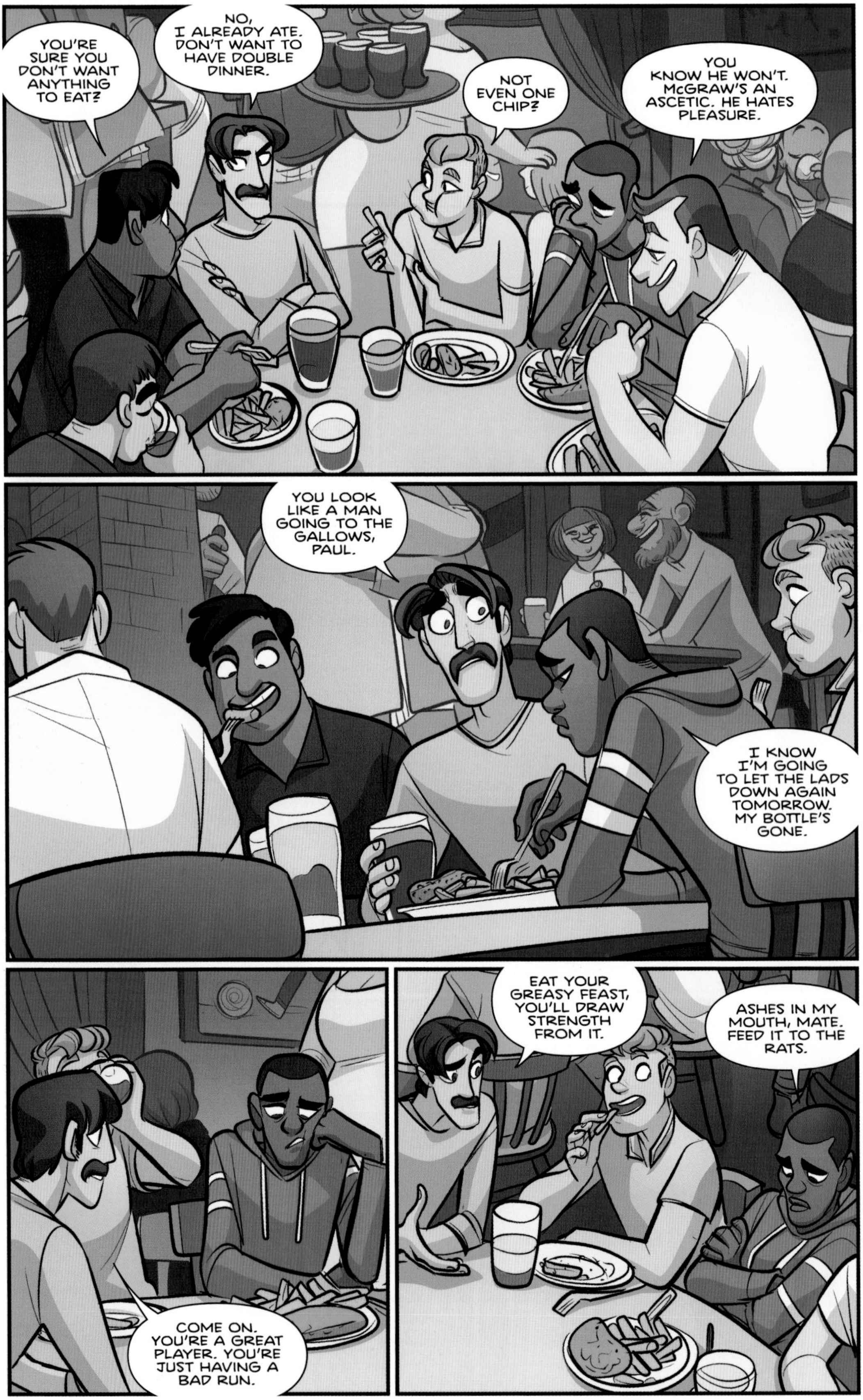
YOU'RE SURE YOU DON'T WANT ANYTHING TO EAT?
NO, I ALREADY ATE. DON'T WANT TO HAVE DOUBLE DINNER.
NOT EVEN ONE CHIP?
YOU KNOW HE WON'T. McGRAW'S AN ASCETIC. HE HATES PLEASURE.
YOU LOOK LIKE A MAN GOING TO THE GALLOWS, PAUL.
I KNOW I'M GOING TO LET THE LADS DOWN AGAIN TOMORROW. MY BOTTLE'S GONE.
COME ON. YOU'RE A GREAT PLAYER. YOU'RE JUST HAVING A BAD RUN.
EAT YOUR GREASY FEAST, YOU'LL DRAW STRENGTH FROM IT.
ASHES IN MY MOUTH, MATE. FEED IT TO THE RATS.

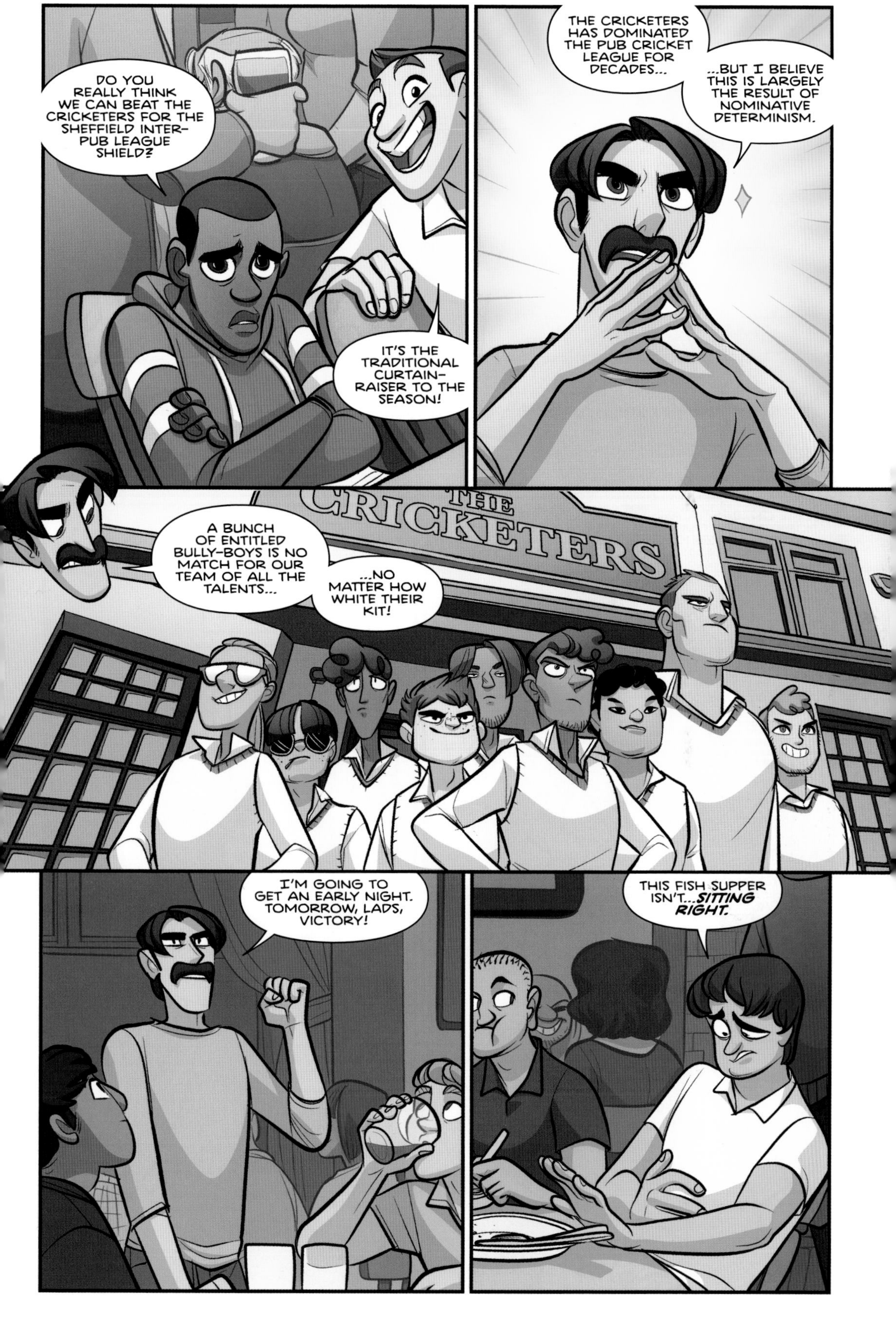
DO YOU REALLY THINK WE CAN BEAT THE CRICKETERS FOR THE SHEFFIELD INTER-PUB LEAGUE SHIELD?
IT'S THE TRADITIONAL CURTAIN-RAISER TO THE SEASON!
THE CRICKETERS HAS DOMINATED THE PUB CRICKET LEAGUE FOR DECADES...
...BUT I BELIEVE THIS IS LARGELY THE RESULT OF NOMINATIVE DETERMINISM.
THE CRICKETERS
A BUNCH OF ENTITLED BULLY-BOYS IS NO MATCH FOR OUR TEAM OF ALL THE TALENTS...
...NO MATTER HOW WHITE THEIR KIT!
I'M GOING TO GET AN EARLY NIGHT. TOMORROW, LADS, VICTORY!
THIS FISH SUPPER ISN'T...*SITTING RIGHT.*

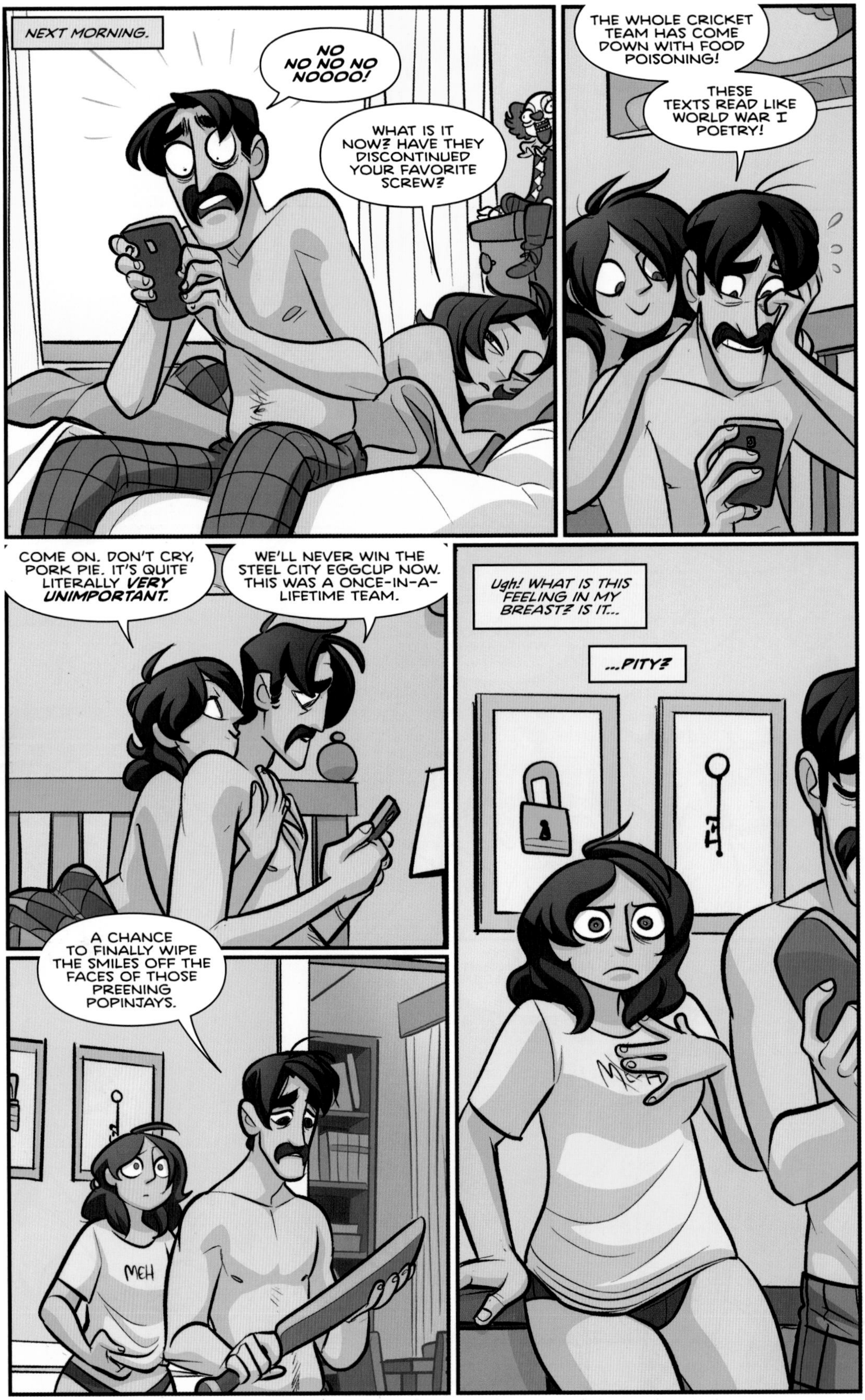
NEXT MORNING.
NO NO NO NO NOOOO!
WHAT IS IT NOW? HAVE THEY DISCONTINUED YOUR FAVORITE SCREW?
THE WHOLE CRICKET TEAM HAS COME DOWN WITH FOOD POISONING!
THESE TEXTS READ LIKE WORLD WAR I POETRY!
COME ON. DON'T CRY, PORK PIE. IT'S QUITE LITERALLY VERY UNIMPORTANT.
WE'LL NEVER WIN THE STEEL CITY EGGCUP NOW. THIS WAS A ONCE-IN-A-LIFETIME TEAM.
A CHANCE TO FINALLY WIPE THE SMILES OFF THE FACES OF THOSE PREENING POPINJAYS.
MEH
Ugh! WHAT IS THIS FEELING IN MY BREAST? IS IT...
...PITY?

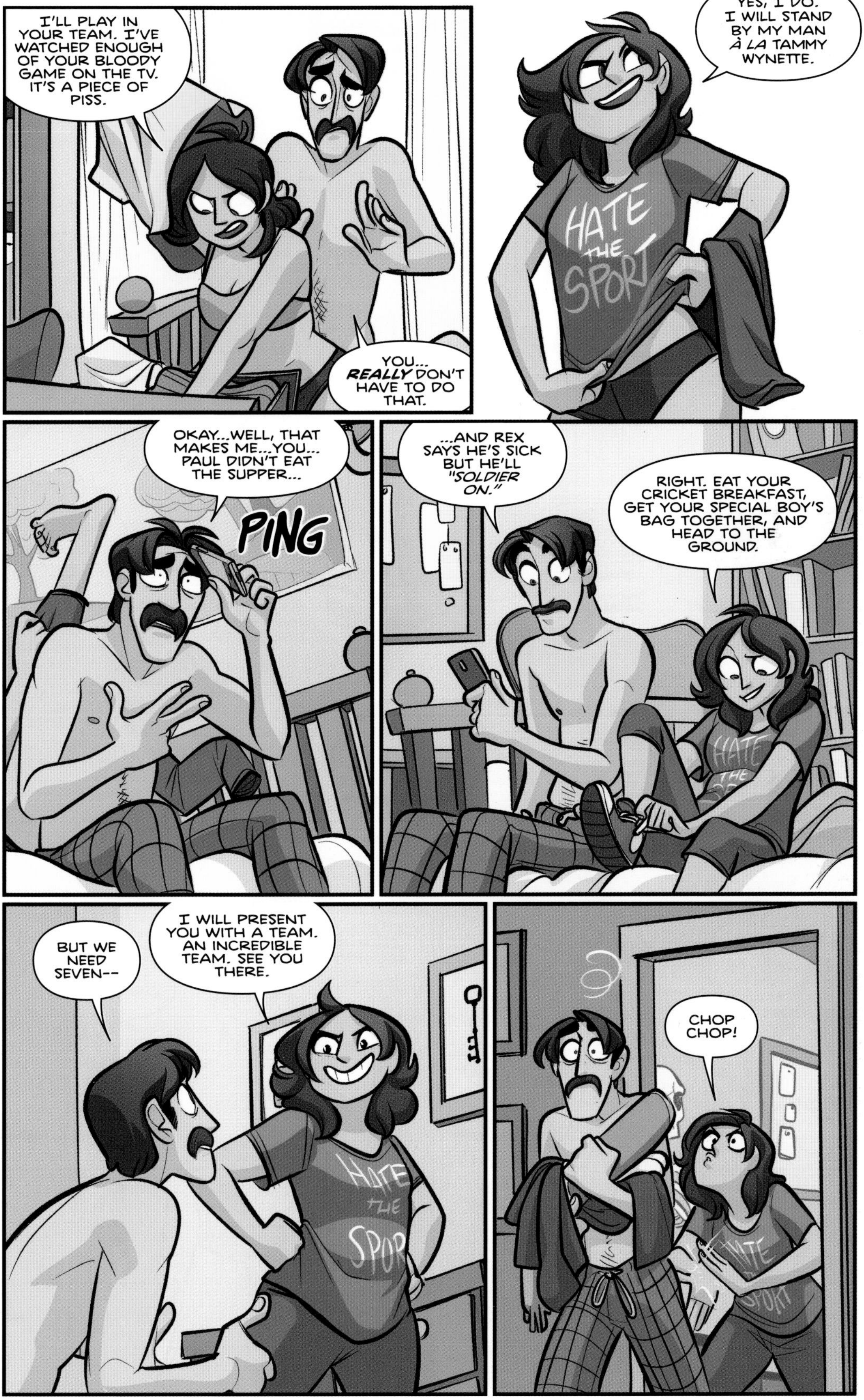
I'LL PLAY IN YOUR TEAM. I'VE WATCHED ENOUGH OF YOUR BLOODY GAME ON THE TV. IT'S A PIECE OF PISS.
YOU... **REALLY** DON'T HAVE TO DO THAT.
YES, I DO. I WILL STAND BY MY MAN *À LA* TAMMY WYNETTE.
HATE THE SPORT
OKAY...WELL, THAT MAKES ME...YOU... PAUL DIDN'T EAT THE SUPPER...
PING
...AND REX SAYS HE'S SICK BUT HE'LL *"SOLDIER ON."*
RIGHT. EAT YOUR CRICKET BREAKFAST, GET YOUR SPECIAL BOY'S BAG TOGETHER, AND HEAD TO THE GROUND.
BUT WE NEED SEVEN--
I WILL PRESENT YOU WITH A TEAM. AN INCREDIBLE TEAM. SEE YOU THERE.
CHOP CHOP!

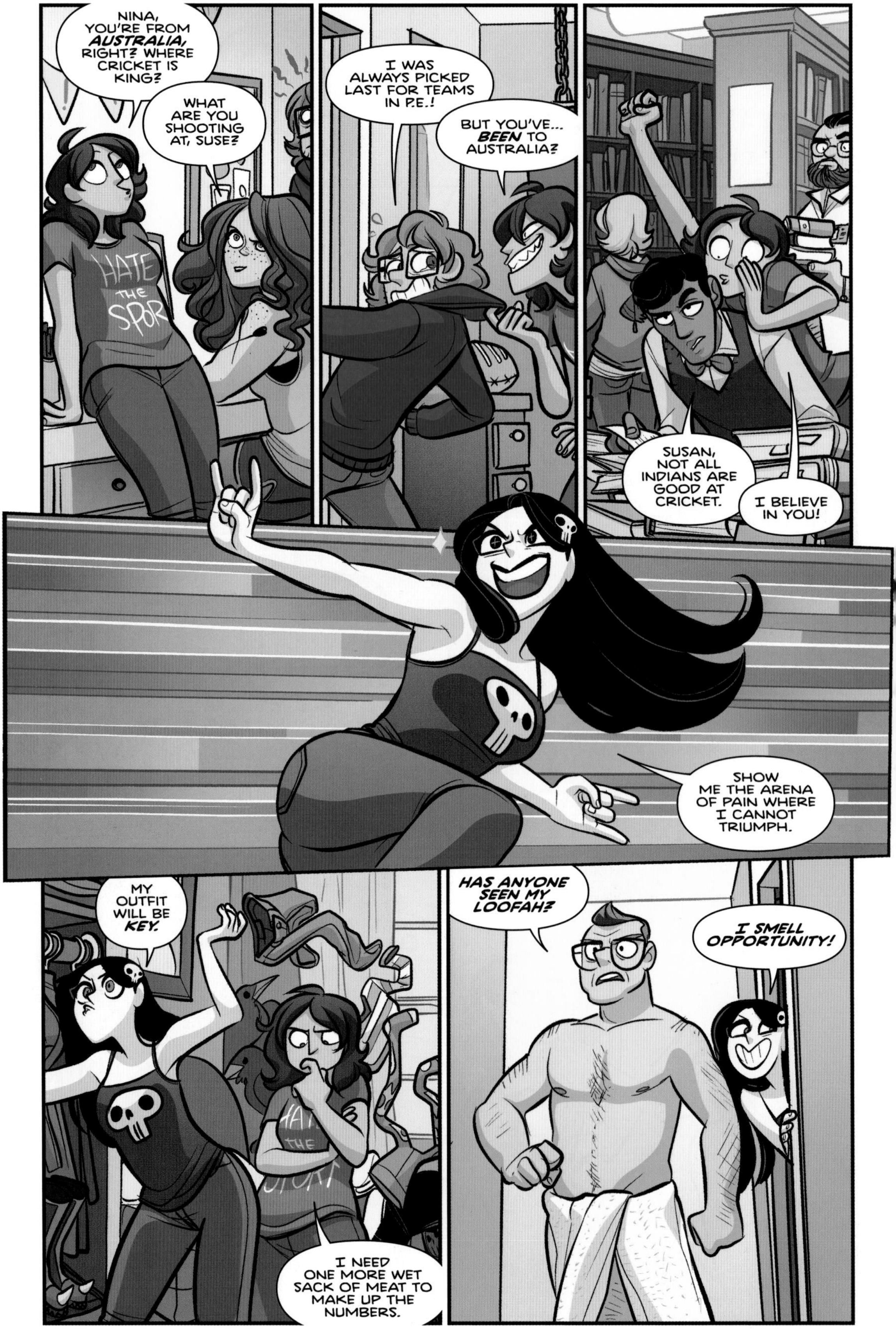
NINA, YOU'RE FROM AUSTRALIA, RIGHT? WHERE CRICKET IS KING?
WHAT ARE YOU SHOOTING AT, SUSE?
I WAS ALWAYS PICKED LAST FOR TEAMS IN P.E.!
BUT YOU'VE... BEEN TO AUSTRALIA?
SUSAN, NOT ALL INDIANS ARE GOOD AT CRICKET.
I BELIEVE IN YOU!
SHOW ME THE ARENA OF PAIN WHERE I CANNOT TRIUMPH.
MY OUTFIT WILL BE KEY.
I NEED ONE MORE WET SACK OF MEAT TO MAKE UP THE NUMBERS.
HAS ANYONE SEEN MY LOOFAH?
I SMELL OPPORTUNITY!

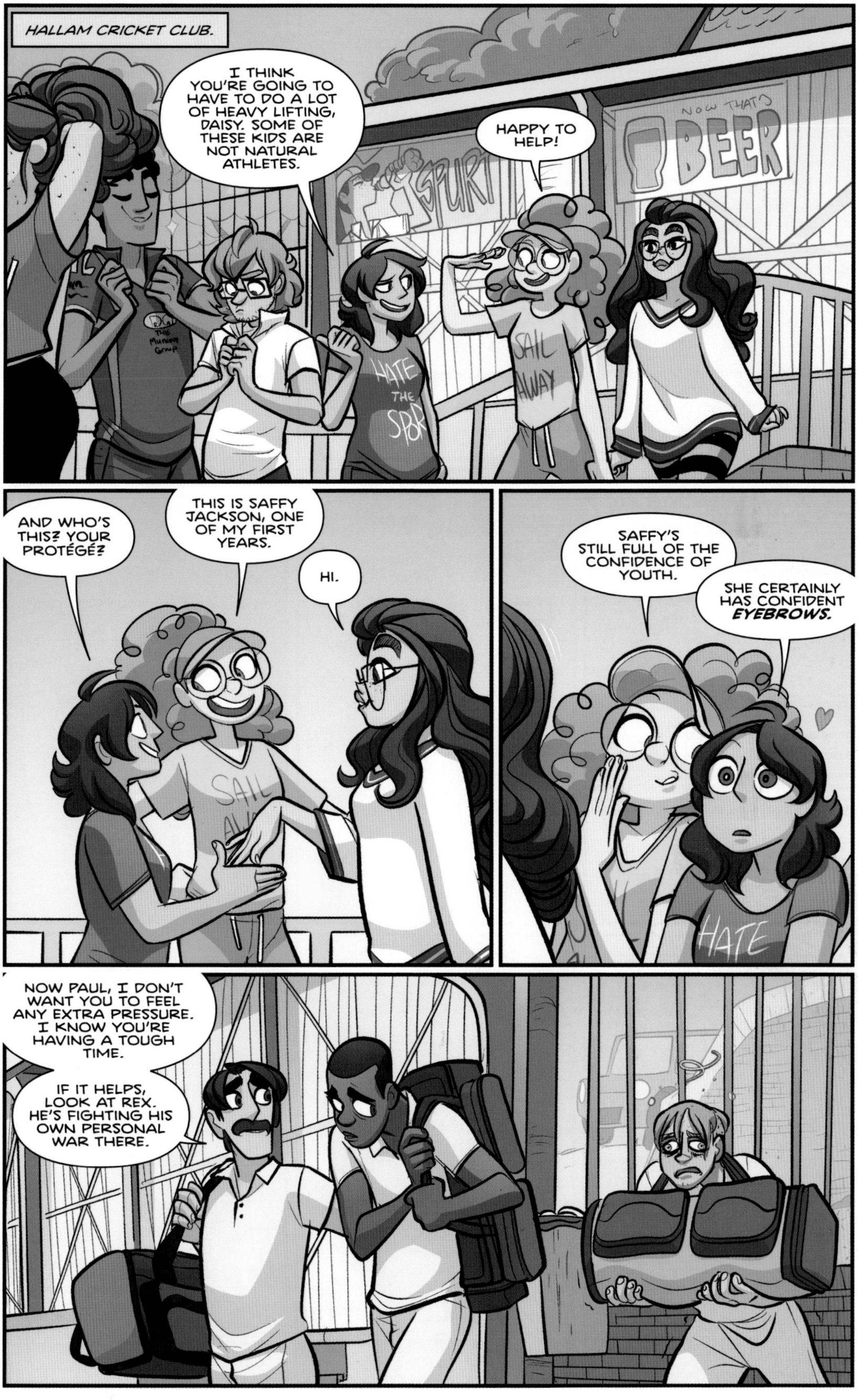
HALLAM CRICKET CLUB.
I THINK YOU'RE GOING TO HAVE TO DO A LOT OF HEAVY LIFTING, DAISY. SOME OF THESE KIDS ARE NOT NATURAL ATHLETES.
HAPPY TO HELP!
NOW THAT'S BEER
SPURT
HATE THE SPBR
SAIL AWAY
AND WHO'S THIS? YOUR PROTÉGÉ?
THIS IS SAFFY JACKSON, ONE OF MY FIRST YEARS.
HI.
SAFFY'S STILL FULL OF THE CONFIDENCE OF YOUTH.
SHE CERTAINLY HAS CONFIDENT ***EYEBROWS.***
HATE
NOW PAUL, I DON'T WANT YOU TO FEEL ANY EXTRA PRESSURE. I KNOW YOU'RE HAVING A TOUGH TIME.
IF IT HELPS, LOOK AT REX. HE'S FIGHTING HIS OWN PERSONAL WAR THERE.

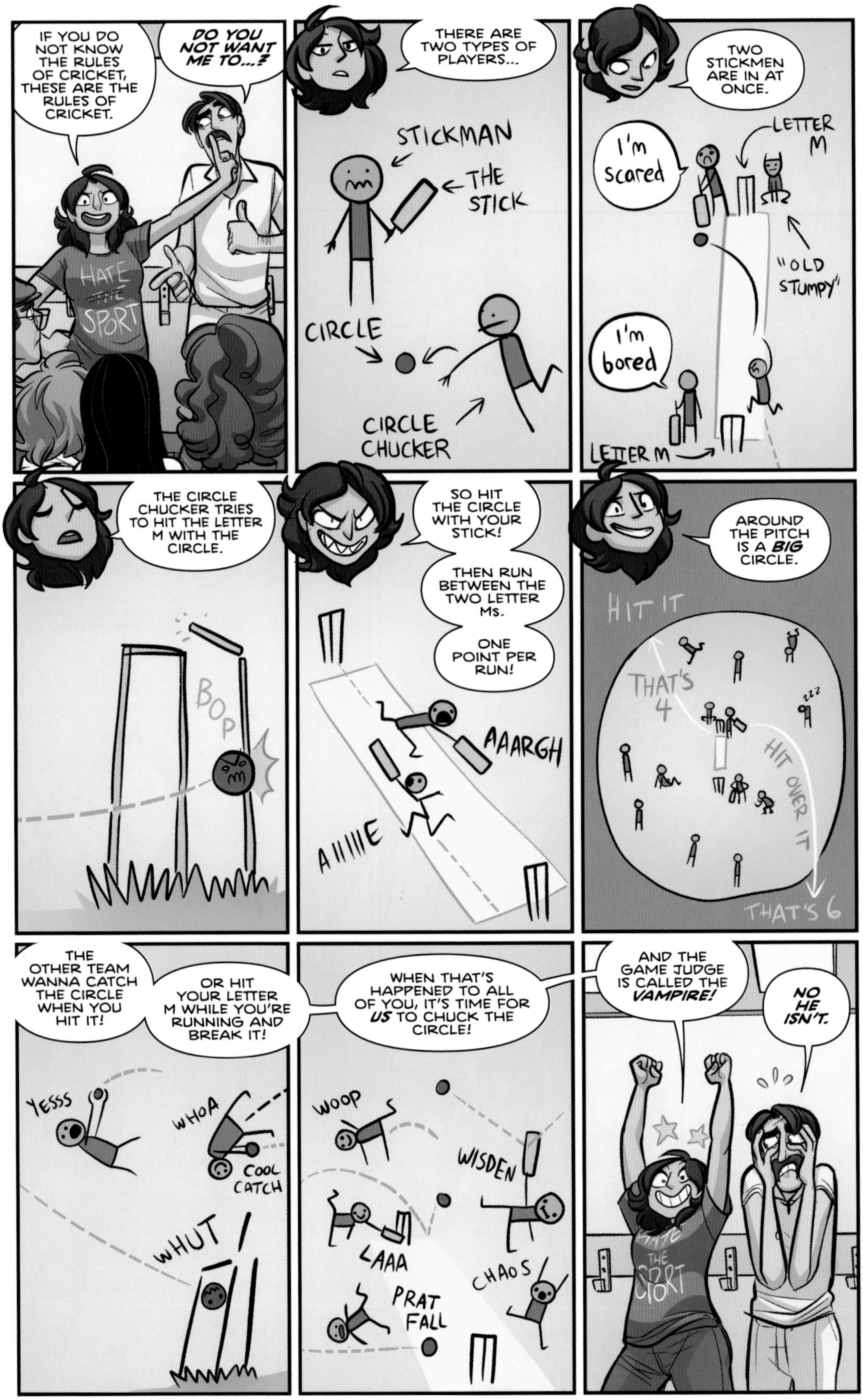
IF YOU DO NOT KNOW THE RULES OF CRICKET, THESE ARE THE RULES OF CRICKET.
DO YOU NOT WANT ME TO...?
HATE THE SPORT
THERE ARE TWO TYPES OF PLAYERS...
STICKMAN
THE STICK
CIRCLE
CIRCLE CHUCKER
TWO STICKMEN ARE IN AT ONCE.
LETTER M
I'm scared
"OLD STUMPY"
I'm bored
LETTER M
THE CIRCLE CHUCKER TRIES TO HIT THE LETTER M WITH THE CIRCLE.
BOP
SO HIT THE CIRCLE WITH YOUR STICK!
THEN RUN BETWEEN THE TWO LETTER Ms.
ONE POINT PER RUN!
AAARGH
AIIIIIE
AROUND THE PITCH IS A BIG CIRCLE.
HIT IT
THAT'S 4
HIT OVER IT
THAT'S 6
THE OTHER TEAM WANNA CATCH THE CIRCLE WHEN YOU HIT IT!
OR HIT YOUR LETTER M WHILE YOU'RE RUNNING AND BREAK IT!
YESSS
WHOA
COOL CATCH
WHUT
WHEN THAT'S HAPPENED TO ALL OF YOU, IT'S TIME FOR US TO CHUCK THE CIRCLE!
WOOP
WISDEN
LAAA
CHAOS
PRAT FALL
AND THE GAME JUDGE IS CALLED THE VAMPIRE!
NO HE ISN'T.
HATE THE SPORT

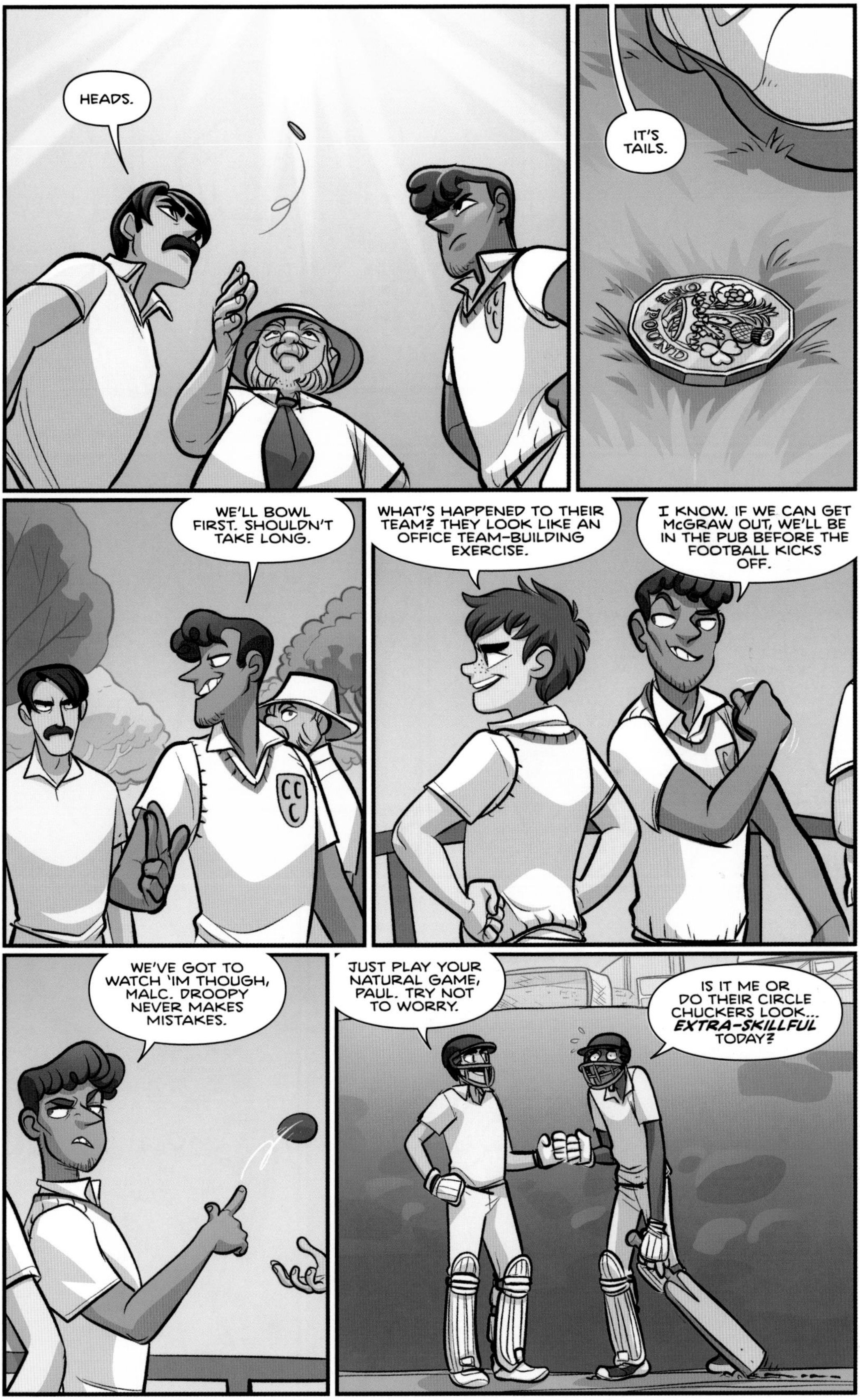
HEADS.
IT'S TAILS.
WE'LL BOWL FIRST. SHOULDN'T TAKE LONG.
WHAT'S HAPPENED TO THEIR TEAM? THEY LOOK LIKE AN OFFICE TEAM-BUILDING EXERCISE.
I KNOW. IF WE CAN GET McGRAW OUT, WE'LL BE IN THE PUB BEFORE THE FOOTBALL KICKS OFF.
WE'VE GOT TO WATCH 'IM THOUGH, MALC. DROOPY NEVER MAKES MISTAKES.
JUST PLAY YOUR NATURAL GAME, PAUL. TRY NOT TO WORRY.
IS IT ME OR DO THEIR CIRCLE CHUCKERS LOOK... *EXTRA-SKILLFUL* TODAY?

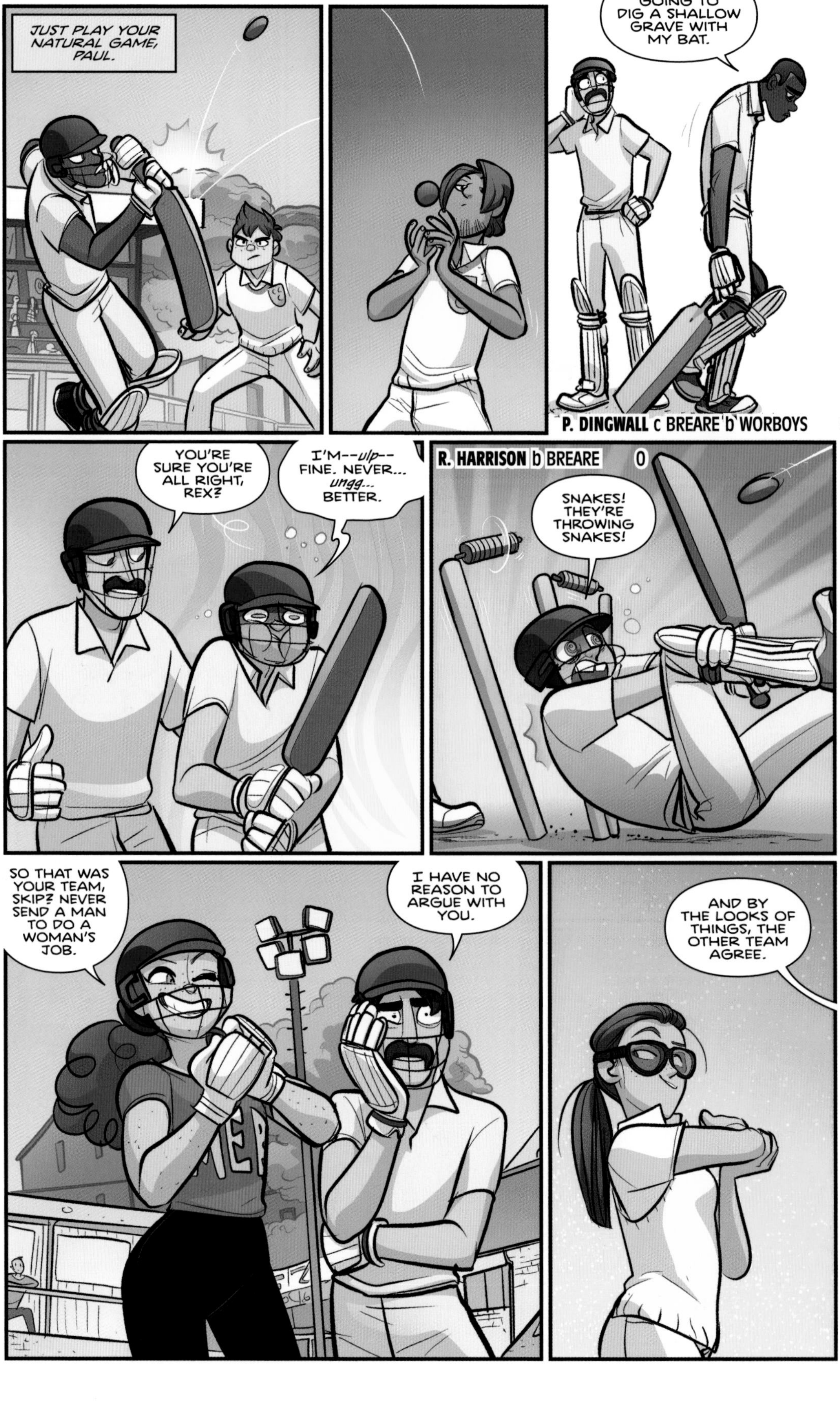
JUST PLAY YOUR NATURAL GAME, PAUL.
I'M GOING TO DIG A SHALLOW GRAVE WITH MY BAT.
P. DINGWALL c BREARE b WORBOYS 0
YOU'RE SURE YOU'RE ALL RIGHT, REX?
I'M--ulp--FINE. NEVER... ungg... BETTER.
R. HARRISON b BREARE 0
SNAKES! THEY'RE THROWING SNAKES!
SO THAT WAS YOUR TEAM, SKIP? NEVER SEND A MAN TO DO A WOMAN'S JOB.
I HAVE NO REASON TO ARGUE WITH YOU.
AND BY THE LOOKS OF THINGS, THE OTHER TEAM AGREE.

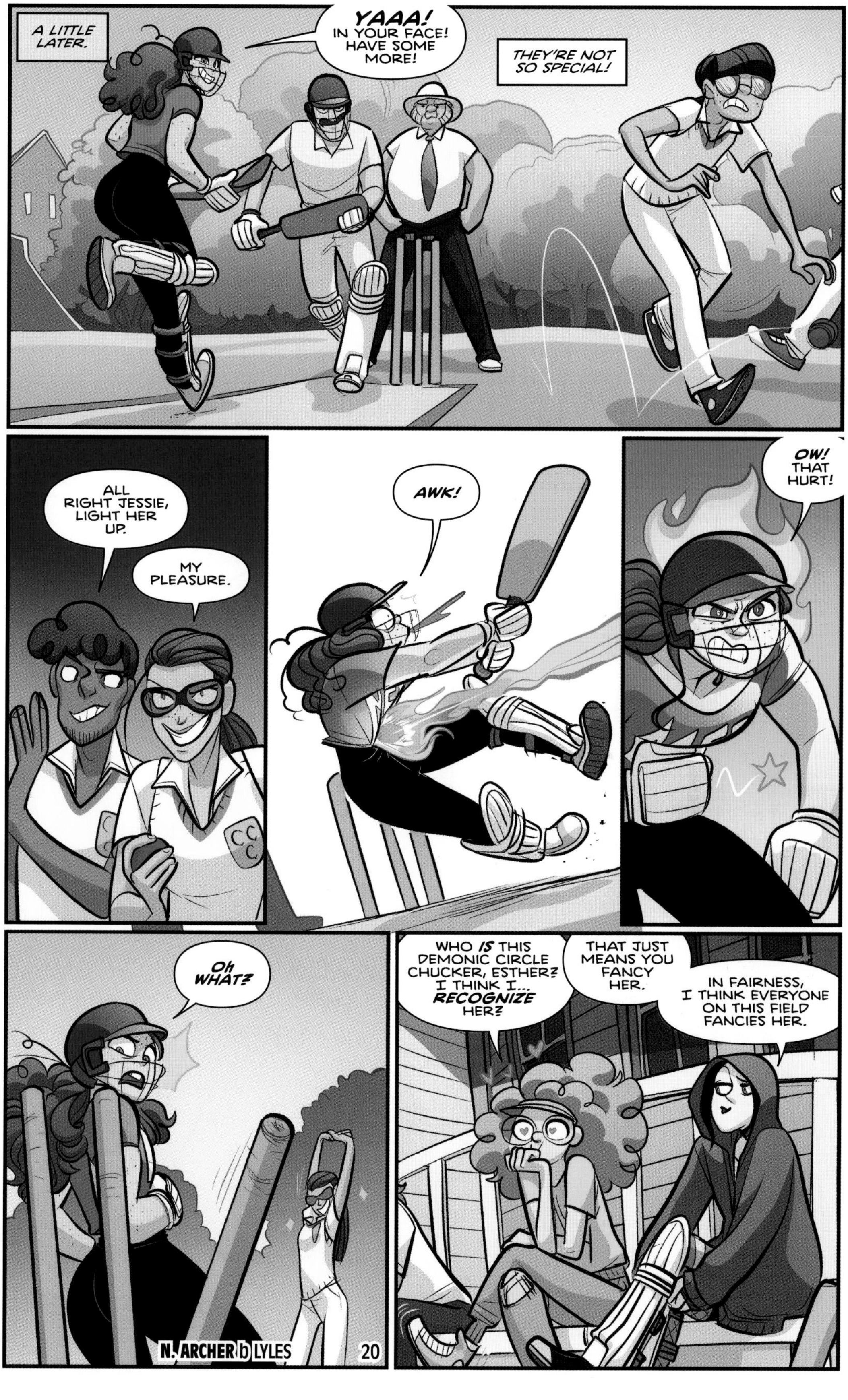
A LITTLE LATER.
YAAA! IN YOUR FACE! HAVE SOME MORE!
THEY'RE NOT SO SPECIAL!
ALL RIGHT JESSIE, LIGHT HER UP.
MY PLEASURE.
AWK!
OW! THAT HURT!
Oh WHAT?
WHO IS THIS DEMONIC CIRCLE CHUCKER, ESTHER? I THINK I... RECOGNIZE HER?
THAT JUST MEANS YOU FANCY HER.
IN FAIRNESS, I THINK EVERYONE ON THIS FIELD FANCIES HER.

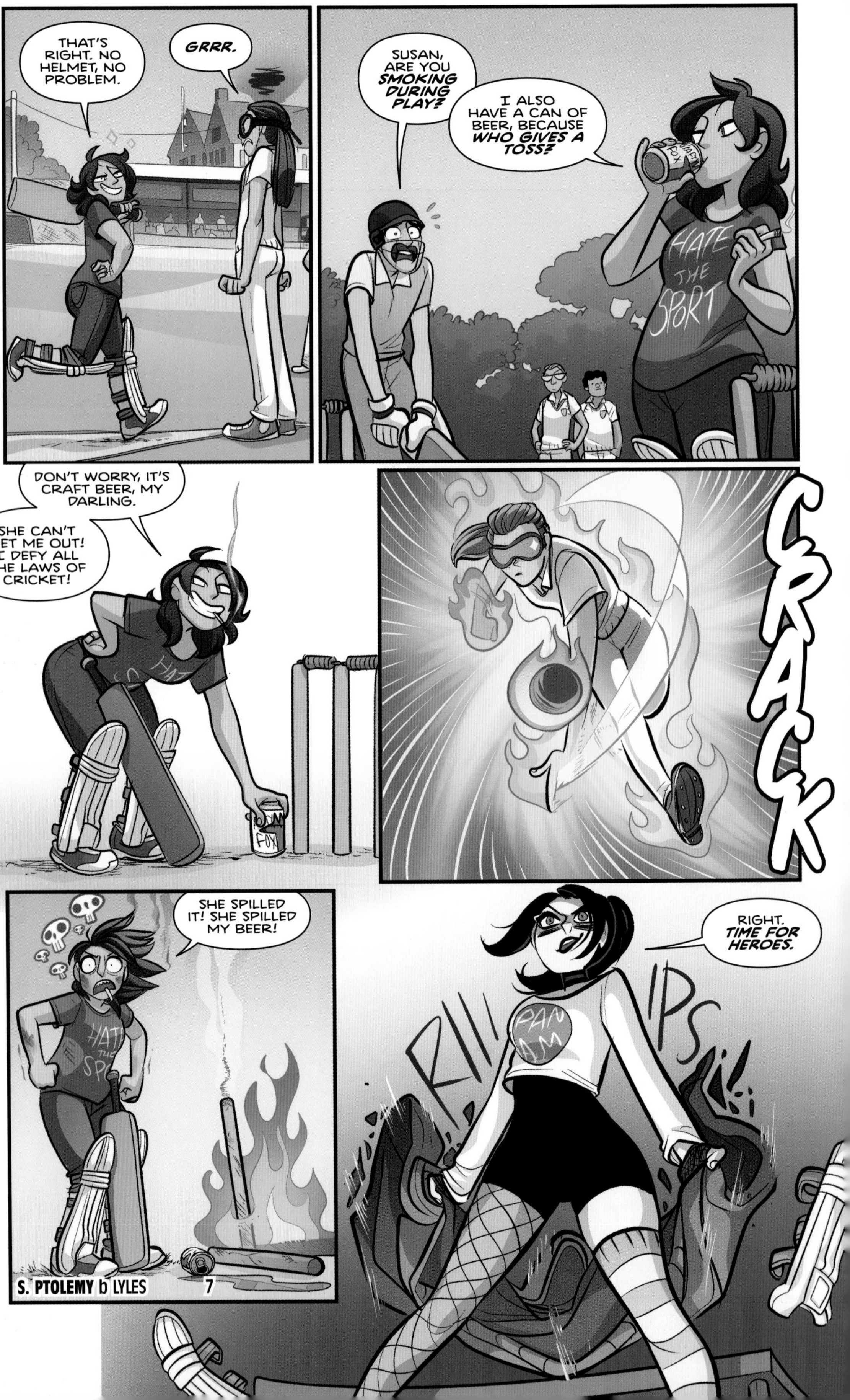
THAT'S RIGHT. NO HELMET, NO PROBLEM.
GRRR.
SUSAN, ARE YOU SMOKING DURING PLAY?
I ALSO HAVE A CAN OF BEER, BECAUSE WHO GIVES A TOSS?
HATE THE SPORT
DON'T WORRY, IT'S CRAFT BEER, MY DARLING.
SHE CAN'T GET ME OUT! I DEFY ALL THE LAWS OF CRICKET!
CRACK
SHE SPILLED IT! SHE SPILLED MY BEER!
RIGHT. TIME FOR HEROES.
PAN AM
S. PTOLEMY b LYLES

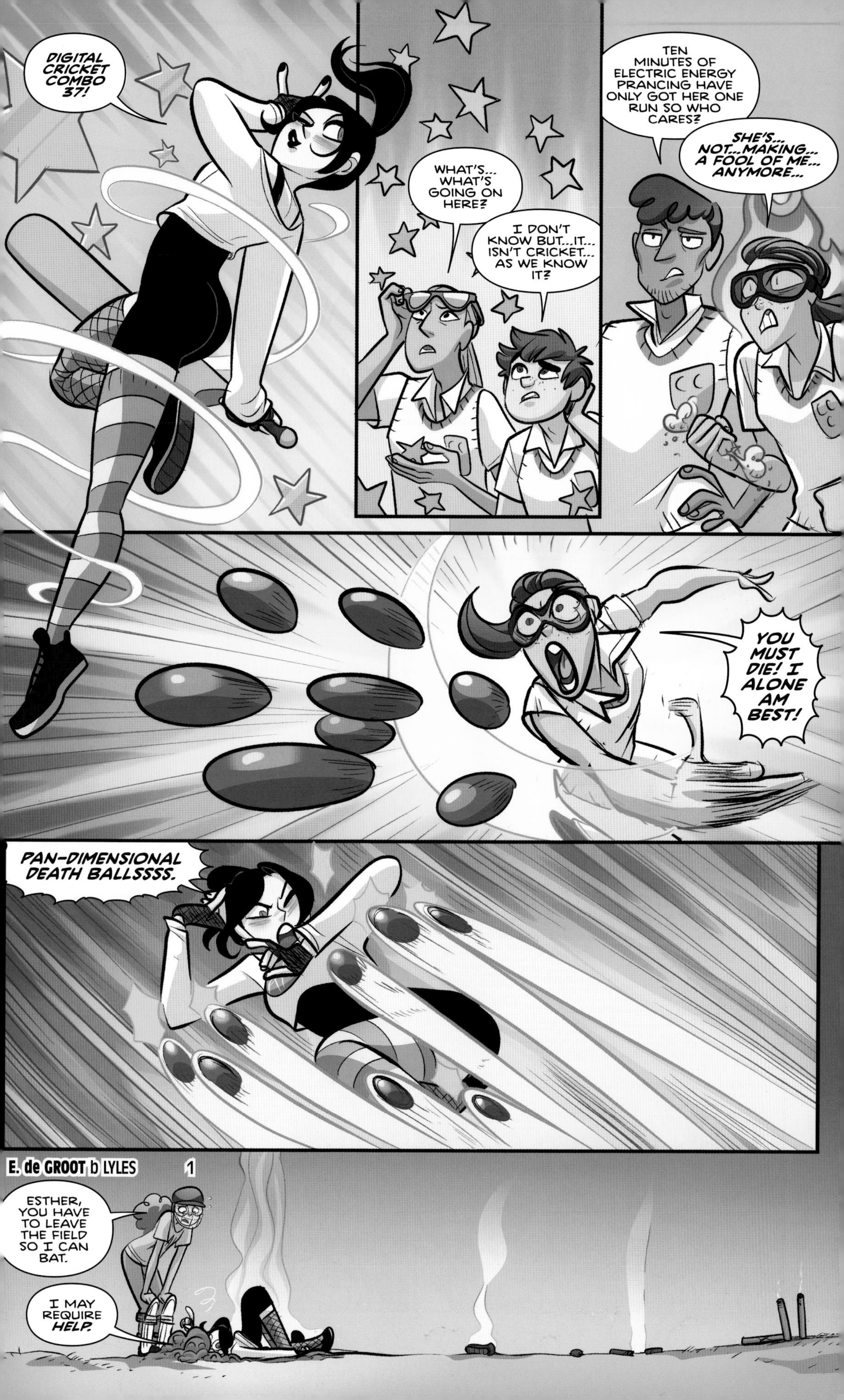
DIGITAL CRICKET COMBO 37!
WHAT'S... WHAT'S GOING ON HERE?
I DON'T KNOW BUT...IT... ISN'T CRICKET... AS WE KNOW IT?
TEN MINUTES OF ELECTRIC ENERGY PRANCING HAVE ONLY GOT HER ONE RUN SO WHO CARES?
SHE'S... NOT...MAKING... A FOOL OF ME... ANYMORE...
YOU MUST DIE! I ALONE AM BEST!
PAN-DIMENSIONAL DEATH BALLSSSS.
E. de GROOT b LYLES 1
ESTHER, YOU HAVE TO LEAVE THE FIELD SO I CAN BAT.
I MAY REQUIRE HELP.

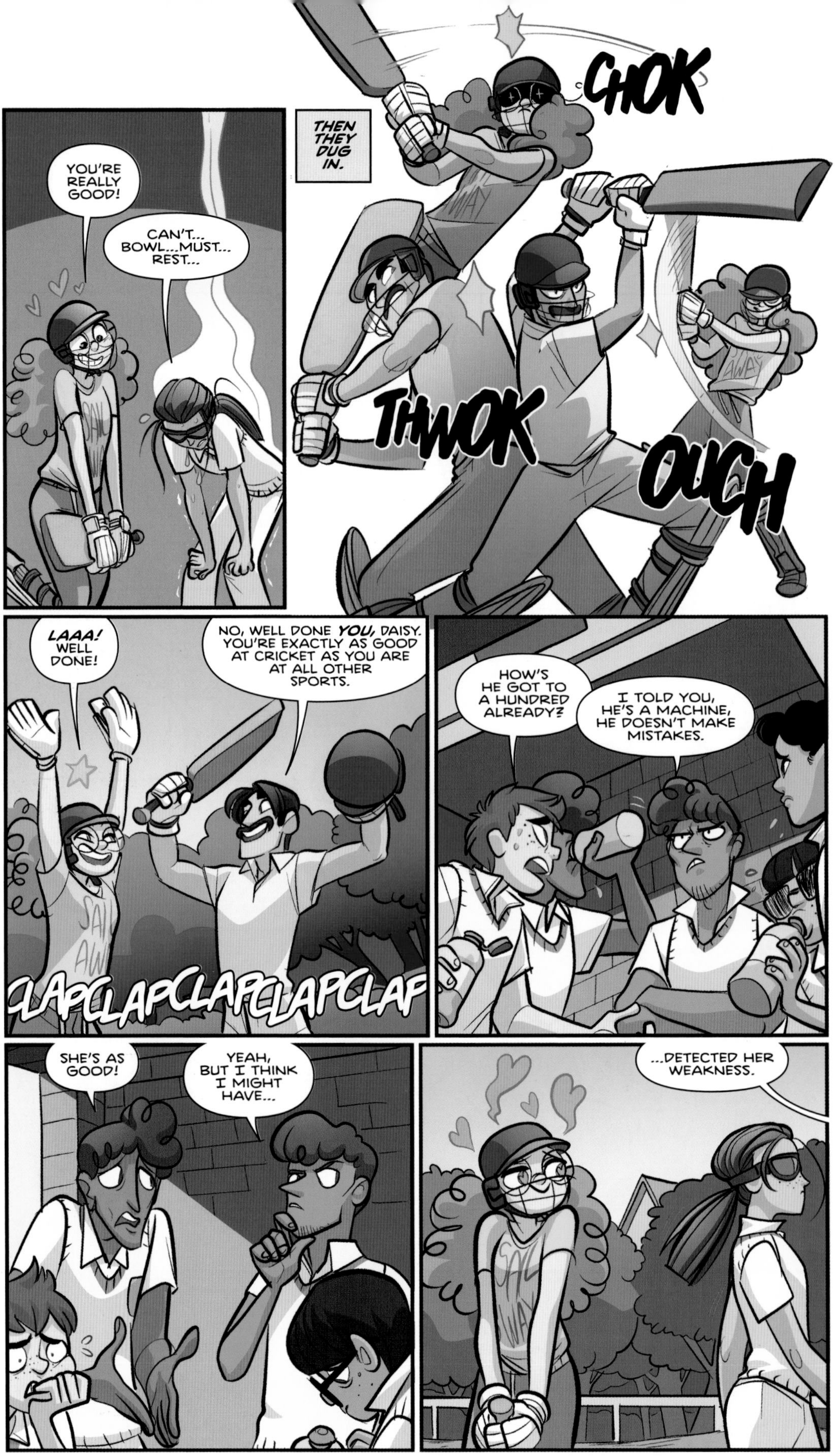
YOU'RE REALLY GOOD!
CAN'T... BOWL...MUST... REST...
THEN THEY DUG IN.
CHOK
THWOK
OUCH
LAAA! WELL DONE!
NO, WELL DONE YOU, DAISY. YOU'RE EXACTLY AS GOOD AT CRICKET AS YOU ARE AT ALL OTHER SPORTS.
CLAPCLAPCLAPCLAPCLAP
HOW'S HE GOT TO A HUNDRED ALREADY?
I TOLD YOU, HE'S A MACHINE, HE DOESN'T MAKE MISTAKES.
SHE'S AS GOOD!
YEAH, BUT I THINK I MIGHT HAVE...
...DETECTED HER WEAKNESS.

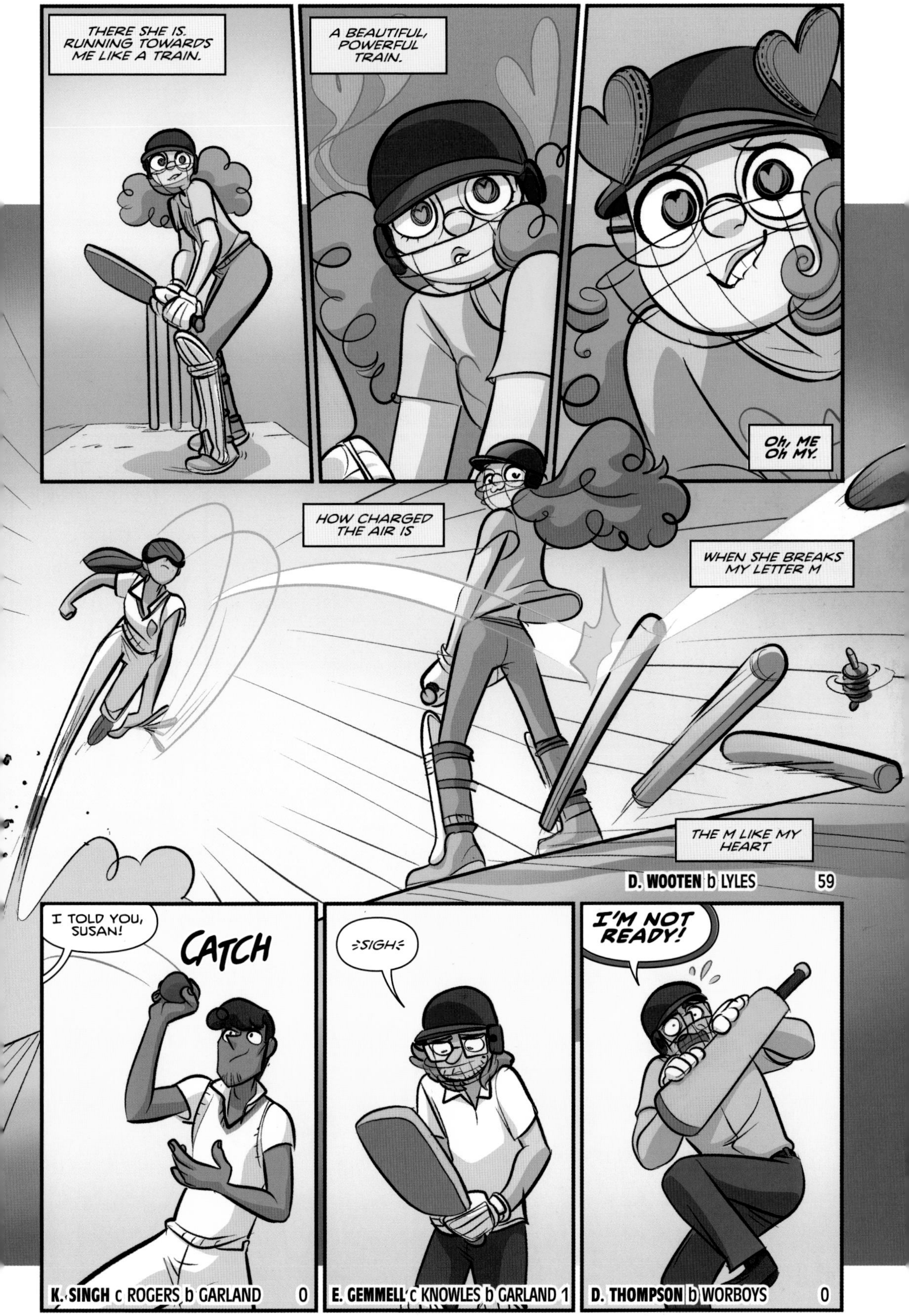
THERE SHE IS. RUNNING TOWARDS ME LIKE A TRAIN.
A BEAUTIFUL, POWERFUL TRAIN.
Oh, ME Oh MY.
HOW CHARGED THE AIR IS
WHEN SHE BREAKS MY LETTER M
THE M LIKE MY HEART
D. WOOTEN b LYLES 59
I TOLD YOU, SUSAN!
CATCH
K. SINGH c ROGERS b GARLAND 0
SIGH
E. GEMMELL c KNOWLES b GARLAND 1
I'M NOT READY!
D. THOMPSON b WORBOYS 0

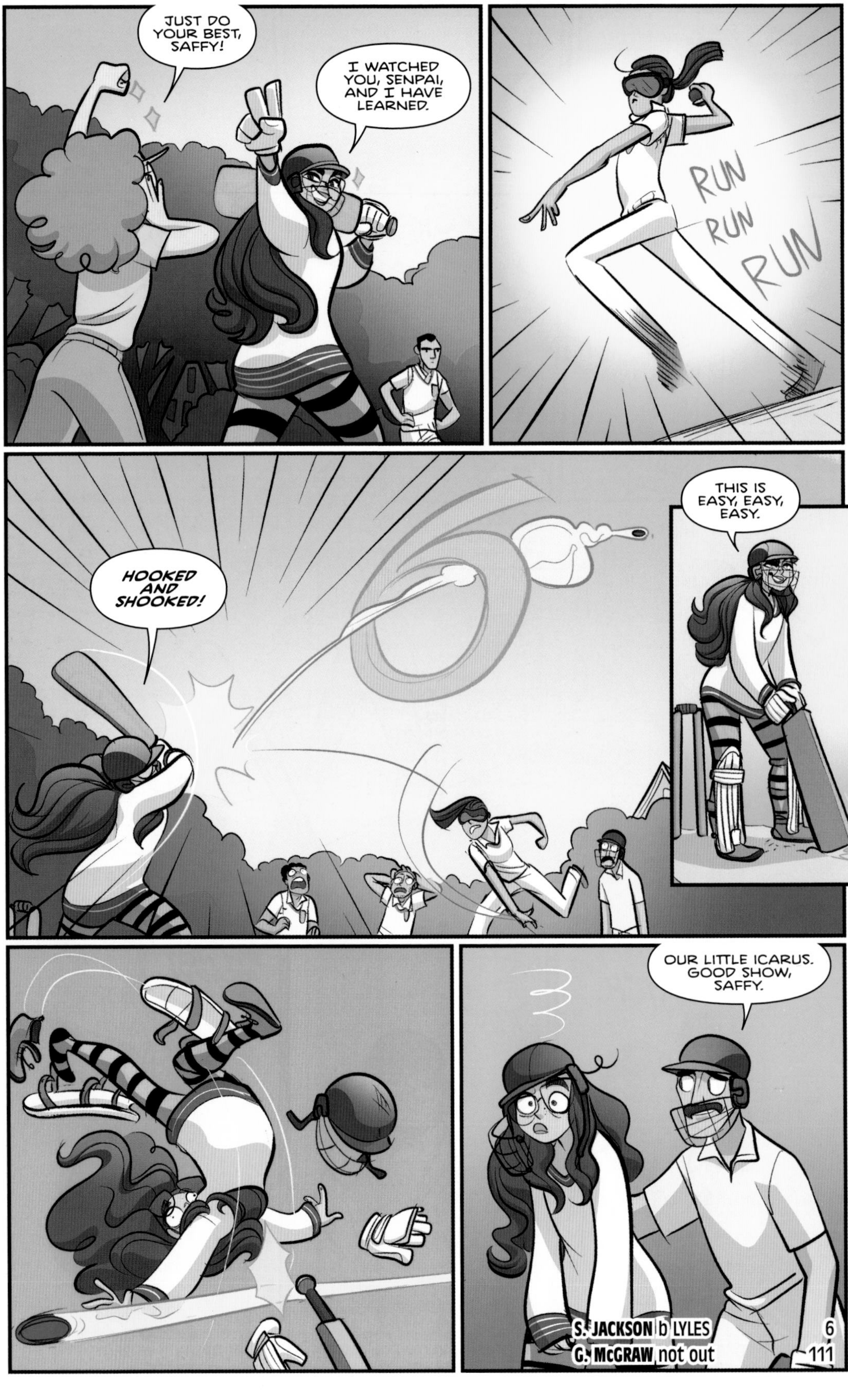
JUST DO YOUR BEST, SAFFY!
I WATCHED YOU, SENPAI, AND I HAVE LEARNED.
RUN
RUN
RUN
HOOKED AND SHOOKED!
THIS IS EASY, EASY, EASY.
OUR LITTLE ICARUS. GOOD SHOW, SAFFY.
S. JACKSON b LYLES 6
G. McGRAW not out 111

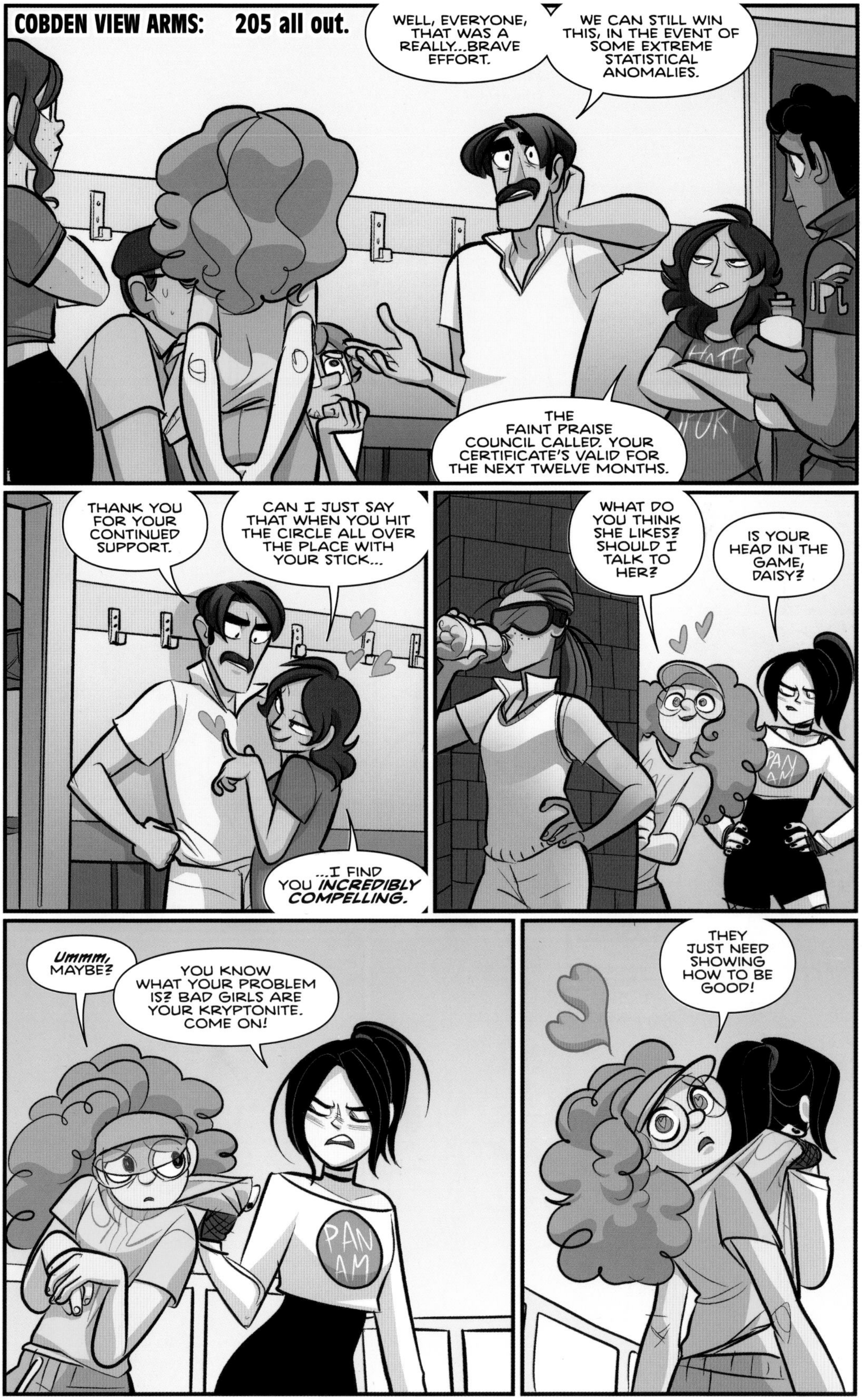
COBDEN VIEW ARMS: 205 all out.
WELL, EVERYONE, THAT WAS A REALLY...BRAVE EFFORT.
WE CAN STILL WIN THIS, IN THE EVENT OF SOME EXTREME STATISTICAL ANOMALIES.
THE FAINT PRAISE COUNCIL CALLED. YOUR CERTIFICATE'S VALID FOR THE NEXT TWELVE MONTHS.
THANK YOU FOR YOUR CONTINUED SUPPORT.
CAN I JUST SAY THAT WHEN YOU HIT THE CIRCLE ALL OVER THE PLACE WITH YOUR STICK...
...I FIND YOU *INCREDIBLY COMPELLING.*
WHAT DO YOU THINK SHE LIKES? SHOULD I TALK TO HER?
IS YOUR HEAD IN THE GAME, DAISY?
Ummm, MAYBE?
YOU KNOW WHAT YOUR PROBLEM IS? BAD GIRLS ARE YOUR KRYPTONITE. COME ON!
THEY JUST NEED SHOWING HOW TO BE GOOD!

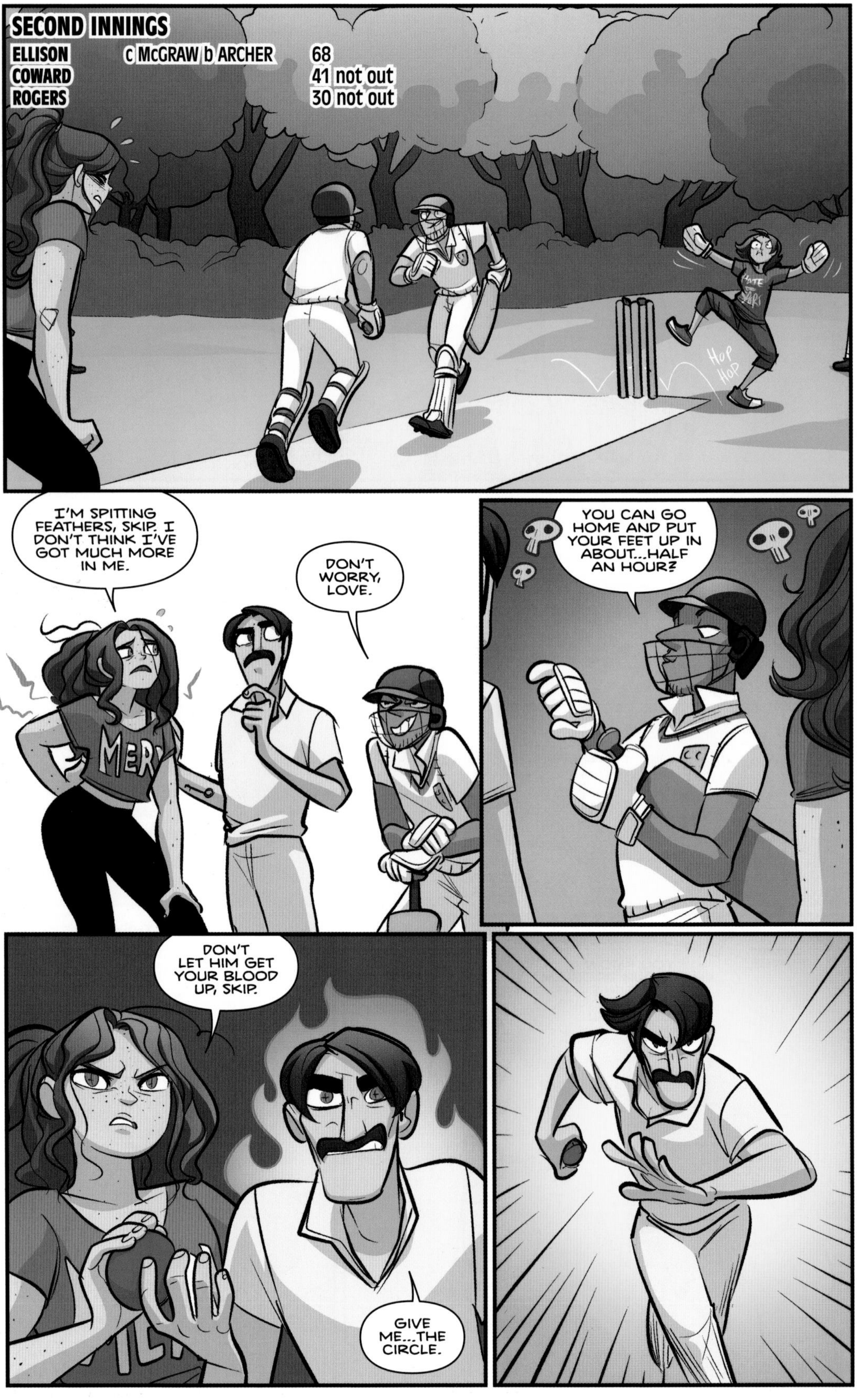
SECOND INNINGS
ELLISON c McGRAW b ARCHER 68
COWARD 41 not out
ROGERS 30 not out
HOP HOP
I'M SPITTING FEATHERS, SKIP. I DON'T THINK I'VE GOT MUCH MORE IN ME.
DON'T WORRY, LOVE.
YOU CAN GO HOME AND PUT YOUR FEET UP IN ABOUT...HALF AN HOUR?
DON'T LET HIM GET YOUR BLOOD UP, SKIP.
GIVE ME...THE CIRCLE.

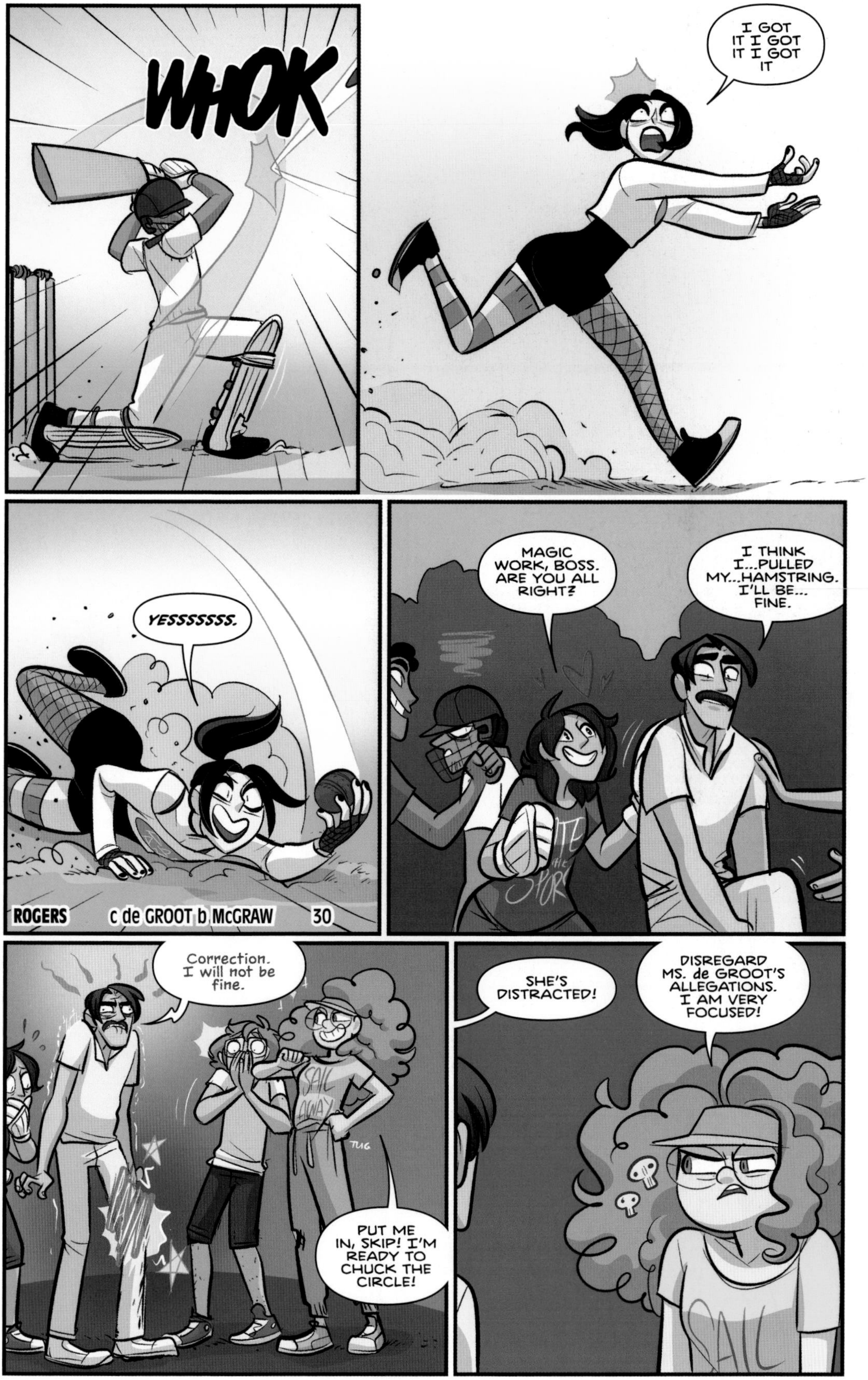
WHOK
I GOT IT I GOT IT I GOT IT
YESSSSSSS.
ROGERS c de GROOT b McGRAW 30
MAGIC WORK, BOSS. ARE YOU ALL RIGHT?
I THINK I...PULLED MY...HAMSTRING. I'LL BE... FINE.
Correction. I will not be fine.
TUG
PUT ME IN, SKIP! I'M READY TO CHUCK THE CIRCLE!
SHE'S DISTRACTED!
DISREGARD MS. de GROOT'S ALLEGATIONS. I AM VERY FOCUSED!

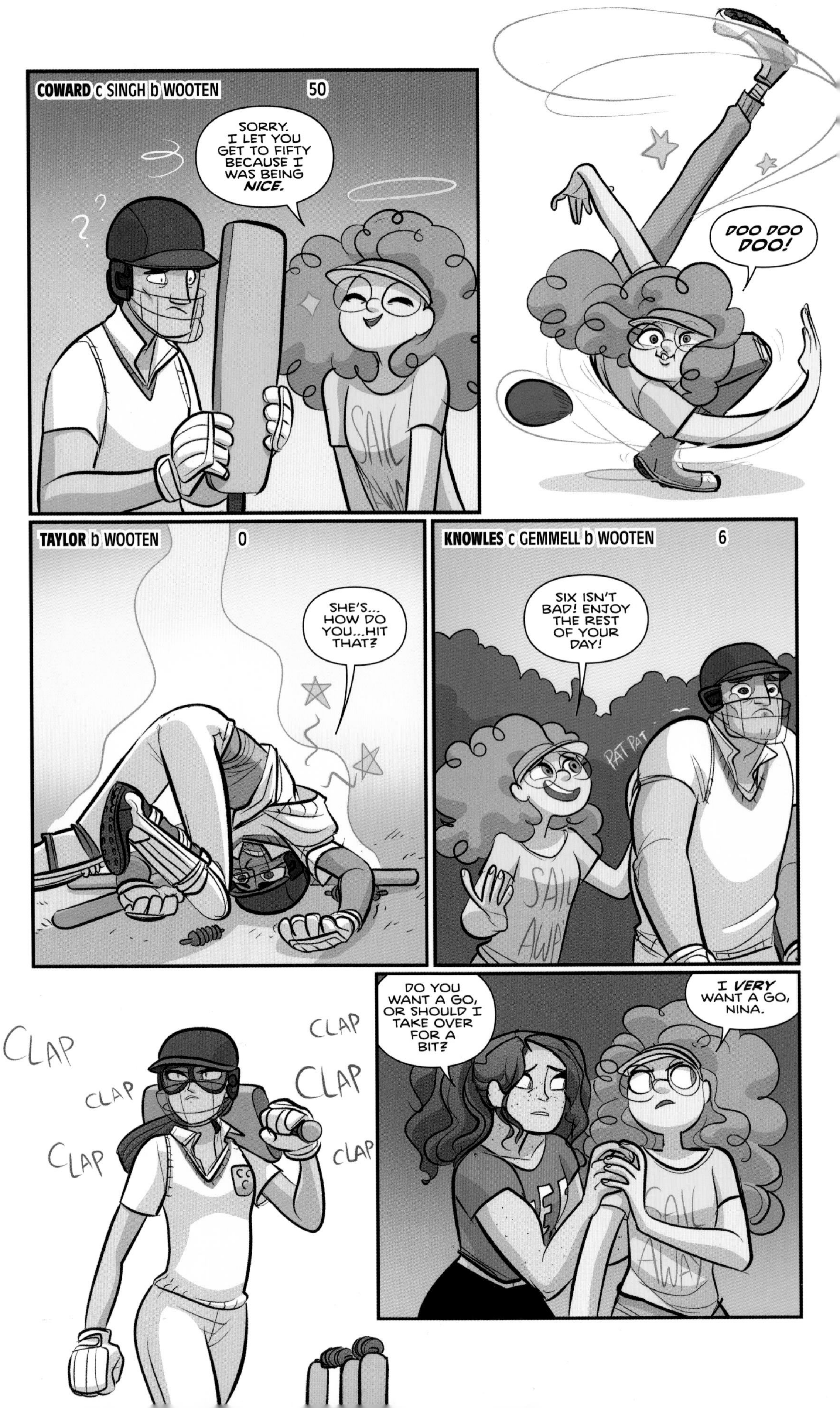

COWARD c SINGH b WOOTEN 50
SORRY. I LET YOU GET TO FIFTY BECAUSE I WAS BEING NICE.
DOO DOO DOO!
SAIL AWAY
TAYLOR b WOOTEN 0
SHE'S... HOW DO YOU...HIT THAT?
KNOWLES c GEMMELL b WOOTEN 6
SIX ISN'T BAD! ENJOY THE REST OF YOUR DAY!
PAT PAT
CLAP
CLAP
CLAP
CLAP
CLAP
CLAP
DO YOU WANT A GO, OR SHOULD I TAKE OVER FOR A BIT?
I VERY WANT A GO, NINA.

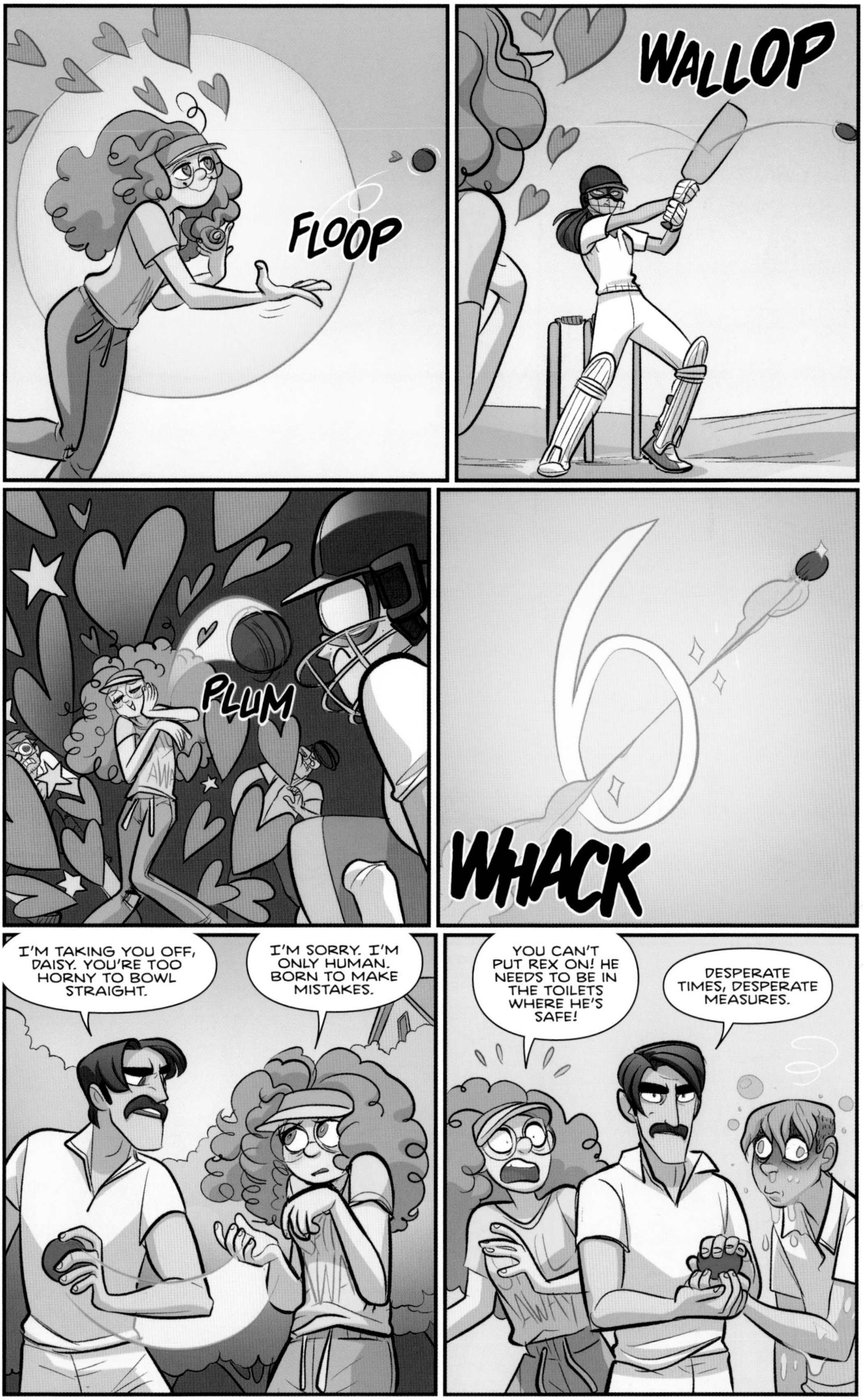
FLOOP
WALLOP
PLUM
WHACK
I'M TAKING YOU OFF, DAISY. YOU'RE TOO HORNY TO BOWL STRAIGHT.
I'M SORRY. I'M ONLY HUMAN. BORN TO MAKE MISTAKES.
YOU CAN'T PUT REX ON! HE NEEDS TO BE IN THE TOILETS WHERE HE'S SAFE!
DESPERATE TIMES, DESPERATE MEASURES.

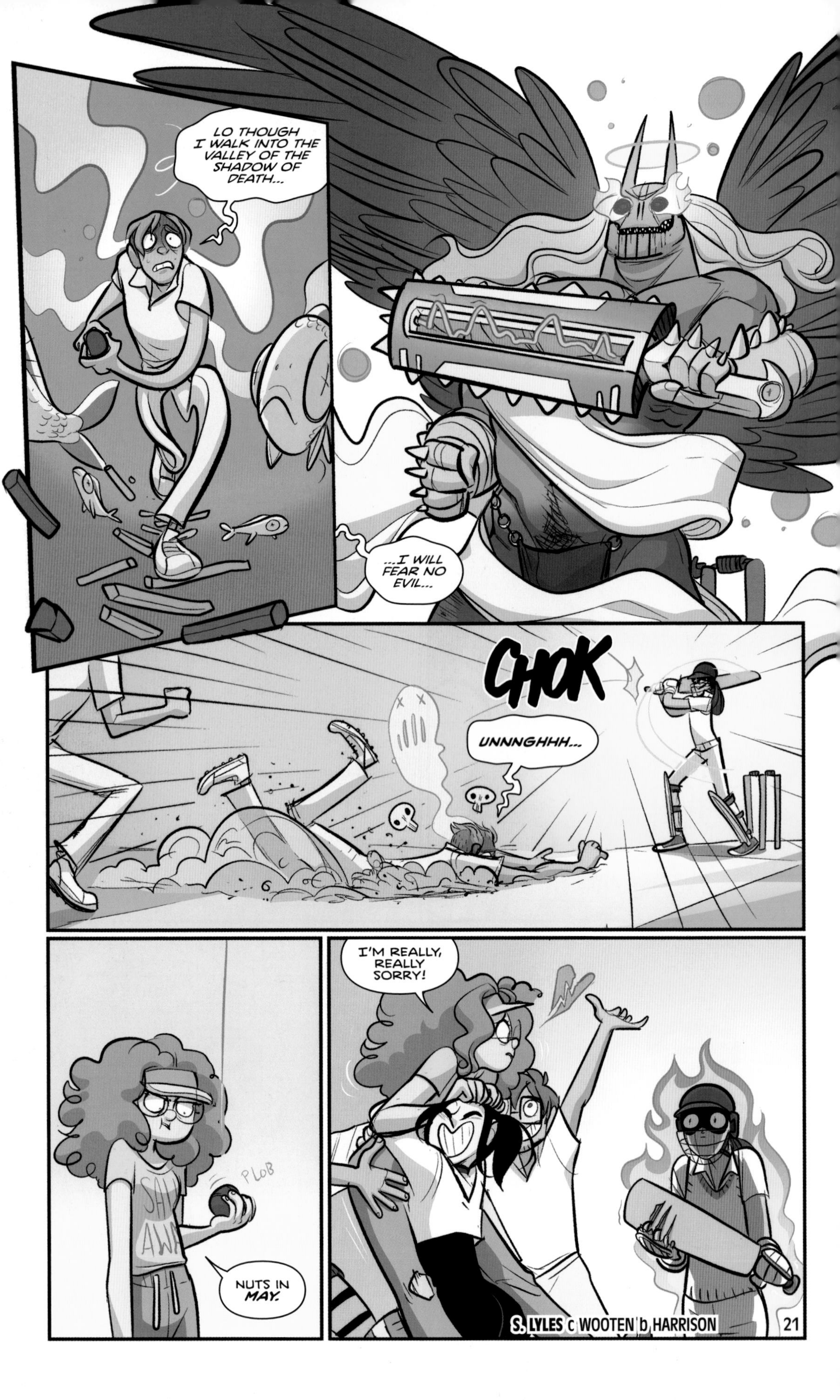
LO THOUGH I WALK INTO THE VALLEY OF THE SHADOW OF DEATH...
...I WILL FEAR NO EVIL...
CHOK
UNNNGHHH...
PLOB
NUTS IN MAY.
I'M REALLY, REALLY SORRY!
S. LYLES c WOOTEN b HARRISON

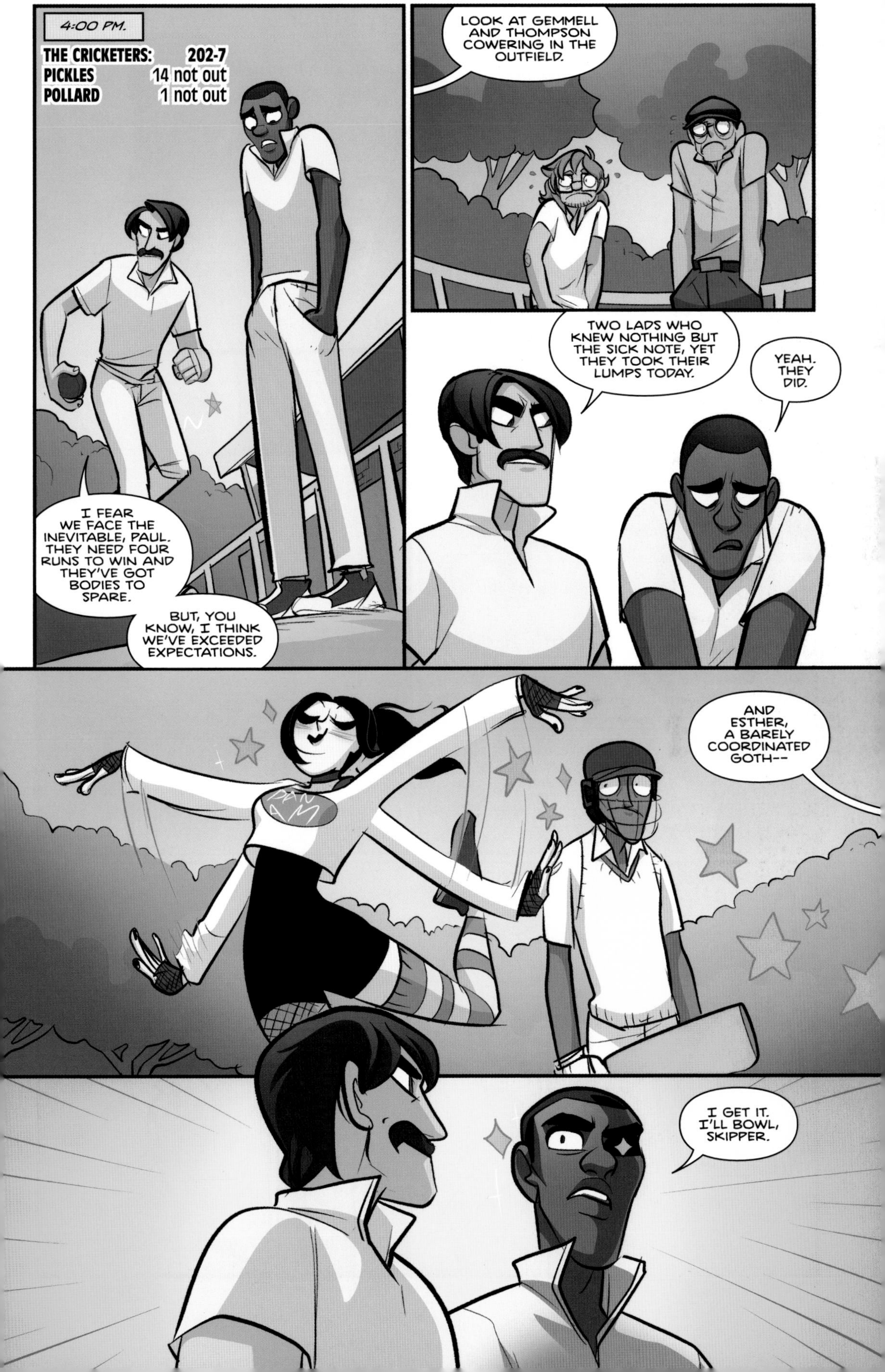
4:00 PM.
THE CRICKETERS: 202-7
PICKLES 14 not out
POLLARD 1 not out
I FEAR WE FACE THE INEVITABLE, PAUL. THEY NEED FOUR RUNS TO WIN AND THEY'VE GOT BODIES TO SPARE.
BUT, YOU KNOW, I THINK WE'VE EXCEEDED EXPECTATIONS.
LOOK AT GEMMELL AND THOMPSON COWERING IN THE OUTFIELD.
TWO LADS WHO KNEW NOTHING BUT THE SICK NOTE, YET THEY TOOK THEIR LUMPS TODAY.
YEAH. THEY DID.
AND ESTHER, A BARELY COORDINATED GOTH--
I GET IT. I'LL BOWL, SKIPPER.

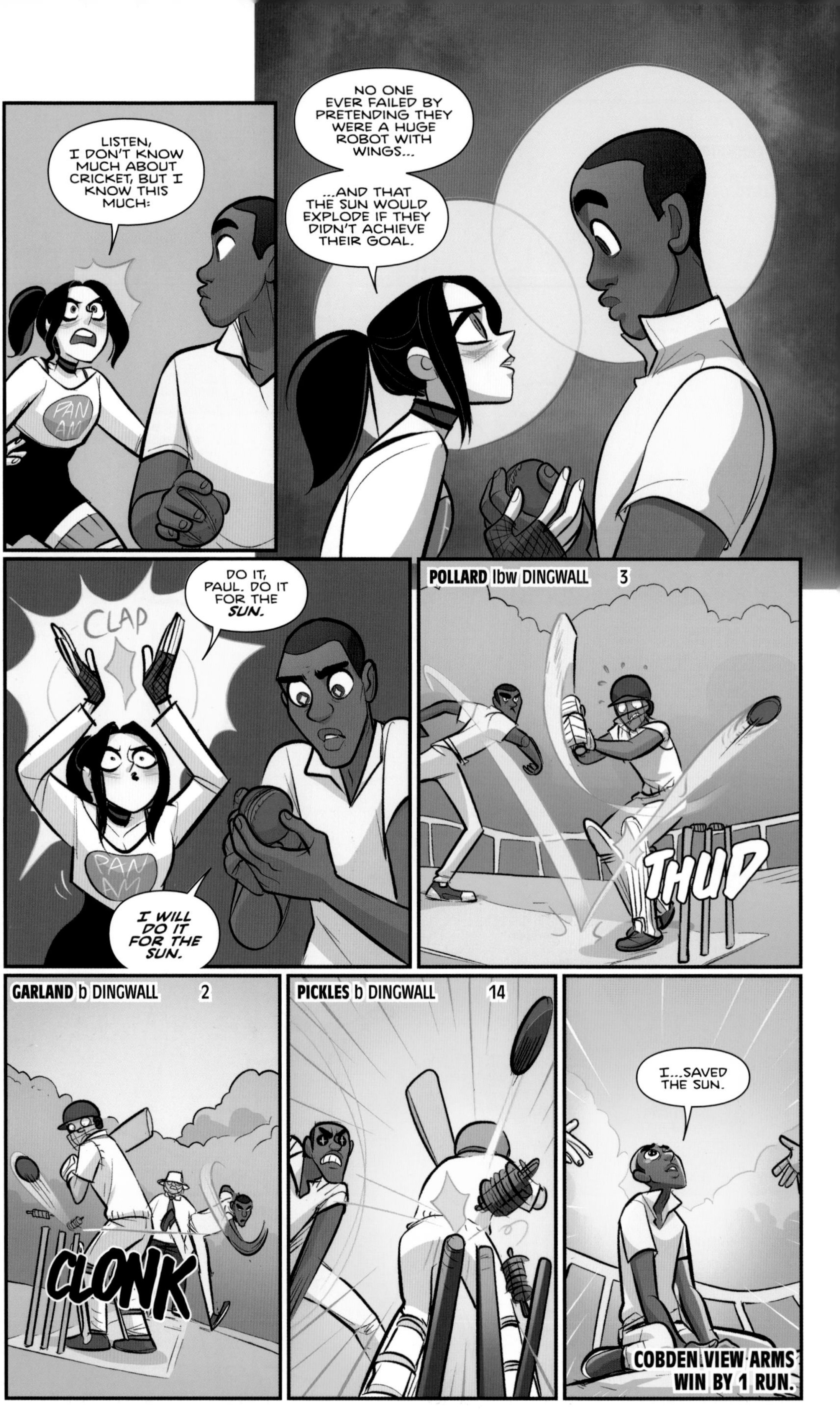

LISTEN, I DON'T KNOW MUCH ABOUT CRICKET, BUT I KNOW THIS MUCH:
NO ONE EVER FAILED BY PRETENDING THEY WERE A HUGE ROBOT WITH WINGS...
...AND THAT THE SUN WOULD EXPLODE IF THEY DIDN'T ACHIEVE THEIR GOAL.
CLAP
DO IT, PAUL. DO IT FOR THE SUN.
I WILL DO IT FOR THE SUN.
POLLARD lbw DINGWALL 3
THUD
GARLAND b DINGWALL 2
CLONK
PICKLES b DINGWALL 14
I...SAVED THE SUN.
COBDEN VIEW ARMS WIN BY 1 RUN.

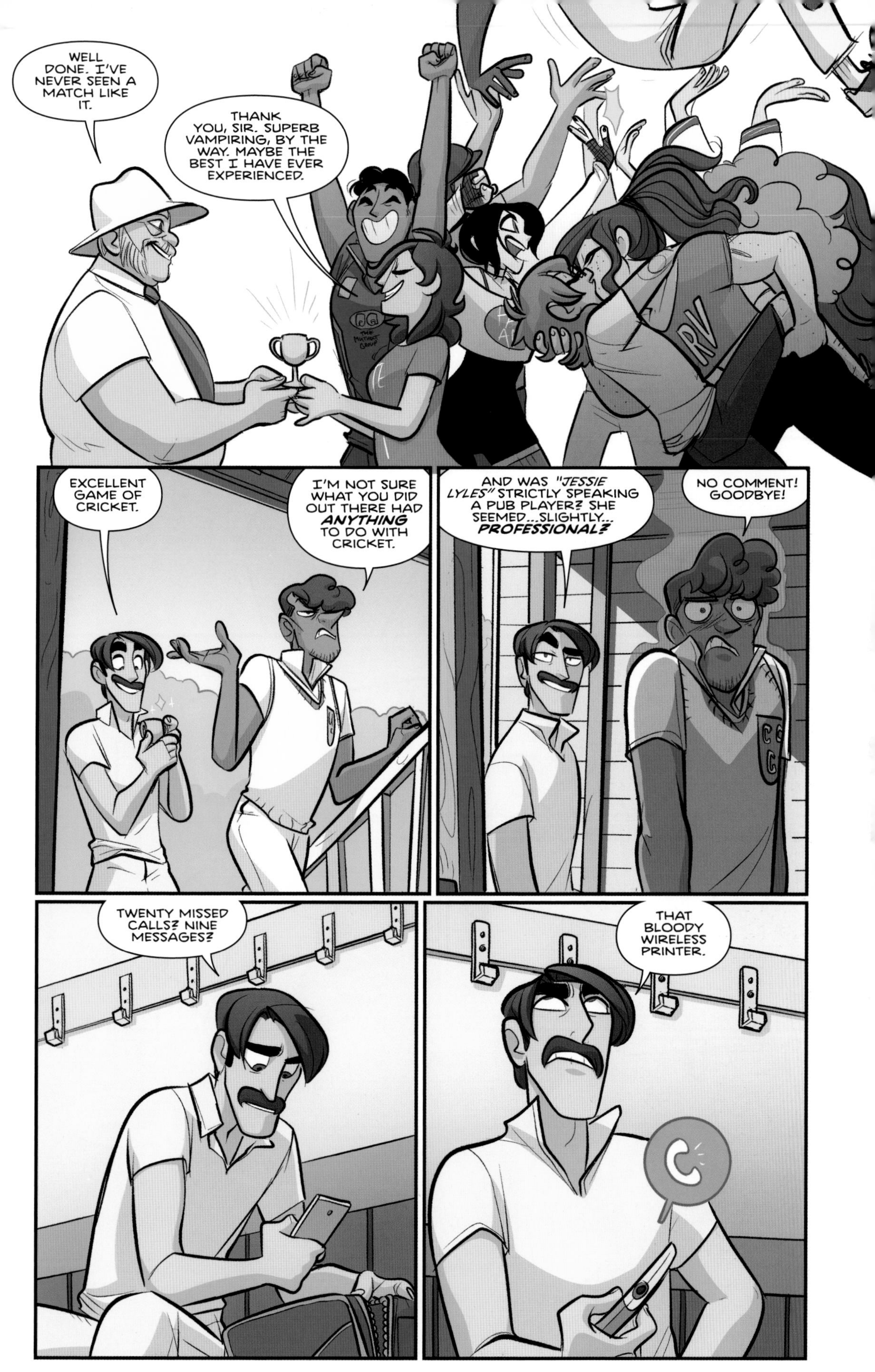
WELL DONE. I'VE NEVER SEEN A MATCH LIKE IT.
THANK YOU, SIR. SUPERB VAMPIRING, BY THE WAY. MAYBE THE BEST I HAVE EVER EXPERIENCED.
EXCELLENT GAME OF CRICKET.
I'M NOT SURE WHAT YOU DID OUT THERE HAD ***ANYTHING*** TO DO WITH CRICKET.
AND WAS *"JESSIE LYLES"* STRICTLY SPEAKING A PUB PLAYER? SHE SEEMED...SLIGHTLY... ***PROFESSIONAL?***
NO COMMENT! GOODBYE!
TWENTY MISSED CALLS? NINE MESSAGES?
THAT BLOODY WIRELESS PRINTER.

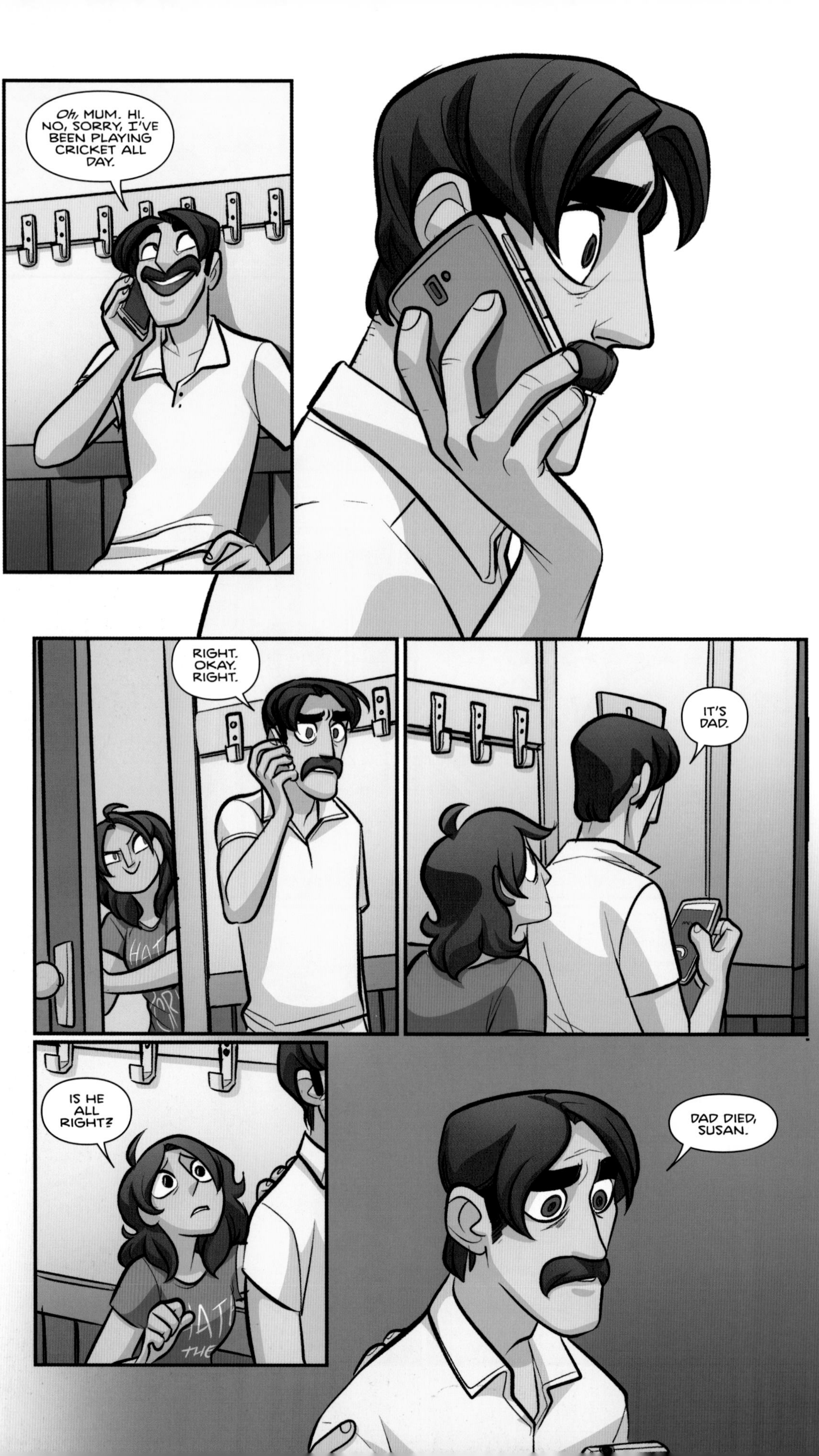
Oh, MUM. HI. NO, SORRY, I'VE BEEN PLAYING CRICKET ALL DAY.
RIGHT. OKAY. RIGHT.
IT'S DAD.
IS HE ALL RIGHT?
DAD DIED, SUSAN.

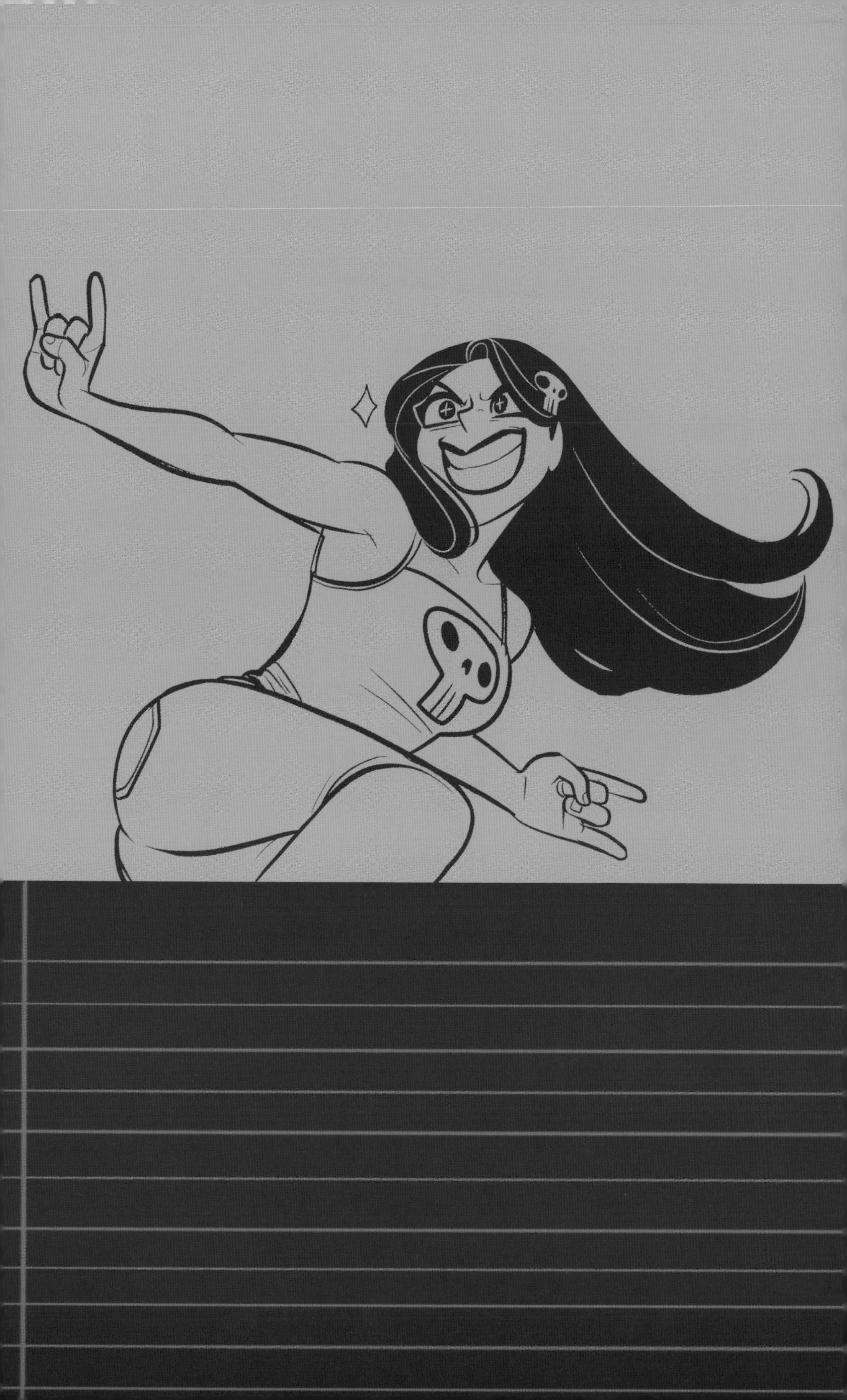

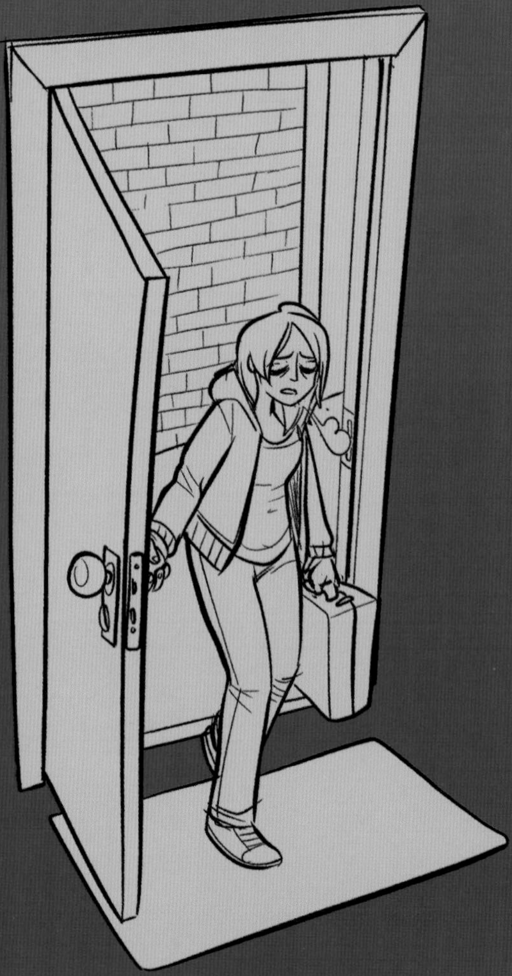

CHAPTER FIFTY-ONE

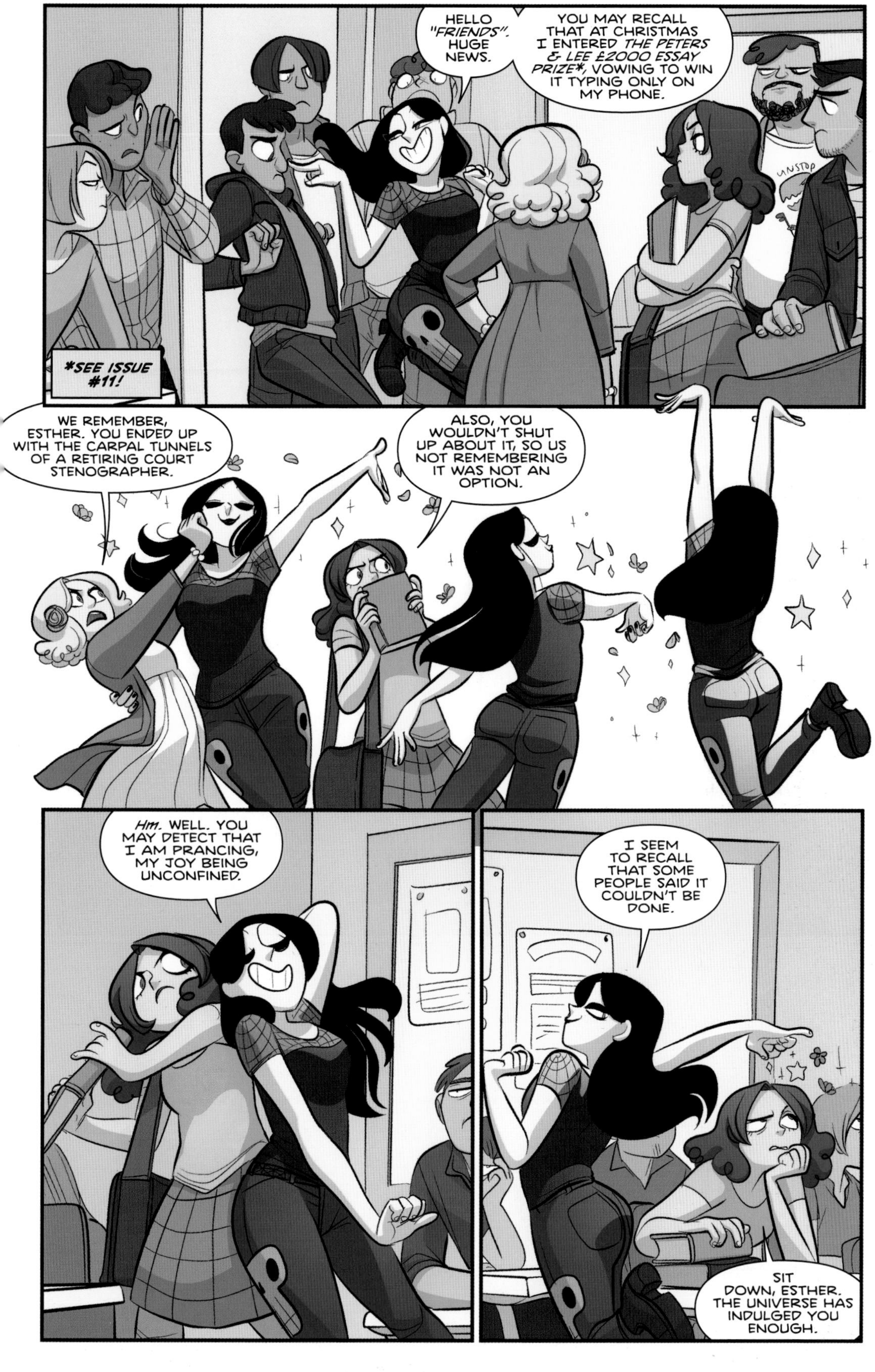
HELLO "FRIENDS". HUGE NEWS.
YOU MAY RECALL THAT AT CHRISTMAS I ENTERED THE PETERS & LEE £2000 ESSAY PRIZE*, VOWING TO WIN IT TYPING ONLY ON MY PHONE.
*SEE ISSUE #11!
WE REMEMBER, ESTHER. YOU ENDED UP WITH THE CARPAL TUNNELS OF A RETIRING COURT STENOGRAPHER.
ALSO, YOU WOULDN'T SHUT UP ABOUT IT, SO US NOT REMEMBERING IT WAS NOT AN OPTION.
Hm. WELL. YOU MAY DETECT THAT I AM PRANCING, MY JOY BEING UNCONFINED.
I SEEM TO RECALL THAT SOME PEOPLE SAID IT COULDN'T BE DONE.
SIT DOWN, ESTHER. THE UNIVERSE HAS INDULGED YOU ENOUGH.

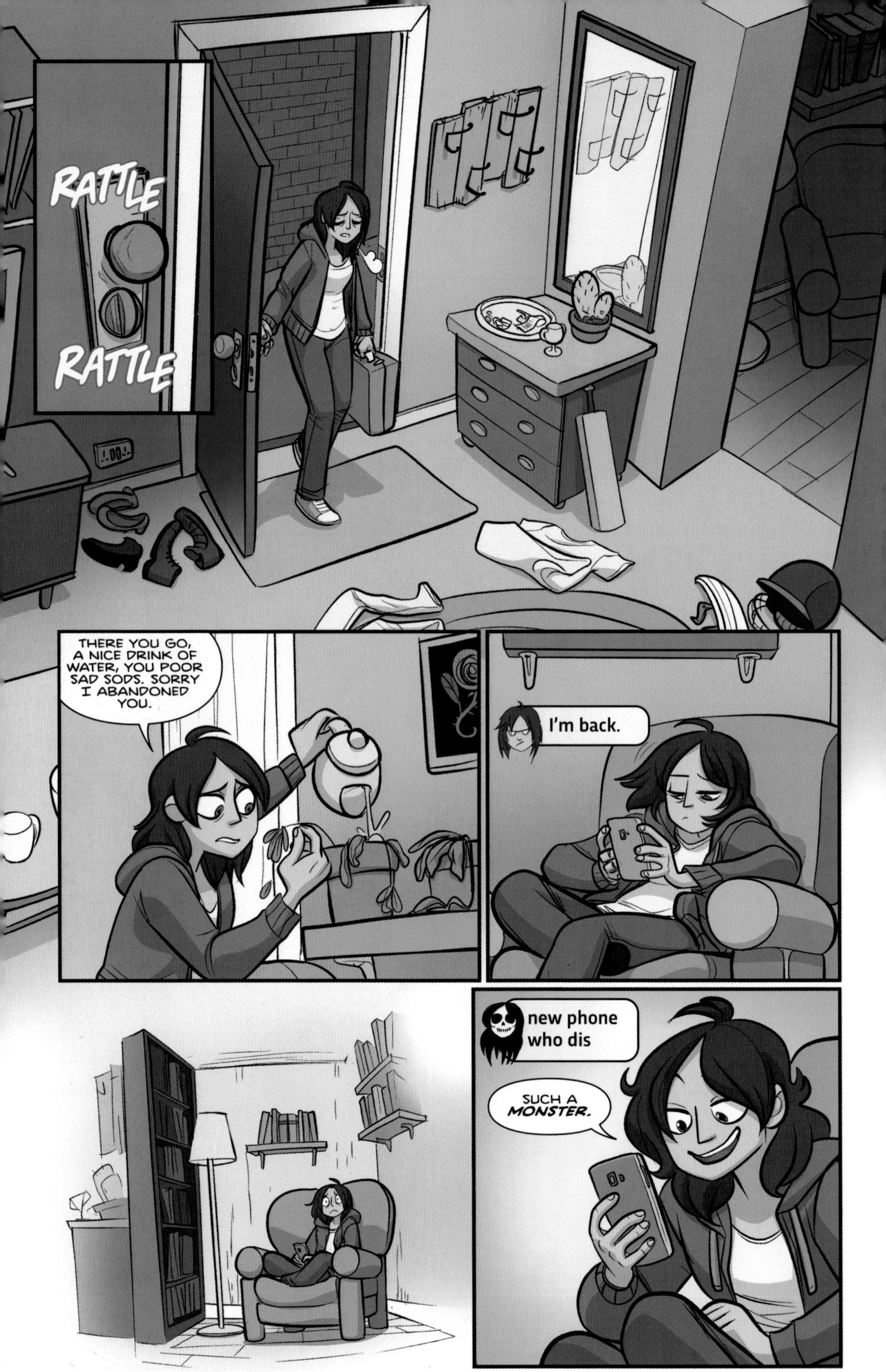
RATTLE
RATTLE
THERE YOU GO, A NICE DRINK OF WATER, YOU POOR SAD SODS. SORRY I ABANDONED YOU.
I'm back.
new phone who dis
SUCH A MONSTER.

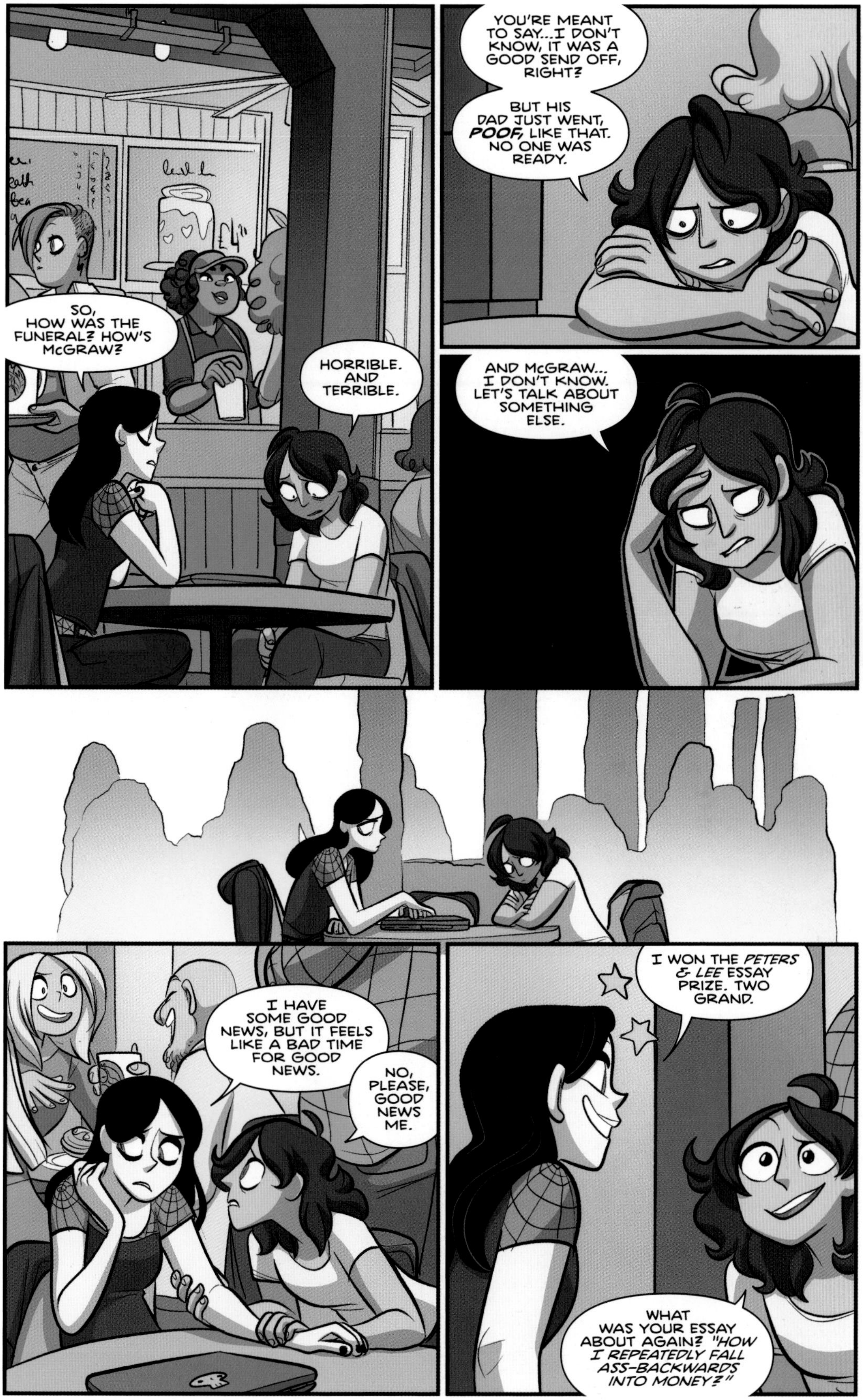
SO, HOW WAS THE FUNERAL? HOW'S McGRAW?
HORRIBLE. AND TERRIBLE.
YOU'RE MEANT TO SAY...I DON'T KNOW, IT WAS A GOOD SEND OFF, RIGHT?
BUT HIS DAD JUST WENT, POOF, LIKE THAT. NO ONE WAS READY.
AND McGRAW... I DON'T KNOW. LET'S TALK ABOUT SOMETHING ELSE.
I HAVE SOME GOOD NEWS, BUT IT FEELS LIKE A BAD TIME FOR GOOD NEWS.
NO, PLEASE, GOOD NEWS ME.
I WON THE PETERS & LEE ESSAY PRIZE. TWO GRAND.
WHAT WAS YOUR ESSAY ABOUT AGAIN? "HOW I REPEATEDLY FALL ASS-BACKWARDS INTO MONEY?"

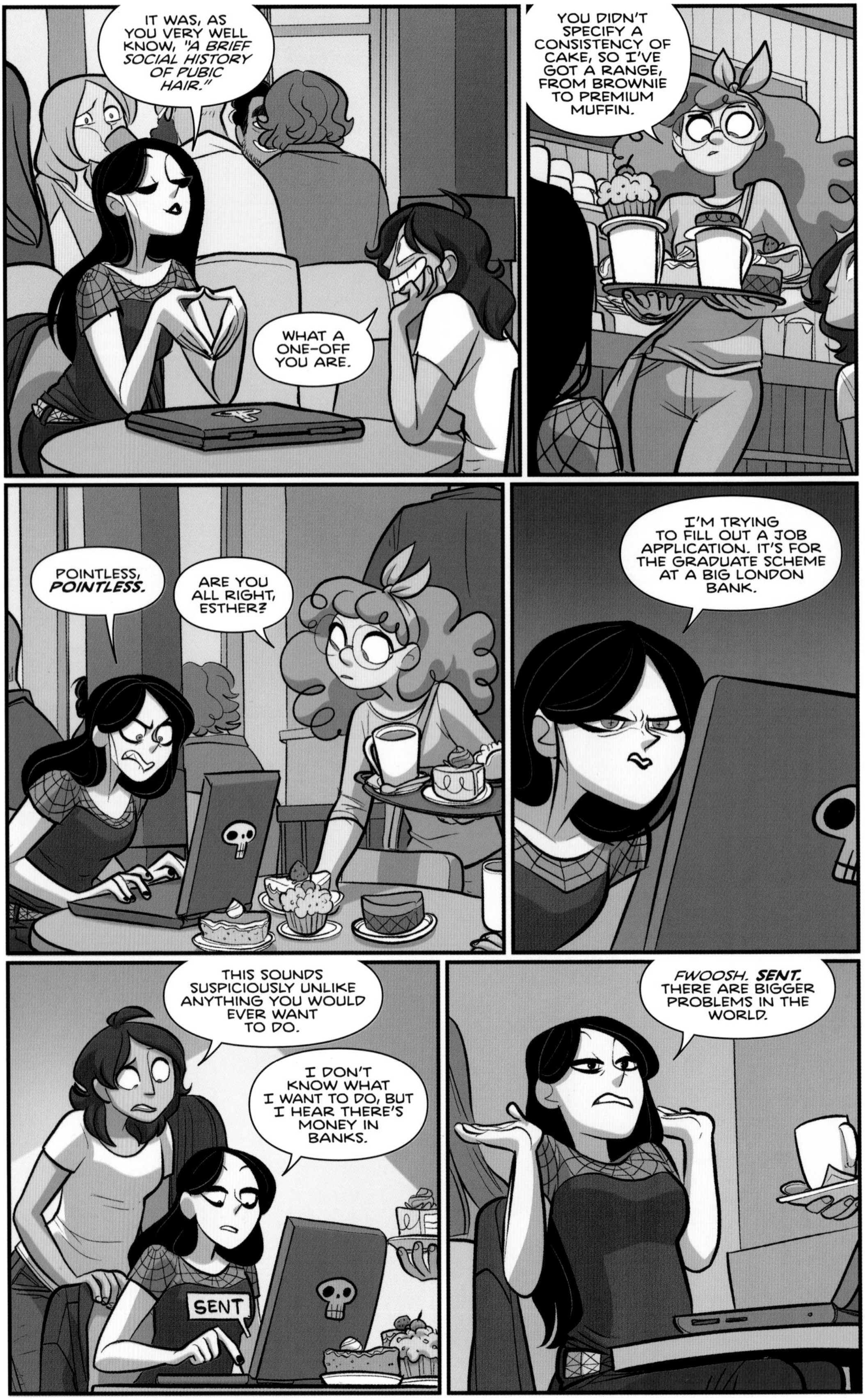
IT WAS, AS YOU VERY WELL KNOW, "A BRIEF SOCIAL HISTORY OF PUBIC HAIR."
WHAT A ONE-OFF YOU ARE.
YOU DIDN'T SPECIFY A CONSISTENCY OF CAKE, SO I'VE GOT A RANGE, FROM BROWNIE TO PREMIUM MUFFIN.
POINTLESS, **POINTLESS.**
ARE YOU ALL RIGHT, ESTHER?
I'M TRYING TO FILL OUT A JOB APPLICATION. IT'S FOR THE GRADUATE SCHEME AT A BIG LONDON BANK.
THIS SOUNDS SUSPICIOUSLY UNLIKE ANYTHING YOU WOULD EVER WANT TO DO.
I DON'T KNOW WHAT I WANT TO DO, BUT I HEAR THERE'S MONEY IN BANKS.
SENT
FWOOSH. ***SENT.*** THERE ARE BIGGER PROBLEMS IN THE WORLD.

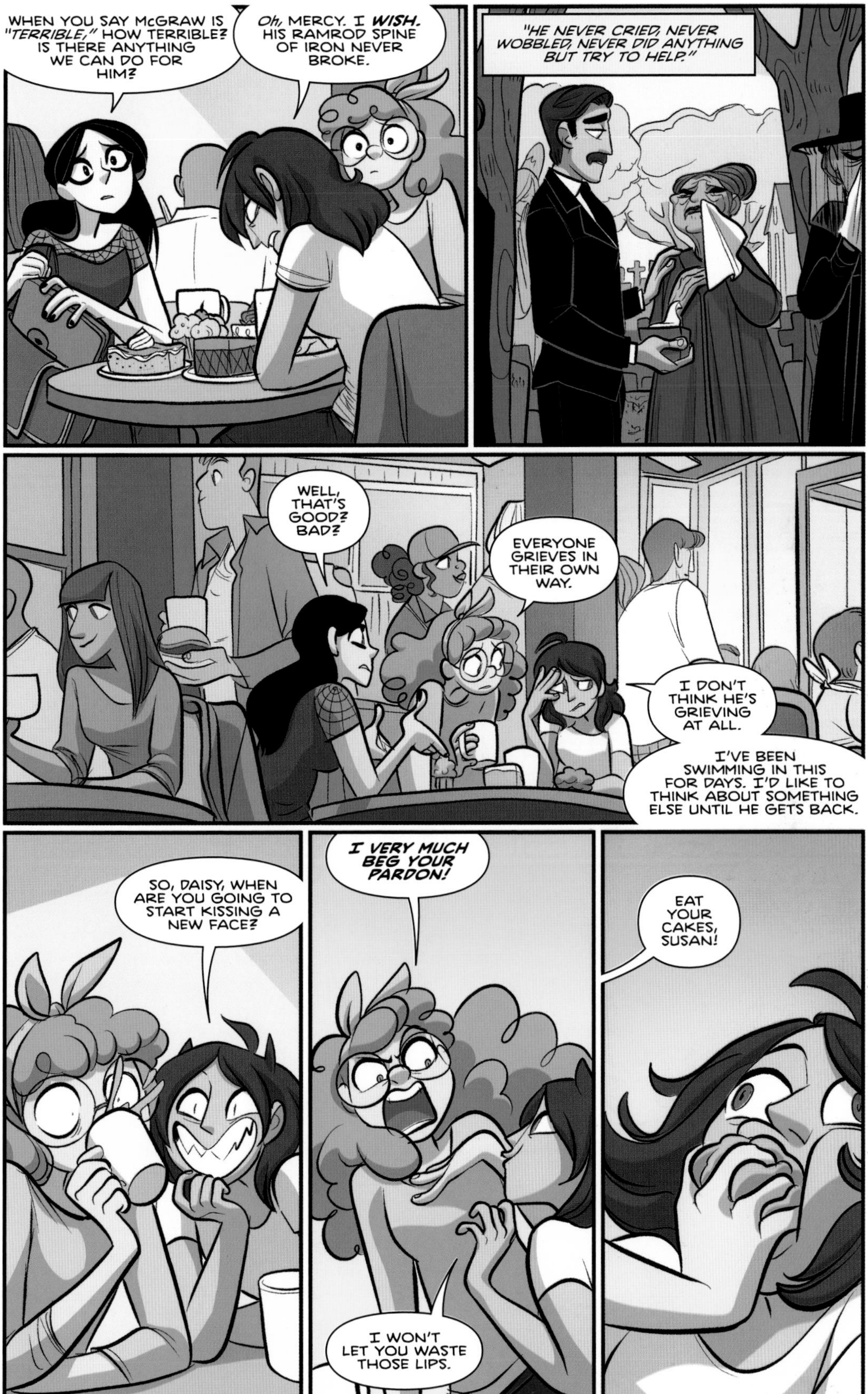
WHEN YOU SAY McGRAW IS "TERRIBLE," HOW TERRIBLE? IS THERE ANYTHING WE CAN DO FOR HIM?
Oh, MERCY. I WISH. HIS RAMROD SPINE OF IRON NEVER BROKE.
"HE NEVER CRIED, NEVER WOBBLED, NEVER DID ANYTHING BUT TRY TO HELP."
WELL, THAT'S GOOD? BAD?
EVERYONE GRIEVES IN THEIR OWN WAY.
I DON'T THINK HE'S GRIEVING AT ALL.
I'VE BEEN SWIMMING IN THIS FOR DAYS. I'D LIKE TO THINK ABOUT SOMETHING ELSE UNTIL HE GETS BACK.
SO, DAISY, WHEN ARE YOU GOING TO START KISSING A NEW FACE?
I VERY MUCH BEG YOUR PARDON!
I WON'T LET YOU WASTE THOSE LIPS.
EAT YOUR CAKES, SUSAN!

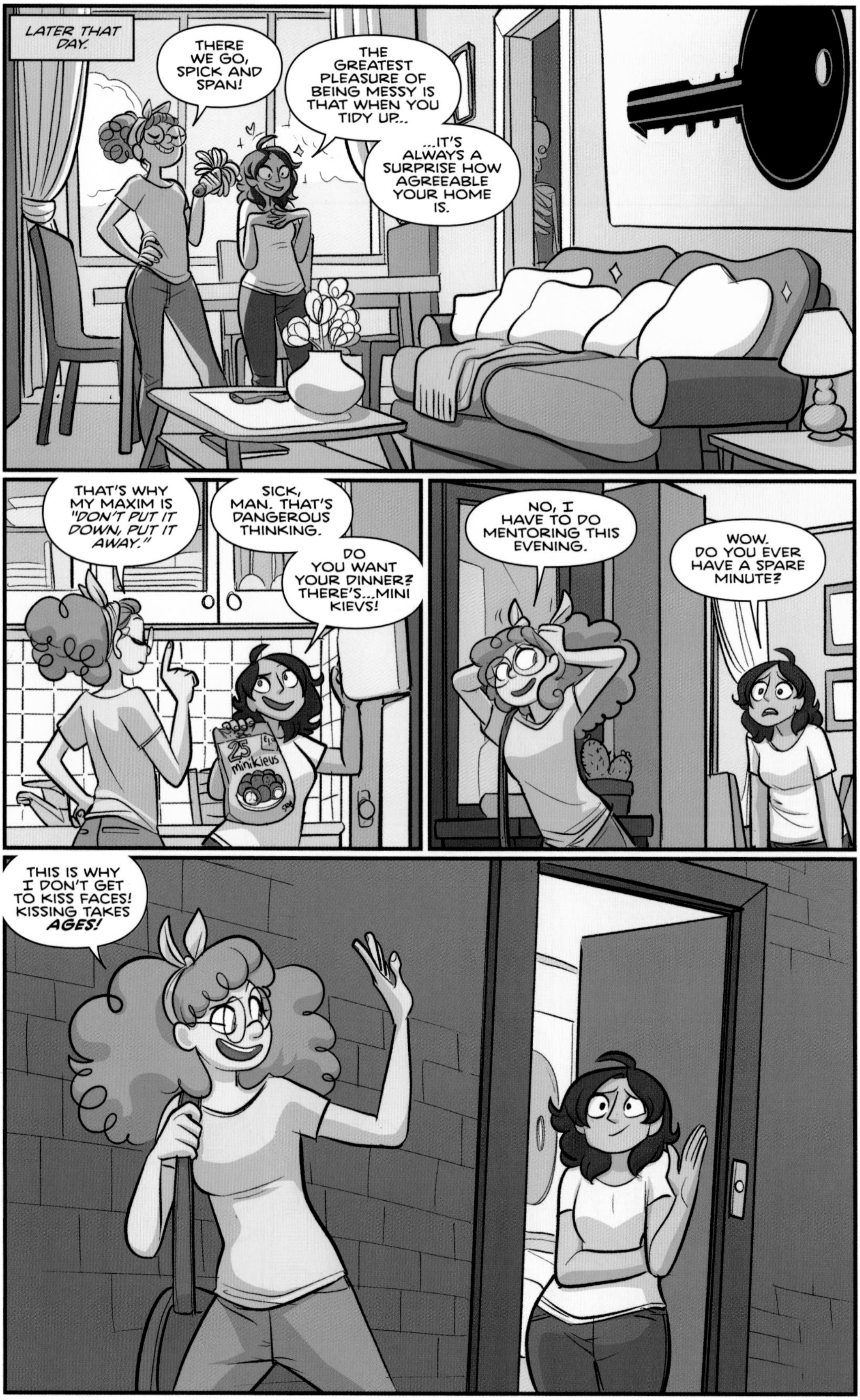
LATER THAT DAY.
THERE WE GO, SPICK AND SPAN!
THE GREATEST PLEASURE OF BEING MESSY IS THAT WHEN YOU TIDY UP...
...IT'S ALWAYS A SURPRISE HOW AGREEABLE YOUR HOME IS.
THAT'S WHY MY MAXIM IS *"DON'T PUT IT DOWN, PUT IT AWAY."*
SICK, MAN. THAT'S DANGEROUS THINKING.
DO YOU WANT YOUR DINNER? THERE'S...MINI KIEVS!
25 minikievs
NO, I HAVE TO DO MENTORING THIS EVENING.
WOW. DO YOU EVER HAVE A SPARE MINUTE?
THIS IS WHY I DON'T GET TO KISS FACES! KISSING TAKES ***AGES!***

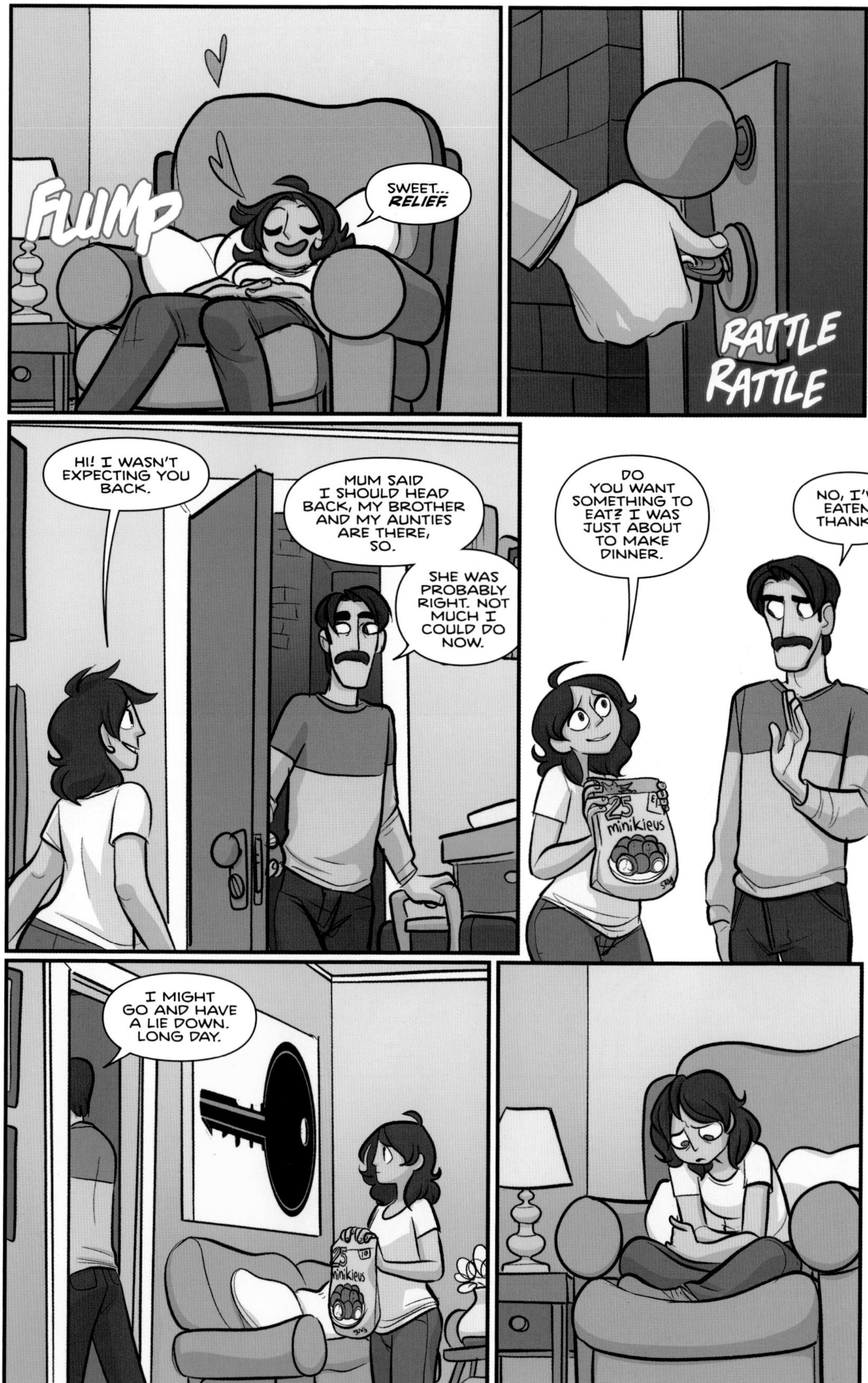
FLUMP
SWEET... RELIEF.
RATTLE RATTLE
HI! I WASN'T EXPECTING YOU BACK.
MUM SAID I SHOULD HEAD BACK, MY BROTHER AND MY AUNTIES ARE THERE, SO.
SHE WAS PROBABLY RIGHT. NOT MUCH I COULD DO NOW.
DO YOU WANT SOMETHING TO EAT? I WAS JUST ABOUT TO MAKE DINNER.
NO, I'VE EATEN. THANKS.
25
minikieus
I MIGHT GO AND HAVE A LIE DOWN. LONG DAY.

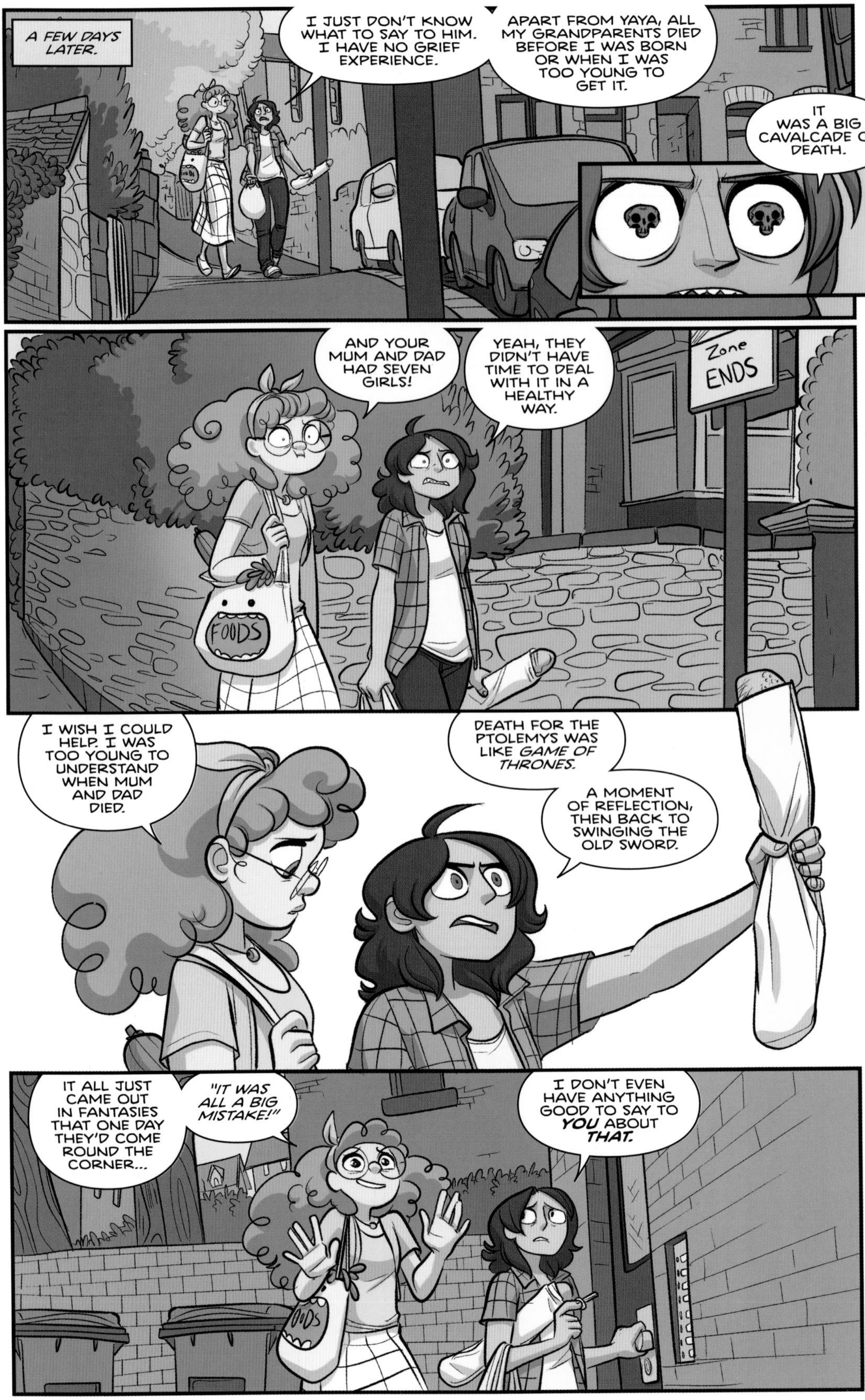
A FEW DAYS LATER.
I JUST DON'T KNOW WHAT TO SAY TO HIM. I HAVE NO GRIEF EXPERIENCE.
APART FROM YAYA, ALL MY GRANDPARENTS DIED BEFORE I WAS BORN OR WHEN I WAS TOO YOUNG TO GET IT.
IT WAS A BIG CAVALCADE OF DEATH.
AND YOUR MUM AND DAD HAD SEVEN GIRLS!
YEAH, THEY DIDN'T HAVE TIME TO DEAL WITH IT IN A HEALTHY WAY.
Zone ENDS
FOODS
I WISH I COULD HELP. I WAS TOO YOUNG TO UNDERSTAND WHEN MUM AND DAD DIED.
DEATH FOR THE PTOLEMYS WAS LIKE *GAME OF THRONES.*
A MOMENT OF REFLECTION, THEN BACK TO SWINGING THE OLD SWORD.
IT ALL JUST CAME OUT IN FANTASIES THAT ONE DAY THEY'D COME ROUND THE CORNER...
"IT WAS ALL A BIG MISTAKE!"
I DON'T EVEN HAVE ANYTHING GOOD TO SAY TO ***YOU*** ABOUT ***THAT.***

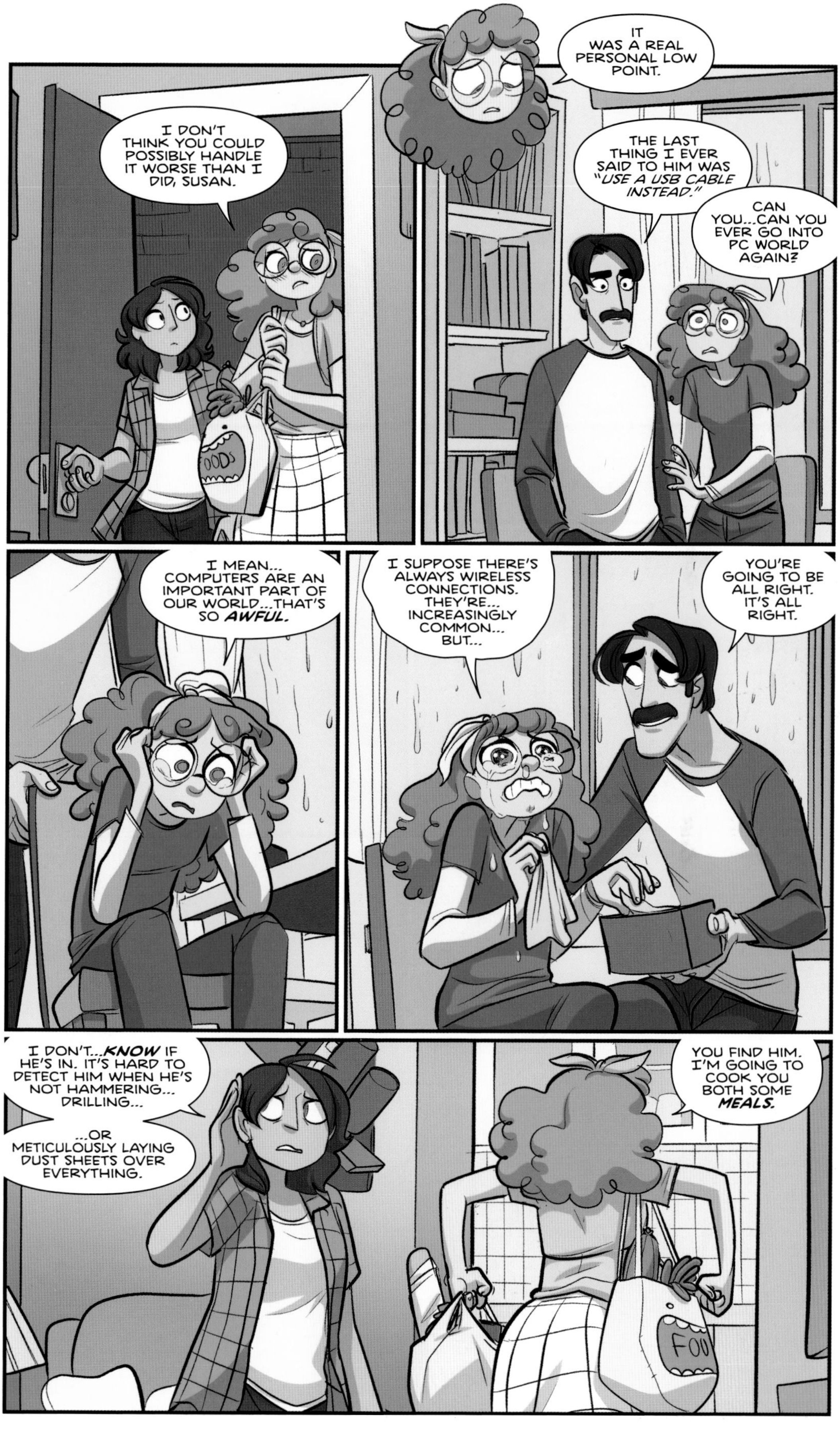
I DON'T THINK YOU COULD POSSIBLY HANDLE IT WORSE THAN I DID, SUSAN.
FOODS
IT WAS A REAL PERSONAL LOW POINT.
THE LAST THING I EVER SAID TO HIM WAS "USE A USB CABLE INSTEAD."
CAN YOU...CAN YOU EVER GO INTO PC WORLD AGAIN?
I MEAN... COMPUTERS ARE AN IMPORTANT PART OF OUR WORLD...THAT'S SO AWFUL.
I SUPPOSE THERE'S ALWAYS WIRELESS CONNECTIONS. THEY'RE... INCREASINGLY COMMON... BUT...
YOU'RE GOING TO BE ALL RIGHT. IT'S ALL RIGHT.
I DON'T...KNOW IF HE'S IN. IT'S HARD TO DETECT HIM WHEN HE'S NOT HAMMERING... DRILLING...
...OR METICULOUSLY LAYING DUST SHEETS OVER EVERYTHING.
YOU FIND HIM. I'M GOING TO COOK YOU BOTH SOME MEALS.
FOO

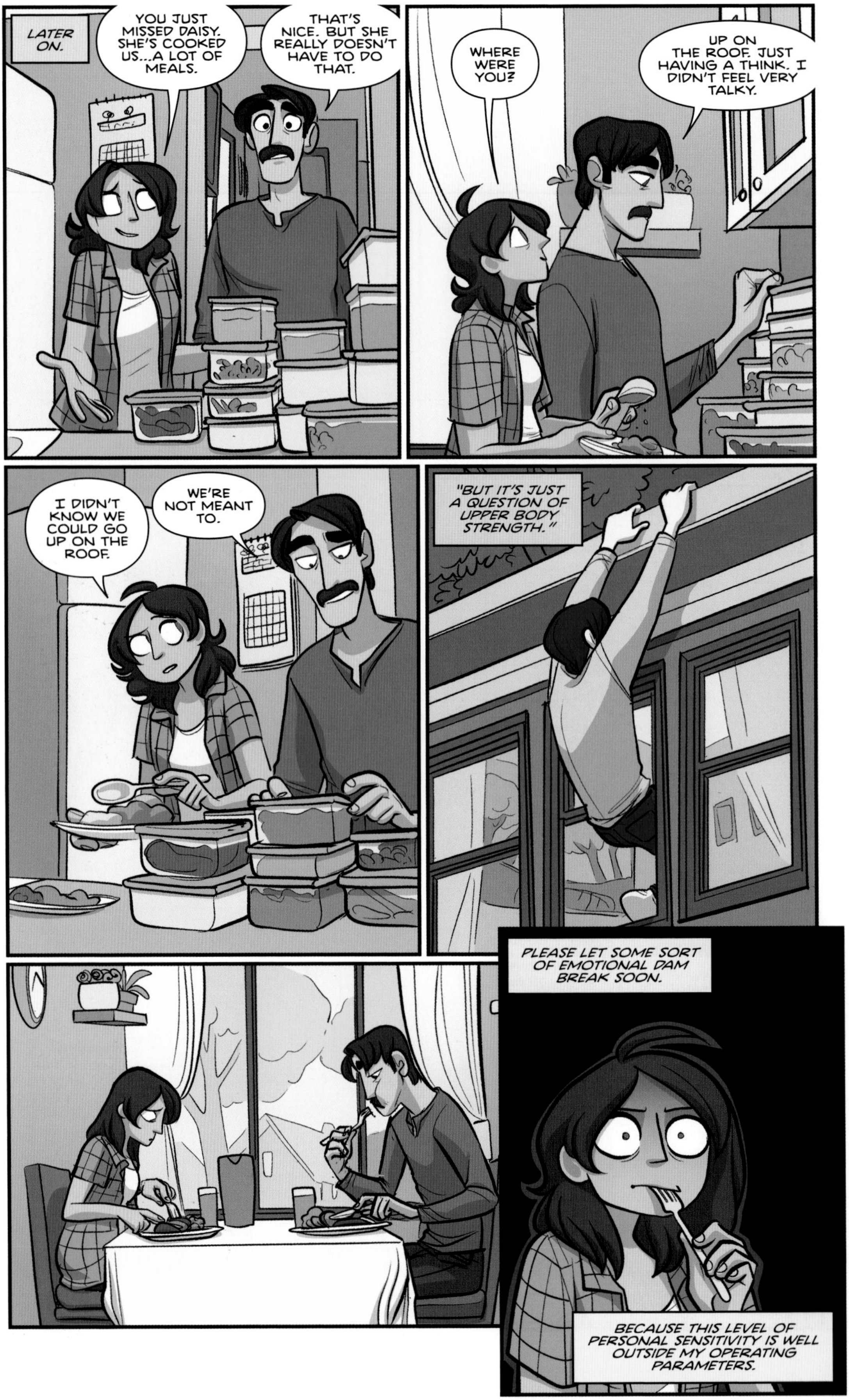
LATER ON.
YOU JUST MISSED DAISY. SHE'S COOKED US...A LOT OF MEALS.
THAT'S NICE. BUT SHE REALLY DOESN'T HAVE TO DO THAT.
WHERE WERE YOU?
UP ON THE ROOF. JUST HAVING A THINK. I DIDN'T FEEL VERY TALKY.
I DIDN'T KNOW WE COULD GO UP ON THE ROOF.
WE'RE NOT MEANT TO.
"BUT IT'S JUST A QUESTION OF UPPER BODY STRENGTH."
PLEASE LET SOME SORT OF EMOTIONAL DAM BREAK SOON.
BECAUSE THIS LEVEL OF PERSONAL SENSITIVITY IS WELL OUTSIDE MY OPERATING PARAMETERS.

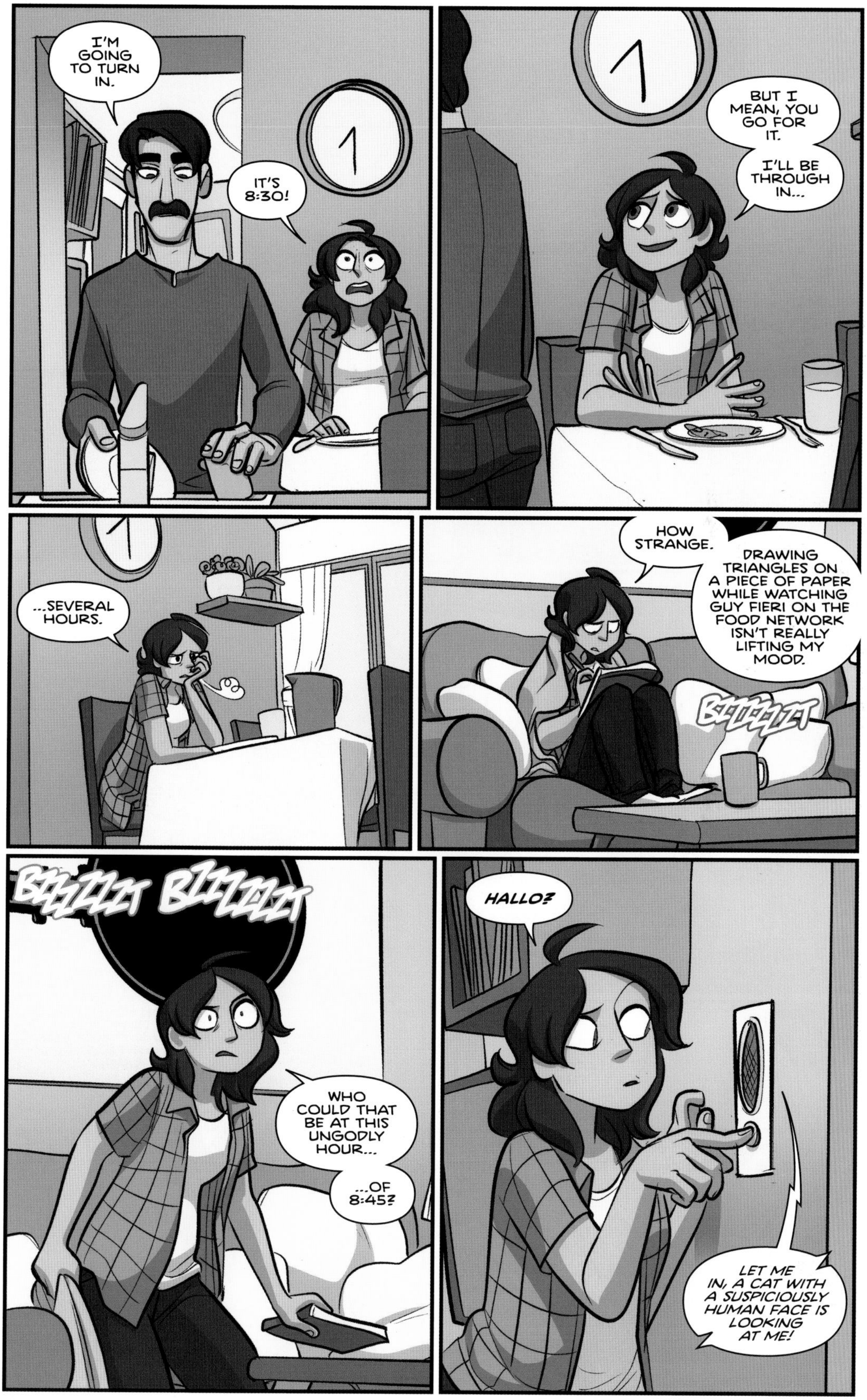
I'M GOING TO TURN IN.
IT'S 8:30!
BUT I MEAN, YOU GO FOR IT.
I'LL BE THROUGH IN...
...SEVERAL HOURS.
HOW STRANGE.
DRAWING TRIANGLES ON A PIECE OF PAPER WHILE WATCHING GUY FIERI ON THE FOOD NETWORK ISN'T REALLY LIFTING MY MOOD.
BZZZZT
BZZZZT BZZZZT
WHO COULD THAT BE AT THIS UNGODLY HOUR...
...OF 8:45?
HALLO?
LET ME IN, A CAT WITH A SUSPICIOUSLY HUMAN FACE IS LOOKING AT ME!

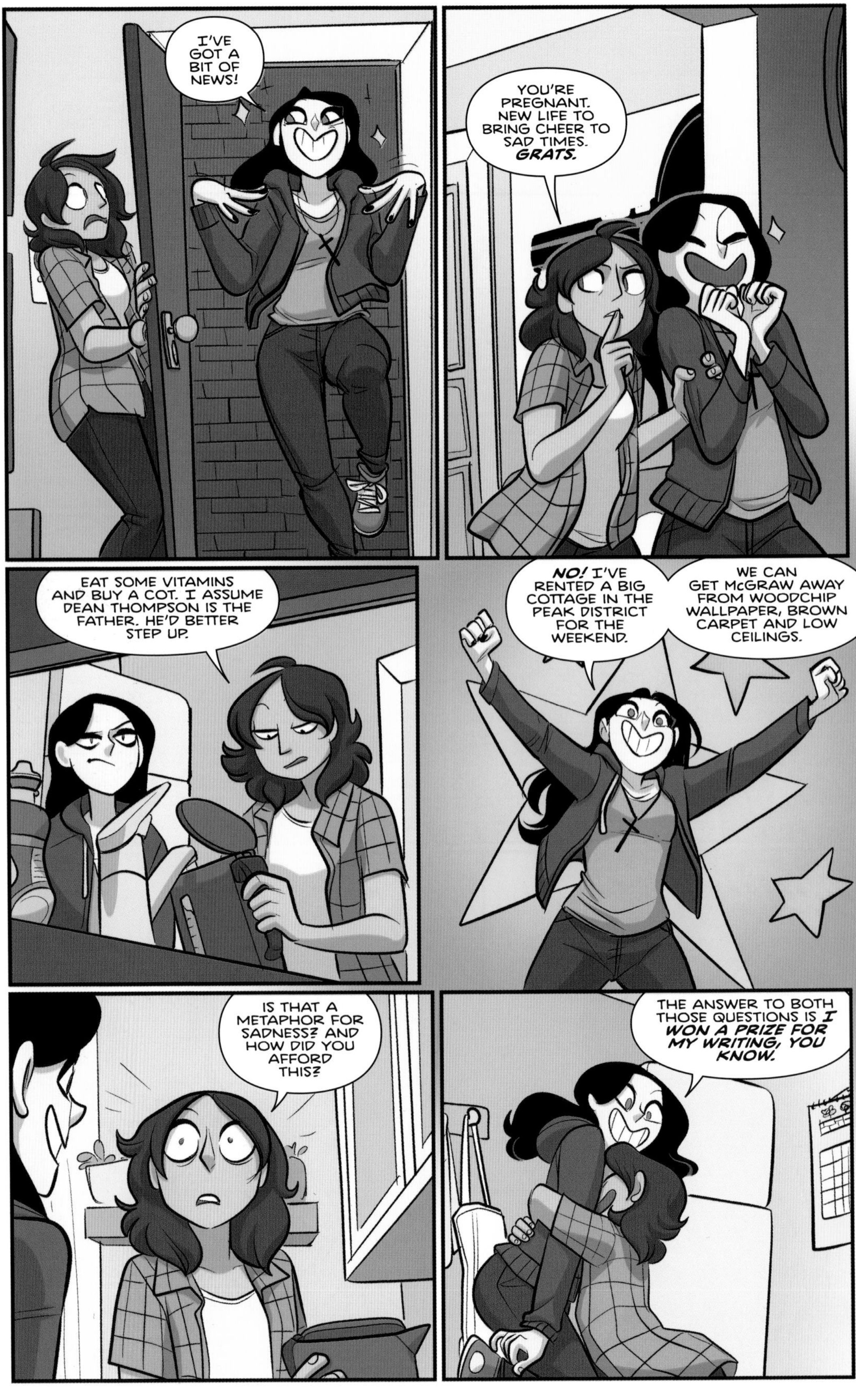
I'VE GOT A BIT OF NEWS!
YOU'RE PREGNANT. NEW LIFE TO BRING CHEER TO SAD TIMES. ***GRATS.***
EAT SOME VITAMINS AND BUY A COT. I ASSUME DEAN THOMPSON IS THE FATHER. HE'D BETTER STEP UP.
NO! I'VE RENTED A BIG COTTAGE IN THE PEAK DISTRICT FOR THE WEEKEND.
WE CAN GET McGRAW AWAY FROM WOODCHIP WALLPAPER, BROWN CARPET AND LOW CEILINGS.
IS THAT A METAPHOR FOR SADNESS? AND HOW DID YOU AFFORD THIS?
THE ANSWER TO BOTH THOSE QUESTIONS IS ***I WON A PRIZE FOR MY WRITING, YOU KNOW.***

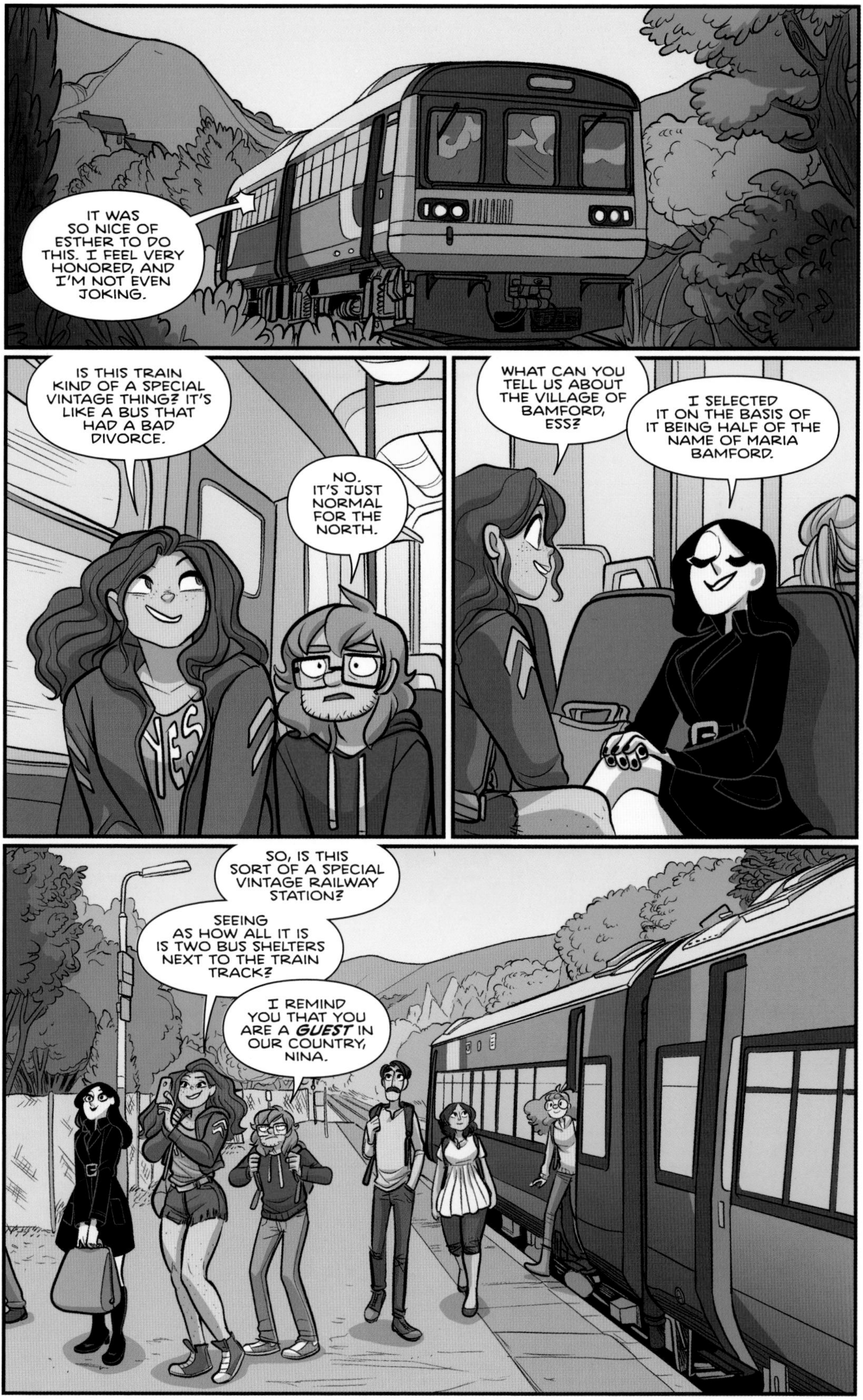
IT WAS SO NICE OF ESTHER TO DO THIS. I FEEL VERY HONORED, AND I'M NOT EVEN JOKING.
IS THIS TRAIN KIND OF A SPECIAL VINTAGE THING? IT'S LIKE A BUS THAT HAD A BAD DIVORCE.
NO. IT'S JUST NORMAL FOR THE NORTH.
WHAT CAN YOU TELL US ABOUT THE VILLAGE OF BAMFORD, ESS?
I SELECTED IT ON THE BASIS OF IT BEING HALF OF THE NAME OF MARIA BAMFORD.
SO, IS THIS SORT OF A SPECIAL VINTAGE RAILWAY STATION?
SEEING AS HOW ALL IT IS IS TWO BUS SHELTERS NEXT TO THE TRAIN TRACK?
I REMIND YOU THAT YOU ARE A ***GUEST*** IN OUR COUNTRY, NINA.
YES

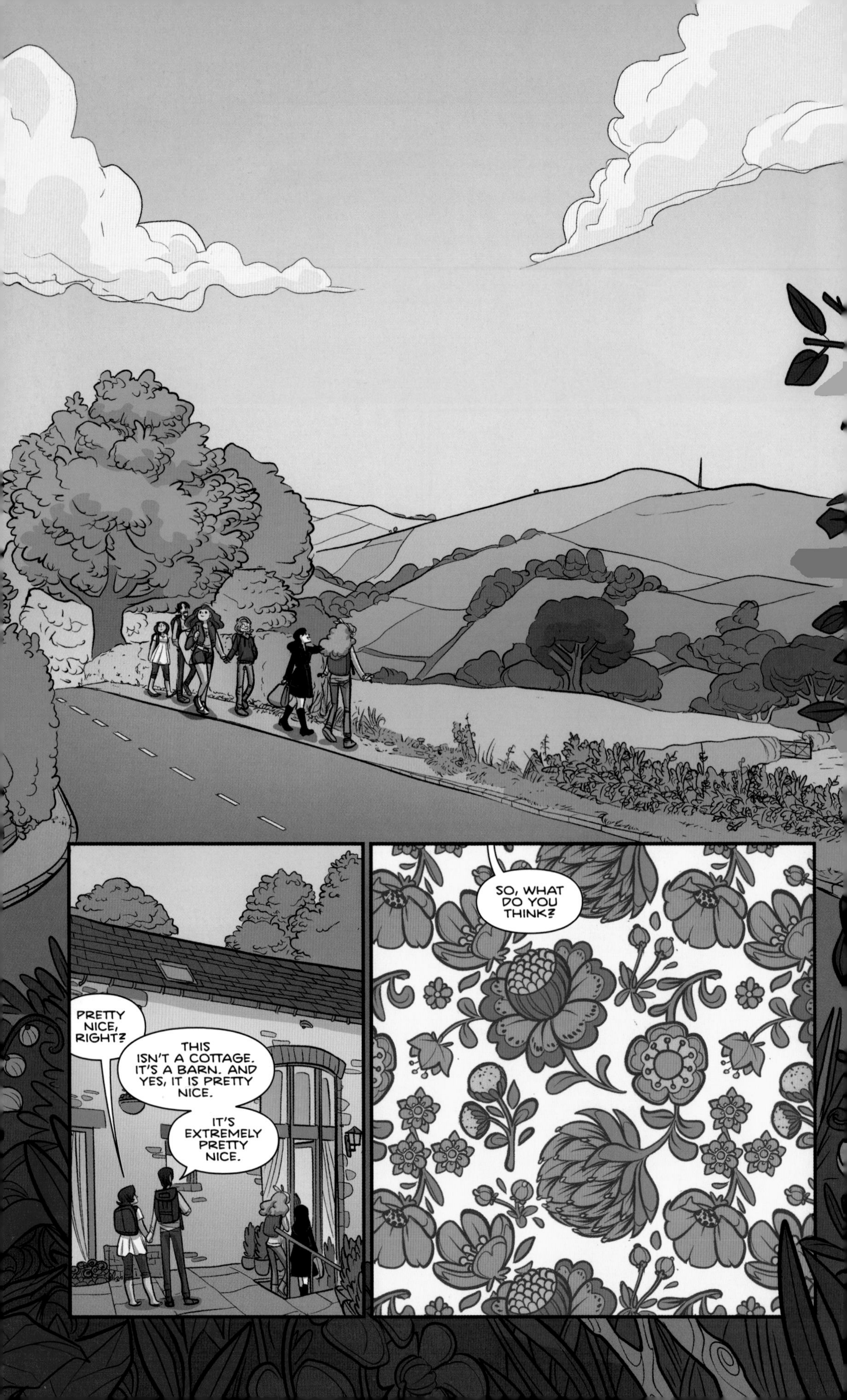
PRETTY NICE, RIGHT?
THIS ISN'T A COTTAGE. IT'S A BARN. AND YES, IT IS PRETTY NICE.
IT'S EXTREMELY PRETTY NICE.
SO, WHAT DO YOU THINK?

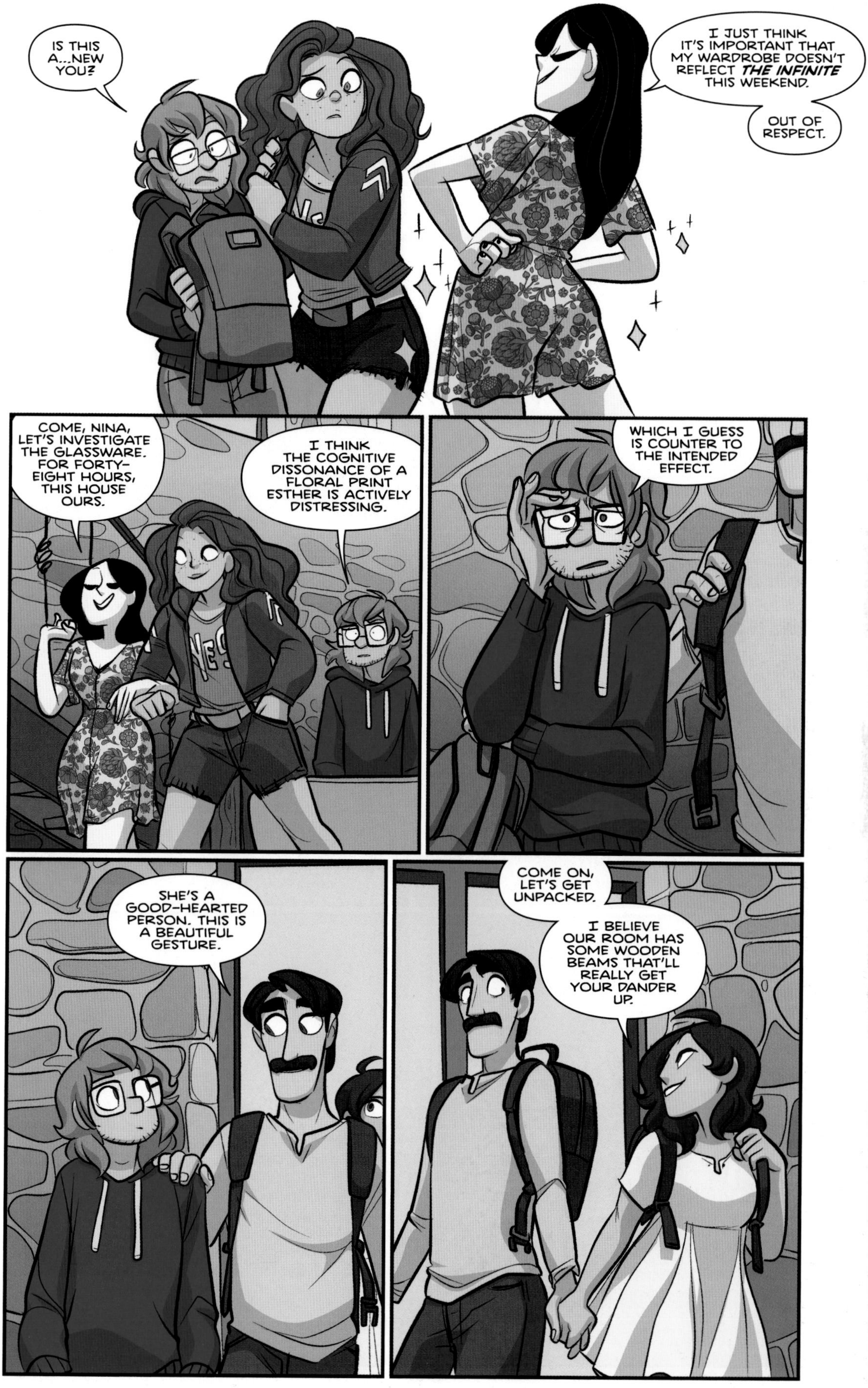
IS THIS A...NEW YOU?
I JUST THINK IT'S IMPORTANT THAT MY WARDROBE DOESN'T REFLECT *THE INFINITE* THIS WEEKEND.
OUT OF RESPECT.
COME, NINA, LET'S INVESTIGATE THE GLASSWARE. FOR FORTY-EIGHT HOURS, THIS HOUSE OURS.
I THINK THE COGNITIVE DISSONANCE OF A FLORAL PRINT ESTHER IS ACTIVELY DISTRESSING.
WHICH I GUESS IS COUNTER TO THE INTENDED EFFECT.
SHE'S A GOOD-HEARTED PERSON. THIS IS A BEAUTIFUL GESTURE.
COME ON, LET'S GET UNPACKED.
I BELIEVE OUR ROOM HAS SOME WOODEN BEAMS THAT'LL REALLY GET YOUR DANDER UP.

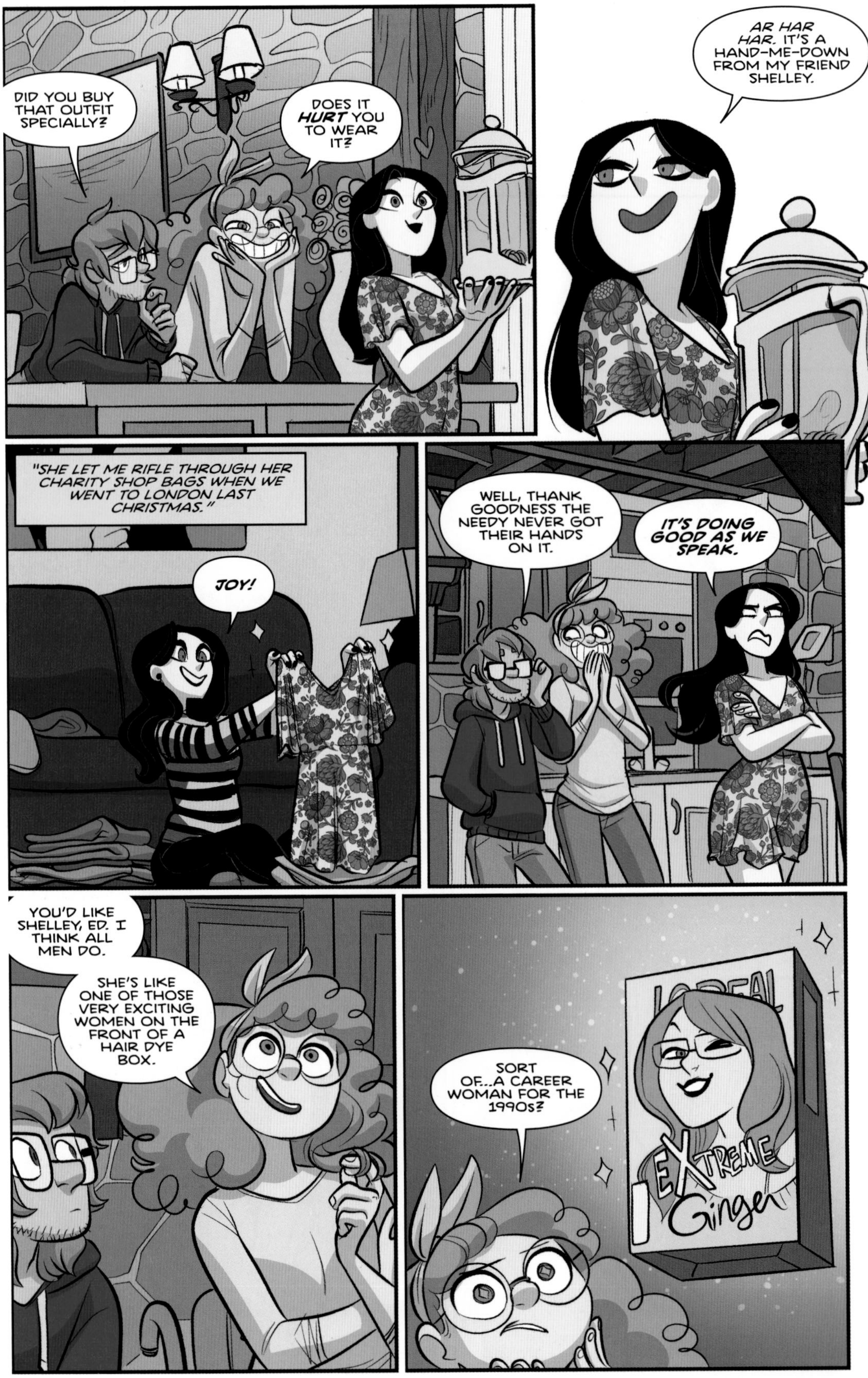
DID YOU BUY THAT OUTFIT SPECIALLY?
DOES IT HURT YOU TO WEAR IT?
AR HAR HAR. IT'S A HAND-ME-DOWN FROM MY FRIEND SHELLEY.
"SHE LET ME RIFLE THROUGH HER CHARITY SHOP BAGS WHEN WE WENT TO LONDON LAST CHRISTMAS."
JOY!
WELL, THANK GOODNESS THE NEEDY NEVER GOT THEIR HANDS ON IT.
IT'S DOING GOOD AS WE SPEAK.
YOU'D LIKE SHELLEY, ED. I THINK ALL MEN DO.
SHE'S LIKE ONE OF THOSE VERY EXCITING WOMEN ON THE FRONT OF A HAIR DYE BOX.
SORT OF...A CAREER WOMAN FOR THE 1990s?
EXTREME
Ginger

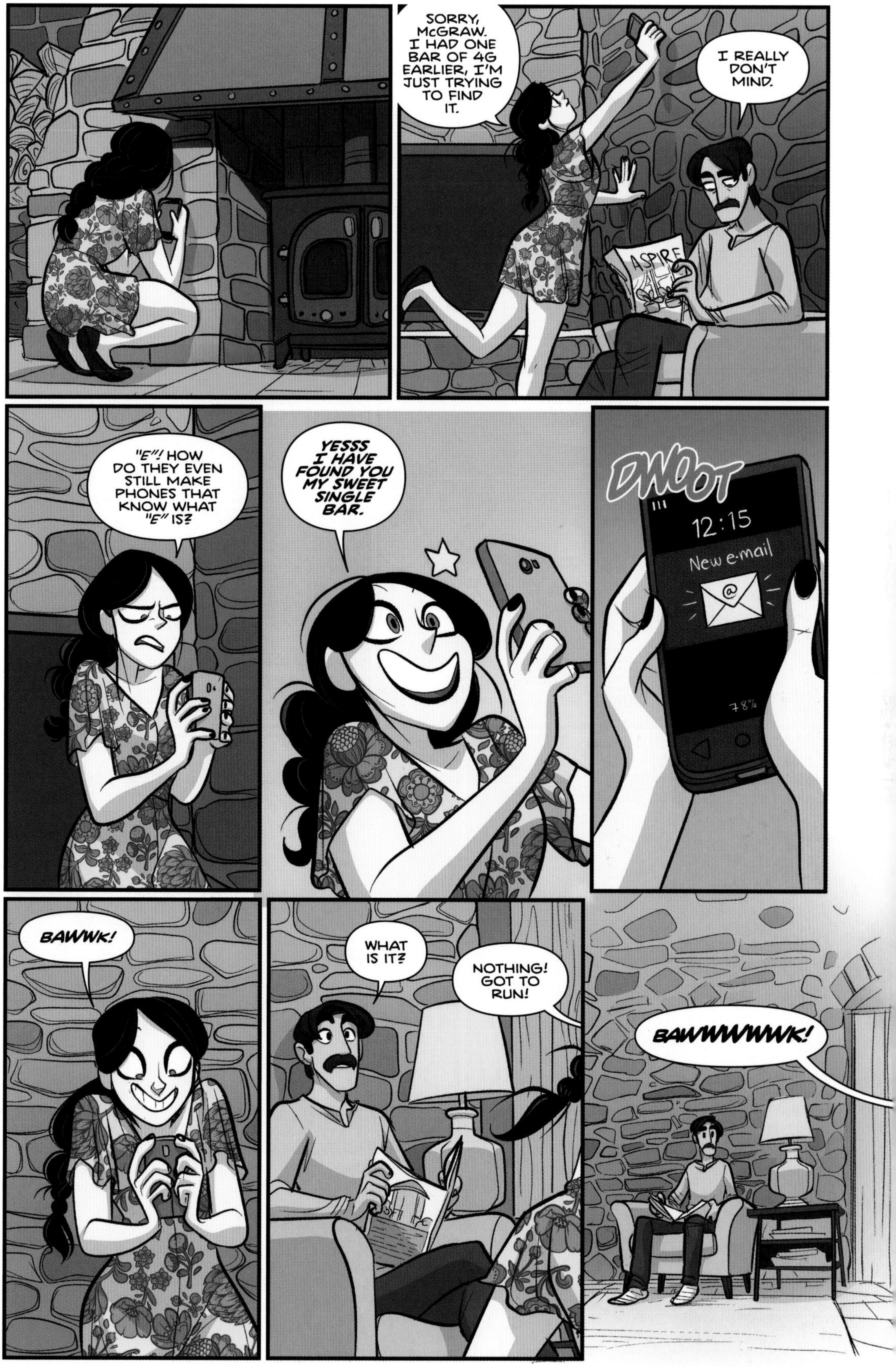

SORRY, McGRAW. I HAD ONE BAR OF 4G EARLIER, I'M JUST TRYING TO FIND IT.
I REALLY DON'T MIND.
ASPIRE
"E"! HOW DO THEY EVEN STILL MAKE PHONES THAT KNOW WHAT "E" IS?
YESSS I HAVE FOUND YOU MY SWEET SINGLE BAR.
DWOOT
12:15
New e-mail
@
78%
BAWWK!
WHAT IS IT?
NOTHING! GOT TO RUN!
BAWWWWWK!

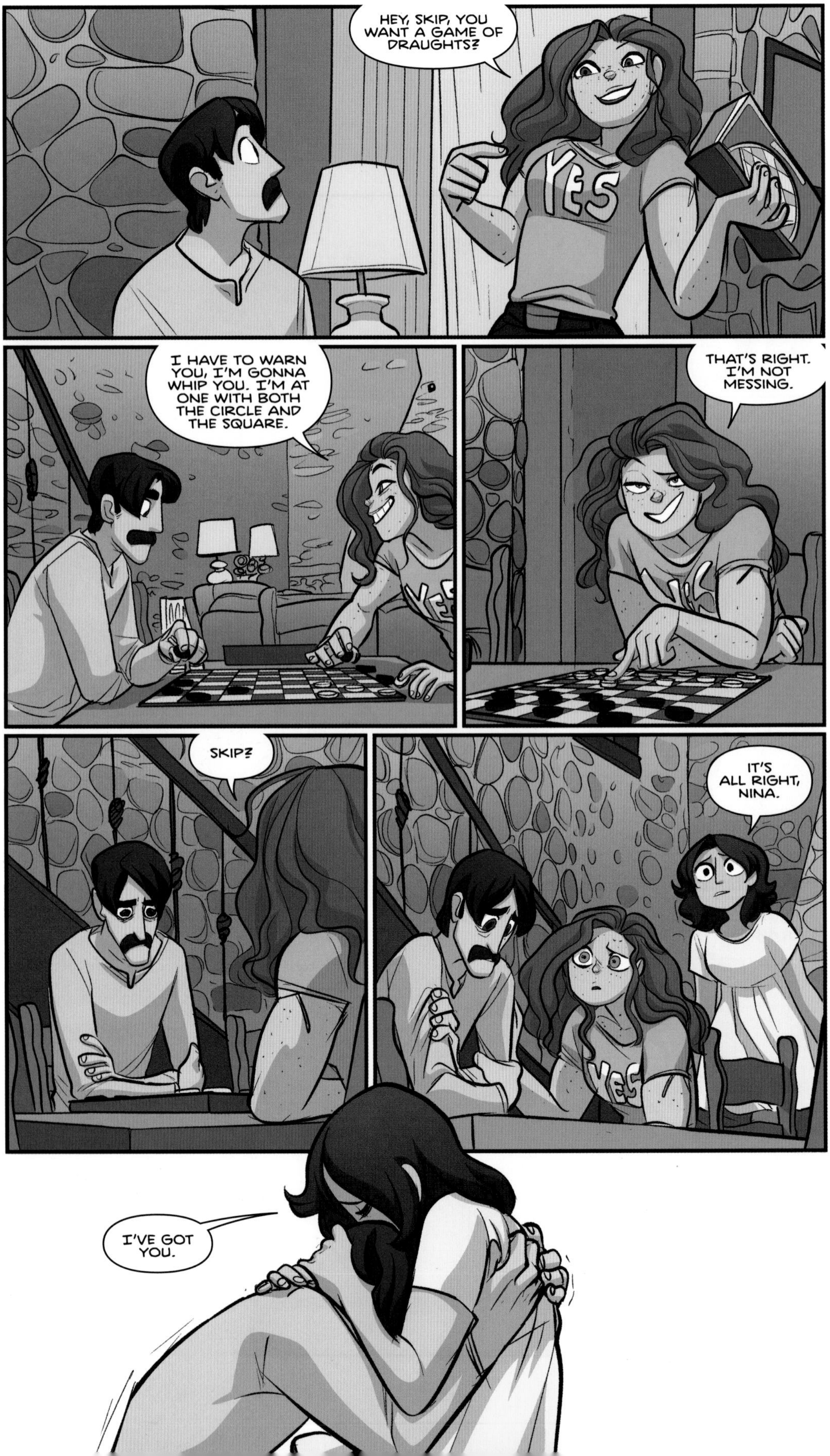

HEY, SKIP, YOU WANT A GAME OF DRAUGHTS?
I HAVE TO WARN YOU, I'M GONNA WHIP YOU. I'M AT ONE WITH BOTH THE CIRCLE AND THE SQUARE.
THAT'S RIGHT. I'M NOT MESSING.
SKIP?
IT'S ALL RIGHT, NINA.
I'VE GOT YOU.

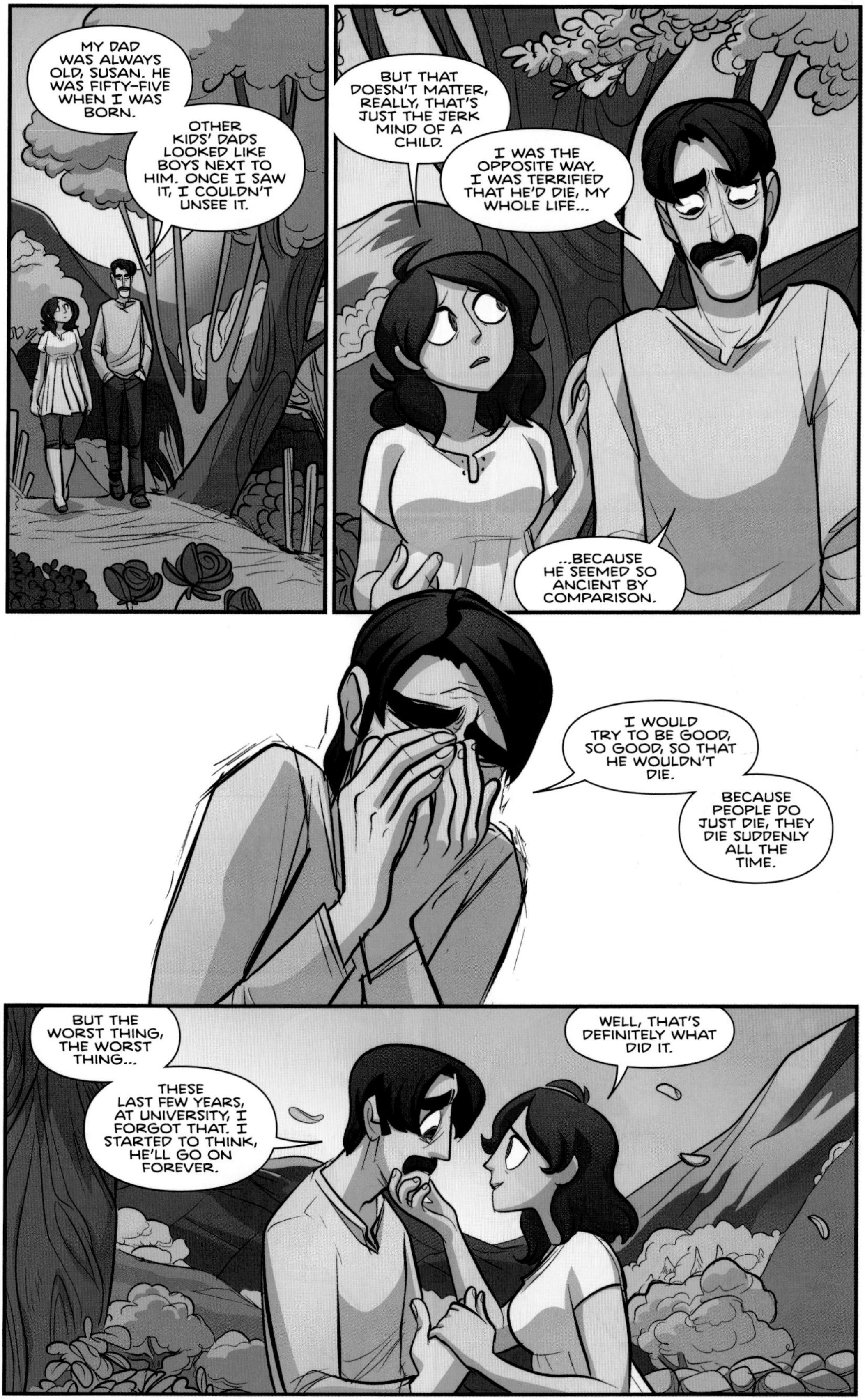

MY DAD WAS ALWAYS OLD, SUSAN. HE WAS FIFTY-FIVE WHEN I WAS BORN.
OTHER KIDS' DADS LOOKED LIKE BOYS NEXT TO HIM. ONCE I SAW IT, I COULDN'T UNSEE IT.
BUT THAT DOESN'T MATTER, REALLY, THAT'S JUST THE JERK MIND OF A CHILD.
I WAS THE OPPOSITE WAY. I WAS TERRIFIED THAT HE'D DIE, MY WHOLE LIFE...
...BECAUSE HE SEEMED SO ANCIENT BY COMPARISON.
I WOULD TRY TO BE GOOD, SO GOOD, SO THAT HE WOULDN'T DIE.
BECAUSE PEOPLE DO JUST DIE, THEY DIE SUDDENLY ALL THE TIME.
BUT THE WORST THING, THE WORST THING...
THESE LAST FEW YEARS, AT UNIVERSITY, I FORGOT THAT. I STARTED TO THINK, HE'LL GO ON FOREVER.
WELL, THAT'S DEFINITELY WHAT DID IT.

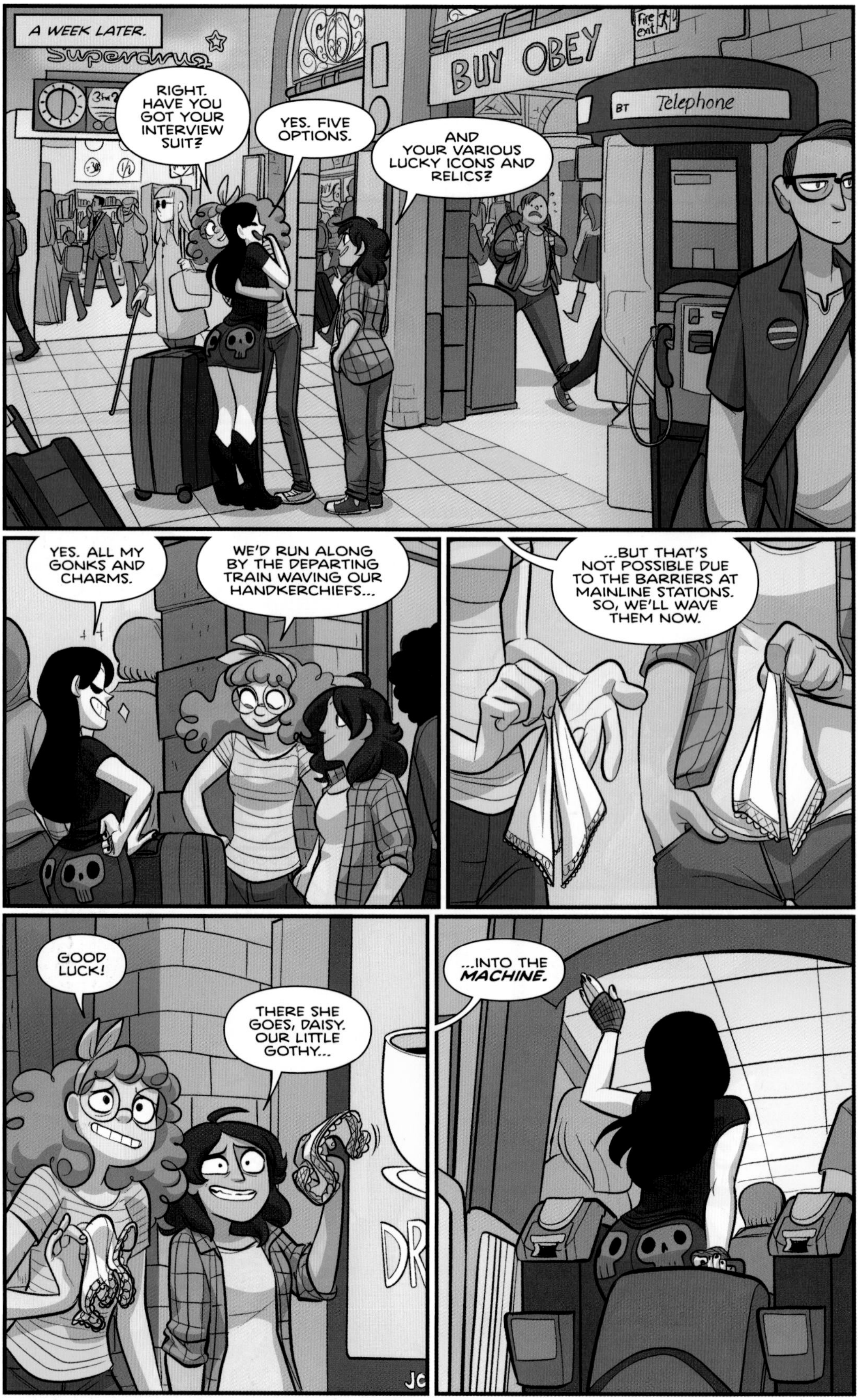
A WEEK LATER.
Superdrug
RIGHT. HAVE YOU GOT YOUR INTERVIEW SUIT?
YES. FIVE OPTIONS.
AND YOUR VARIOUS LUCKY ICONS AND RELICS?
BUY OBEY
Fire exit
BT Telephone
YES. ALL MY GONKS AND CHARMS.
WE'D RUN ALONG BY THE DEPARTING TRAIN WAVING OUR HANDKERCHIEFS...
...BUT THAT'S NOT POSSIBLE DUE TO THE BARRIERS AT MAINLINE STATIONS. SO, WE'LL WAVE THEM NOW.
GOOD LUCK!
THERE SHE GOES, DAISY. OUR LITTLE GOTHY...
...INTO THE *MACHINE.*

CHAPTER
FIFTY-TWO

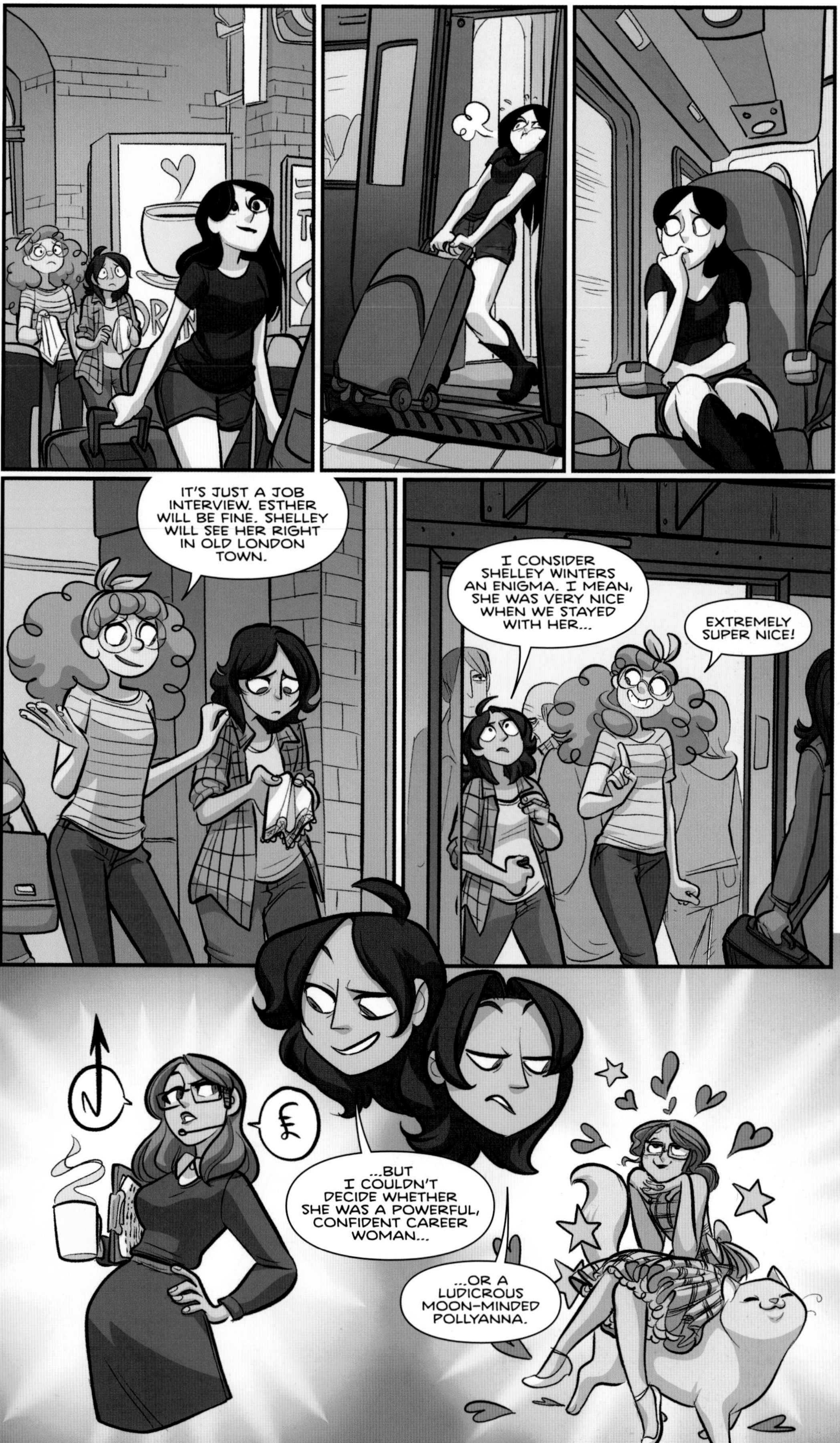
IT'S JUST A JOB INTERVIEW. ESTHER WILL BE FINE. SHELLEY WILL SEE HER RIGHT IN OLD LONDON TOWN.
I CONSIDER SHELLEY WINTERS AN ENIGMA. I MEAN, SHE WAS VERY NICE WHEN WE STAYED WITH HER...
EXTREMELY SUPER NICE!
...BUT I COULDN'T DECIDE WHETHER SHE WAS A POWERFUL, CONFIDENT CAREER WOMAN...
...OR A LUDICROUS MOON-MINDED POLLYANNA.

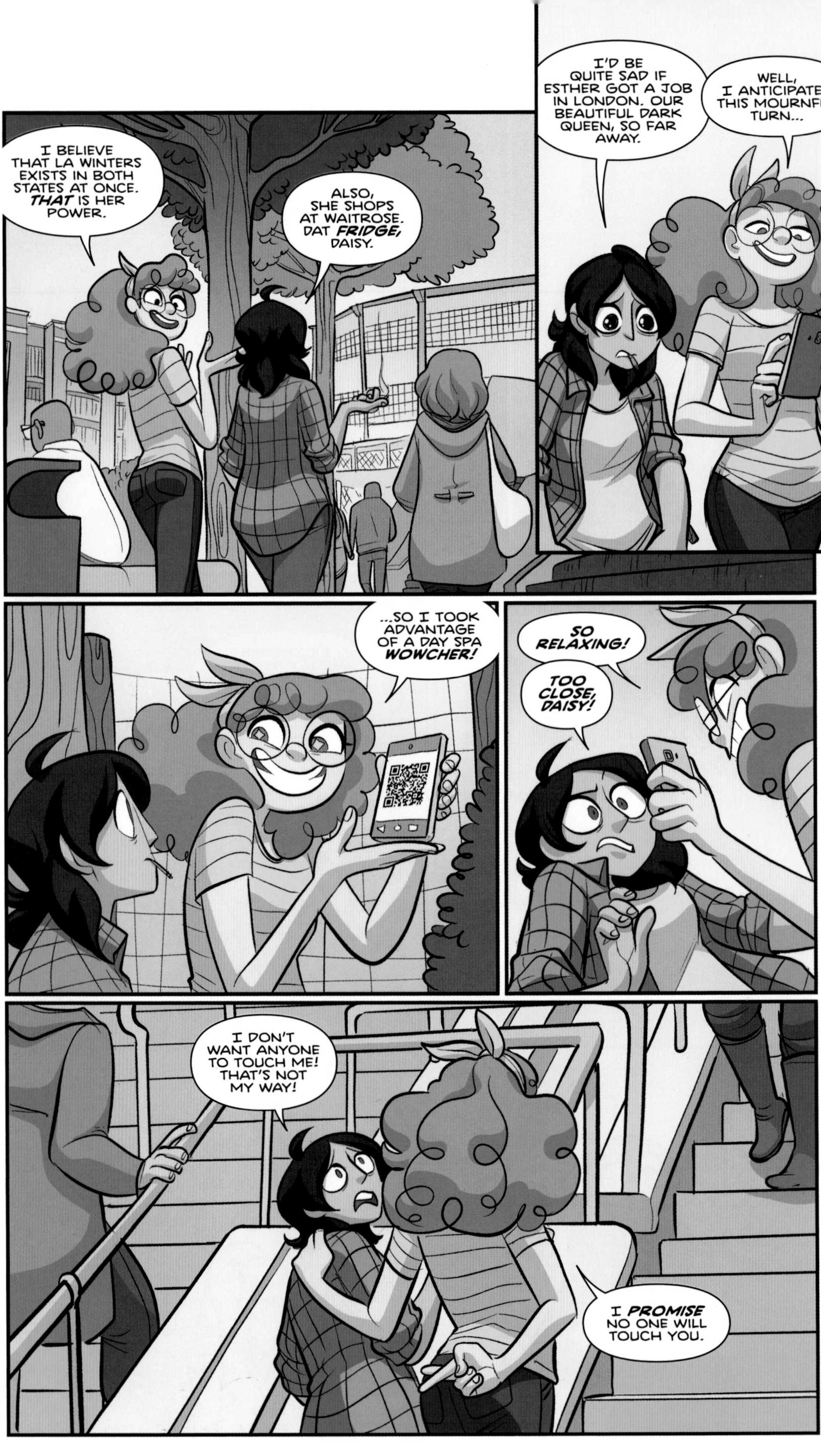
I BELIEVE THAT LA WINTERS EXISTS IN BOTH STATES AT ONCE. *THAT* IS HER POWER.
ALSO, SHE SHOPS AT WAITROSE. DAT *FRIDGE,* DAISY.
I'D BE QUITE SAD IF ESTHER GOT A JOB IN LONDON. OUR BEAUTIFUL DARK QUEEN, SO FAR AWAY.
WELL, I ANTICIPATED THIS MOURNFUL TURN...
...SO I TOOK ADVANTAGE OF A DAY SPA *WOWCHER!*
SO RELAXING!
TOO CLOSE, DAISY!
I DON'T WANT ANYONE TO TOUCH ME! THAT'S NOT MY WAY!
I *PROMISE* NO ONE WILL TOUCH YOU.

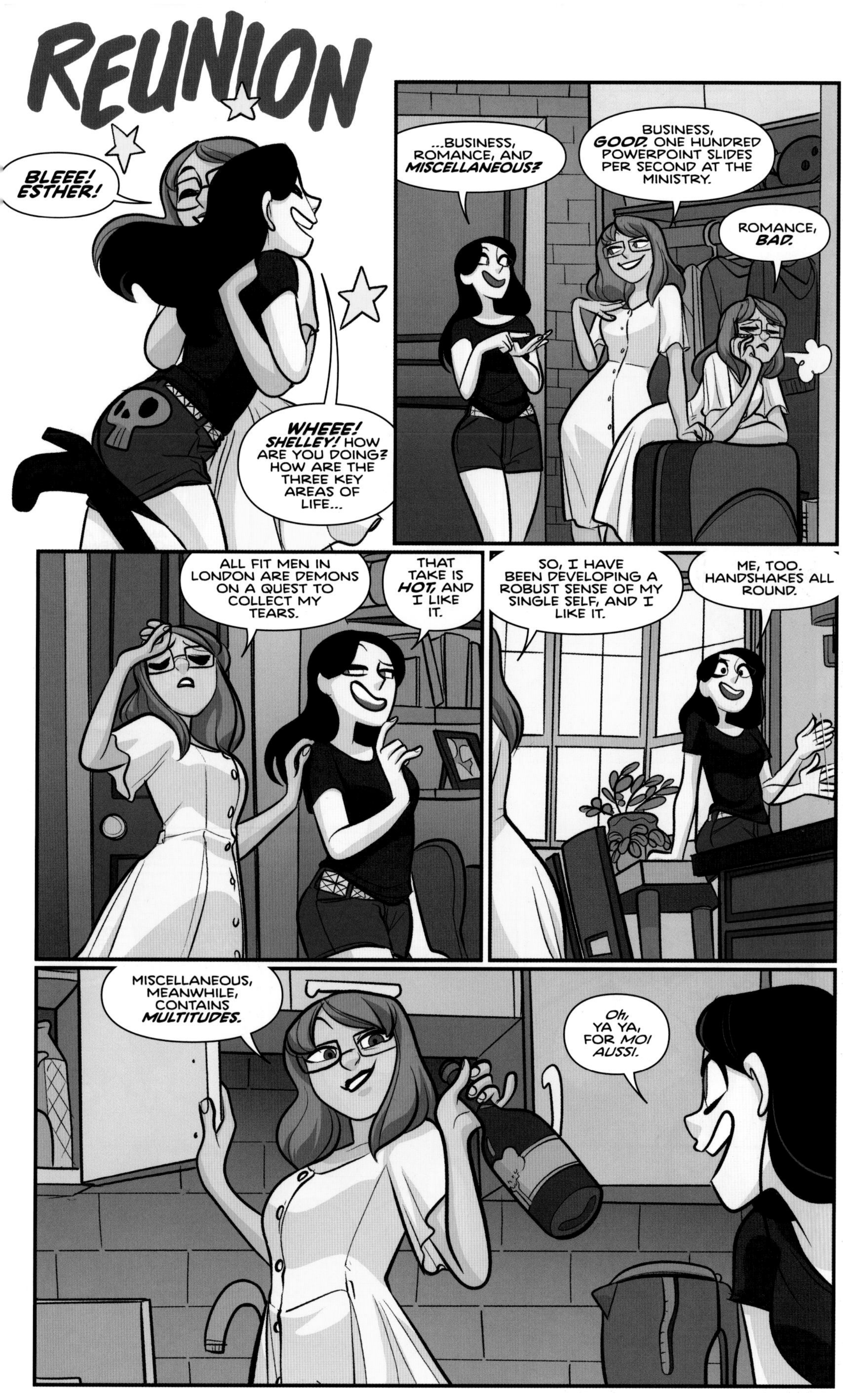
REUNION
BLEEE! ESTHER!
WHEEE! SHELLEY! HOW ARE YOU DOING? HOW ARE THE THREE KEY AREAS OF LIFE...
...BUSINESS, ROMANCE, AND MISCELLANEOUS?
BUSINESS, GOOD. ONE HUNDRED POWERPOINT SLIDES PER SECOND AT THE MINISTRY.
ROMANCE, BAD.
ALL FIT MEN IN LONDON ARE DEMONS ON A QUEST TO COLLECT MY TEARS.
THAT TAKE IS HOT, AND I LIKE IT.
SO, I HAVE BEEN DEVELOPING A ROBUST SENSE OF MY SINGLE SELF, AND I LIKE IT.
ME, TOO. HANDSHAKES ALL ROUND.
MISCELLANEOUS, MEANWHILE, CONTAINS MULTITUDES.
Oh, YA YA, FOR MOI AUSSI.

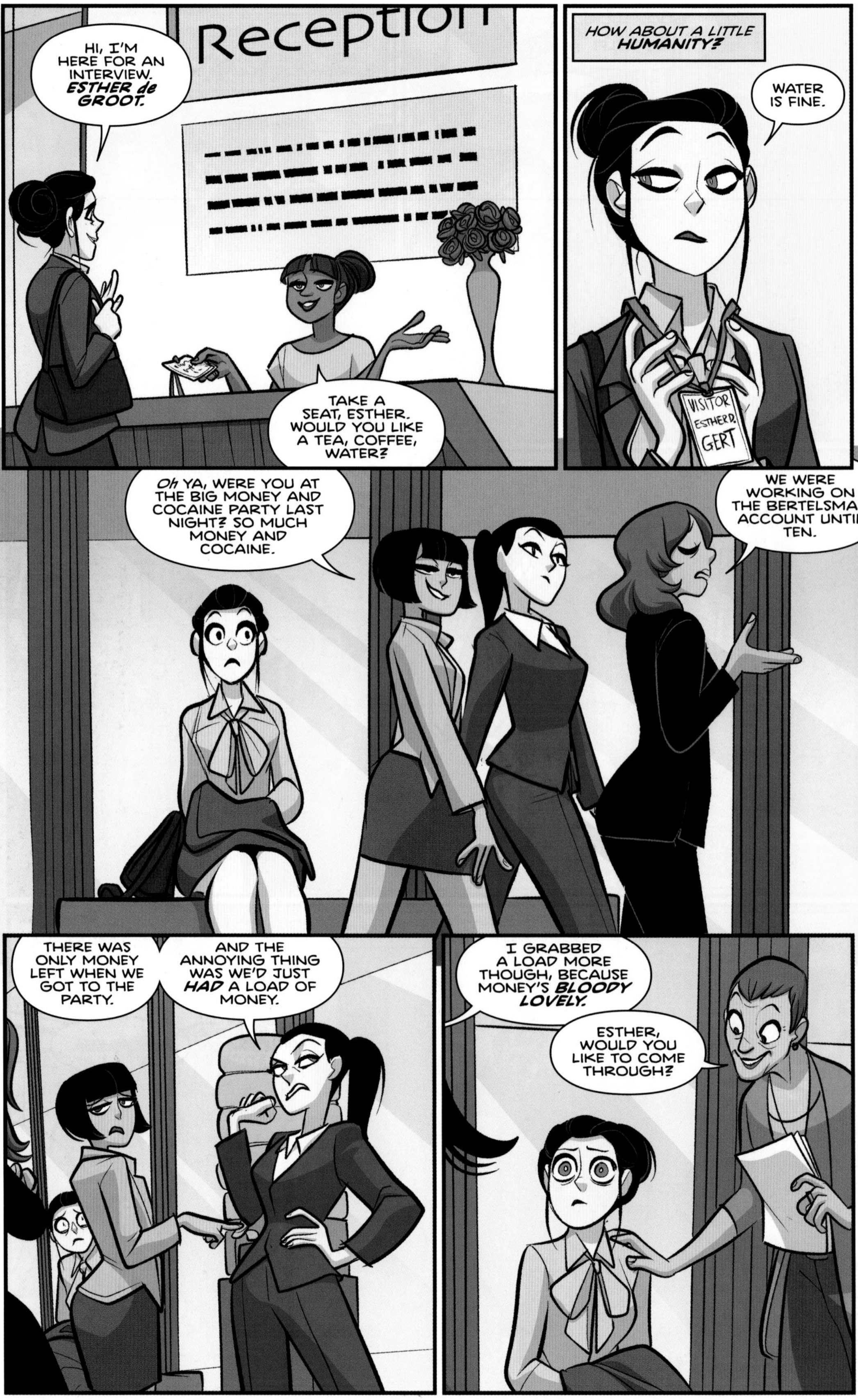
Reception
HI, I'M HERE FOR AN INTERVIEW. ***ESTHER de GROOT.***
TAKE A SEAT, ESTHER. WOULD YOU LIKE A TEA, COFFEE, WATER?
HOW ABOUT A LITTLE ***HUMANITY?***
WATER IS FINE.
VISITOR ESTHER D. GERT
Oh YA, WERE YOU AT THE BIG MONEY AND COCAINE PARTY LAST NIGHT? SO MUCH MONEY AND COCAINE.
WE WERE WORKING ON THE BERTELSMAN ACCOUNT UNTIL TEN.
THERE WAS ONLY MONEY LEFT WHEN WE GOT TO THE PARTY.
AND THE ANNOYING THING WAS WE'D JUST ***HAD*** A LOAD OF MONEY.
I GRABBED A LOAD MORE THOUGH, BECAUSE MONEY'S ***BLOODY LOVELY.***
ESTHER, WOULD YOU LIKE TO COME THROUGH?

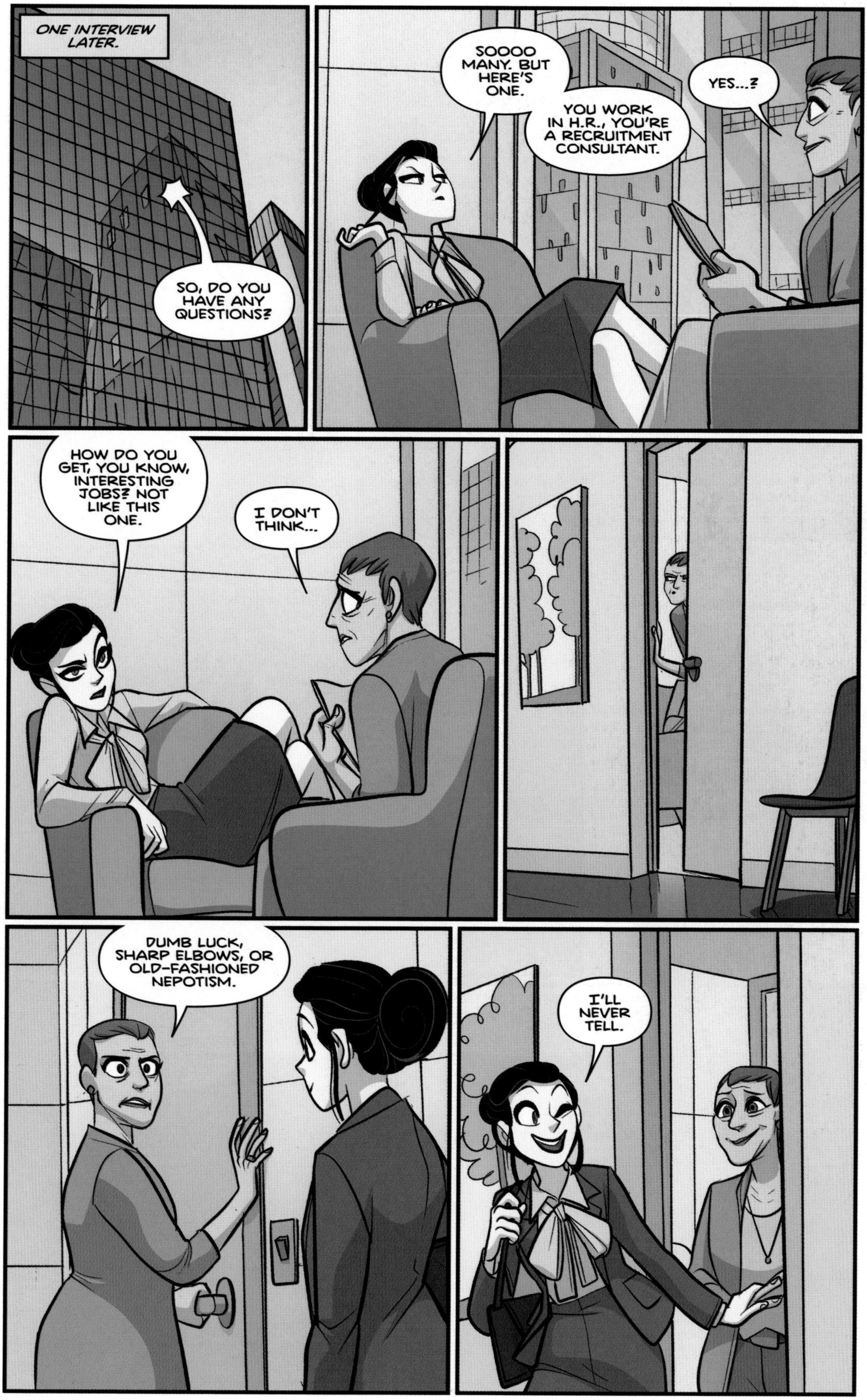
ONE INTERVIEW LATER.
SO, DO YOU HAVE ANY QUESTIONS?
SOOOO MANY. BUT HERE'S ONE.
YES...?
YOU WORK IN H.R., YOU'RE A RECRUITMENT CONSULTANT.
HOW DO YOU GET, YOU KNOW, INTERESTING JOBS? NOT LIKE THIS ONE.
I DON'T THINK...
DUMB LUCK, SHARP ELBOWS, OR OLD-FASHIONED NEPOTISM.
I'LL NEVER TELL.

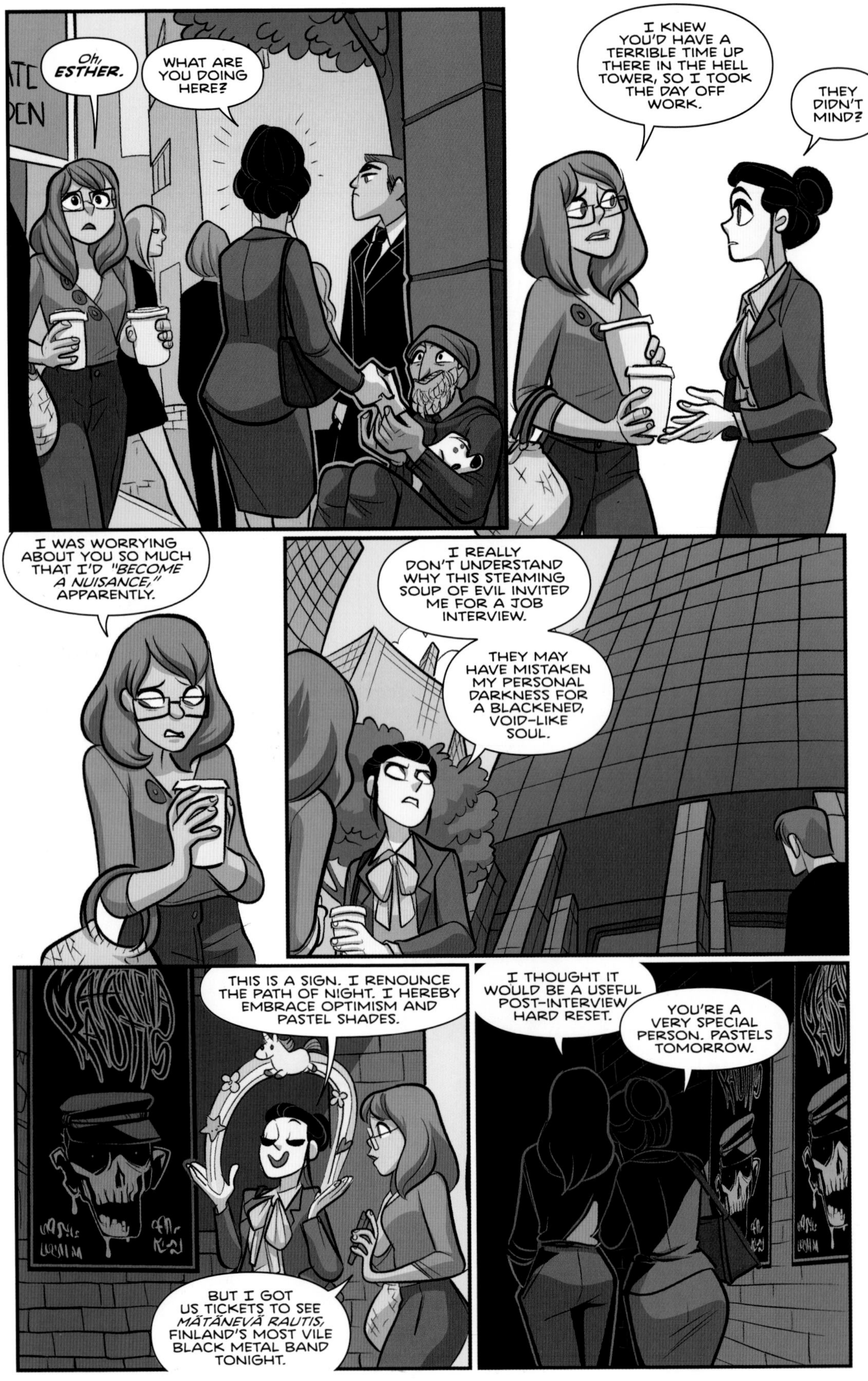
Oh, ESTHER.
WHAT ARE YOU DOING HERE?
I KNEW YOU'D HAVE A TERRIBLE TIME UP THERE IN THE HELL TOWER, SO I TOOK THE DAY OFF WORK.
THEY DIDN'T MIND?
I WAS WORRYING ABOUT YOU SO MUCH THAT I'D "BECOME A NUISANCE," APPARENTLY.
I REALLY DON'T UNDERSTAND WHY THIS STEAMING SOUP OF EVIL INVITED ME FOR A JOB INTERVIEW.
THEY MAY HAVE MISTAKEN MY PERSONAL DARKNESS FOR A BLACKENED, VOID-LIKE SOUL.
THIS IS A SIGN. I RENOUNCE THE PATH OF NIGHT. I HEREBY EMBRACE OPTIMISM AND PASTEL SHADES.
BUT I GOT US TICKETS TO SEE MÄTÄNEVÄ RAUTIS, FINLAND'S MOST VILE BLACK METAL BAND TONIGHT.
I THOUGHT IT WOULD BE A USEFUL POST-INTERVIEW HARD RESET.
YOU'RE A VERY SPECIAL PERSON. PASTELS TOMORROW.

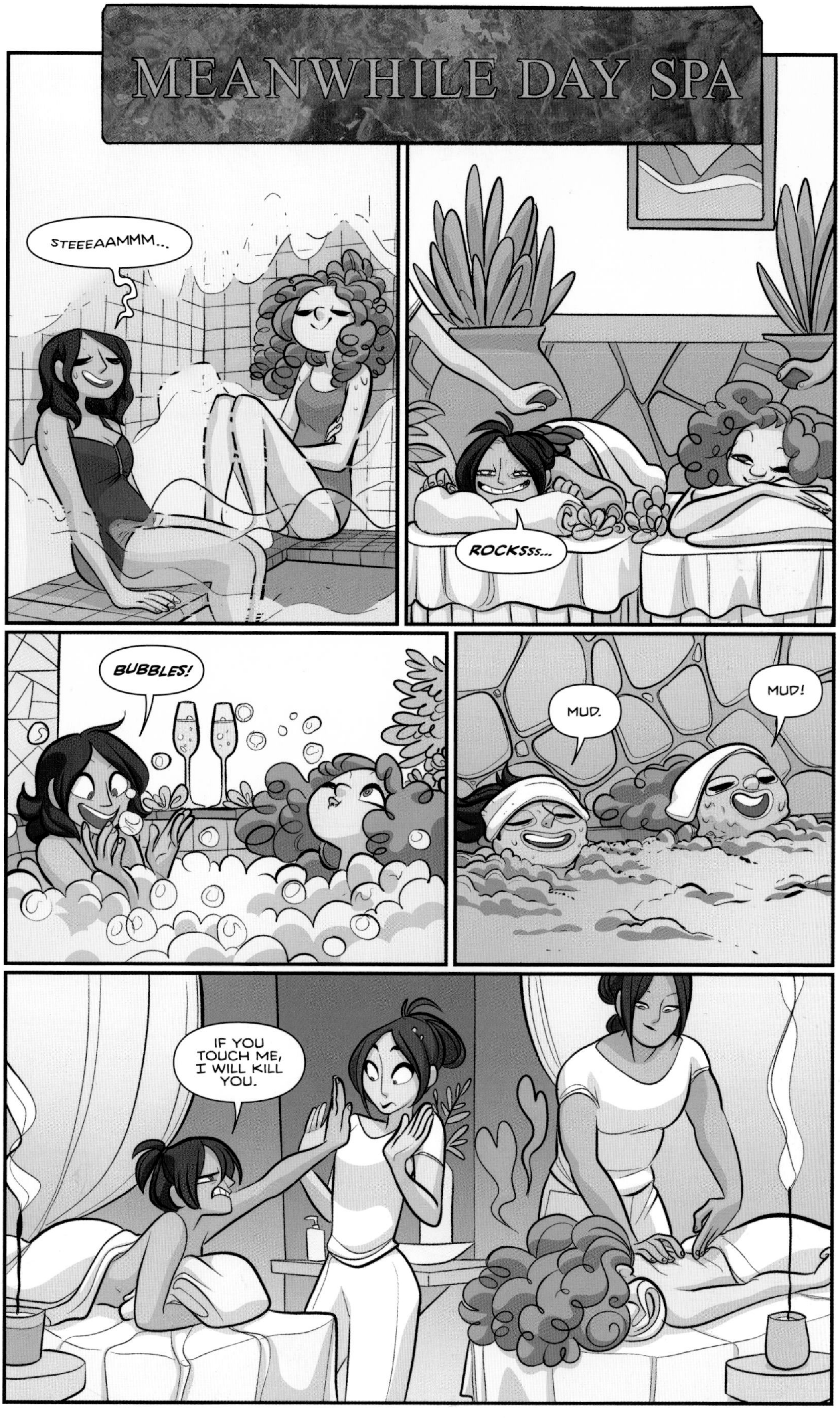
MEANWHILE DAY SPA
STEEEAAMMM...
ROCKSSS...
BUBBLES!
MUD.
MUD!
IF YOU TOUCH ME, I WILL KILL YOU.

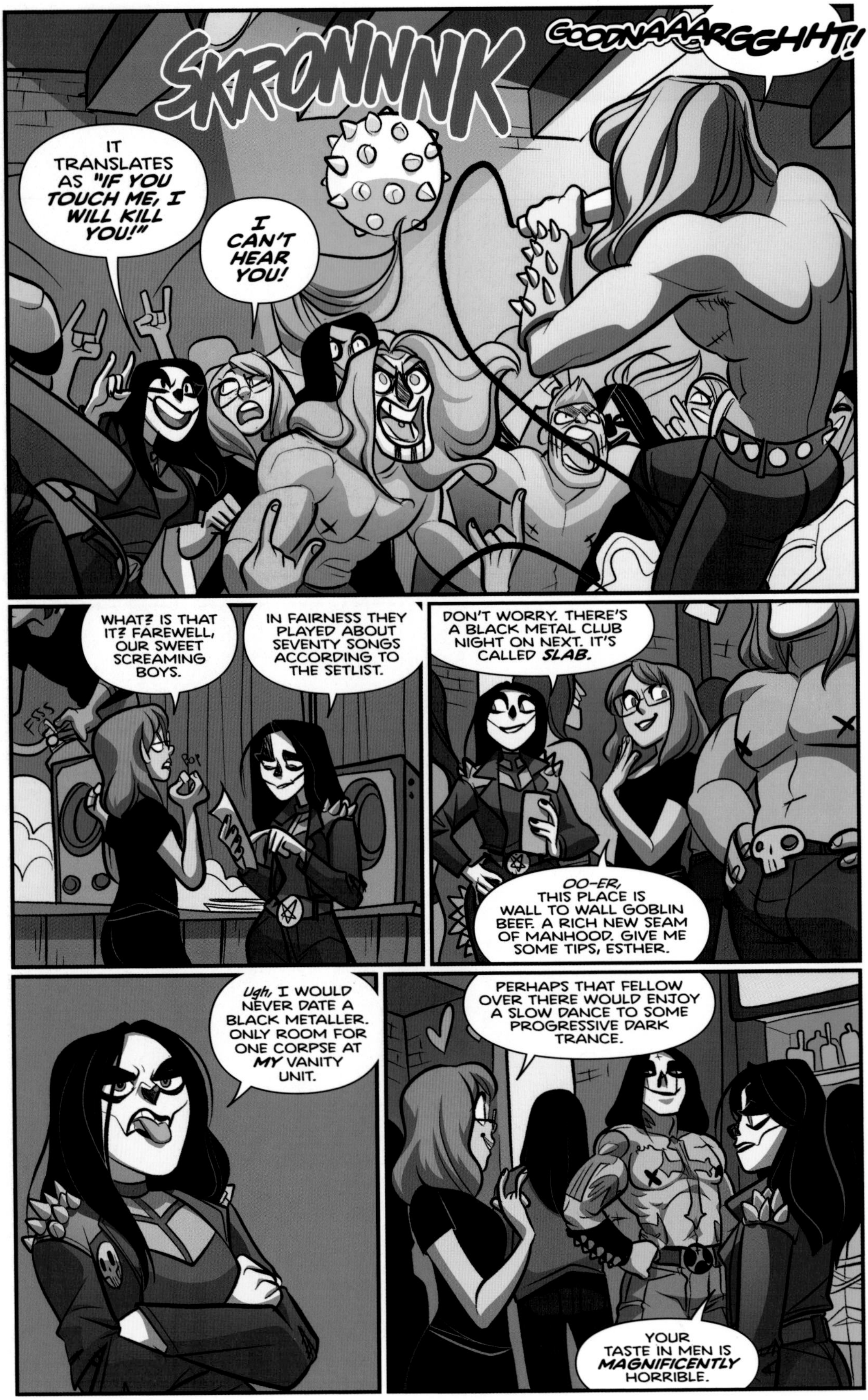

SKRONNNK
GOODNAAAARGGHHT!
IT TRANSLATES AS "IF YOU TOUCH ME, I WILL KILL YOU!"
I CAN'T HEAR YOU!
WHAT? IS THAT IT? FAREWELL, OUR SWEET SCREAMING BOYS.
IN FAIRNESS THEY PLAYED ABOUT SEVENTY SONGS ACCORDING TO THE SETLIST.
DON'T WORRY. THERE'S A BLACK METAL CLUB NIGHT ON NEXT. IT'S CALLED SLAB.
OO-ER, THIS PLACE IS WALL TO WALL GOBLIN BEEF. A RICH NEW SEAM OF MANHOOD. GIVE ME SOME TIPS, ESTHER.
Ugh, I WOULD NEVER DATE A BLACK METALLER. ONLY ROOM FOR ONE CORPSE AT MY VANITY UNIT.
PERHAPS THAT FELLOW OVER THERE WOULD ENJOY A SLOW DANCE TO SOME PROGRESSIVE DARK TRANCE.
YOUR TASTE IN MEN IS MAGNIFICENTLY HORRIBLE.

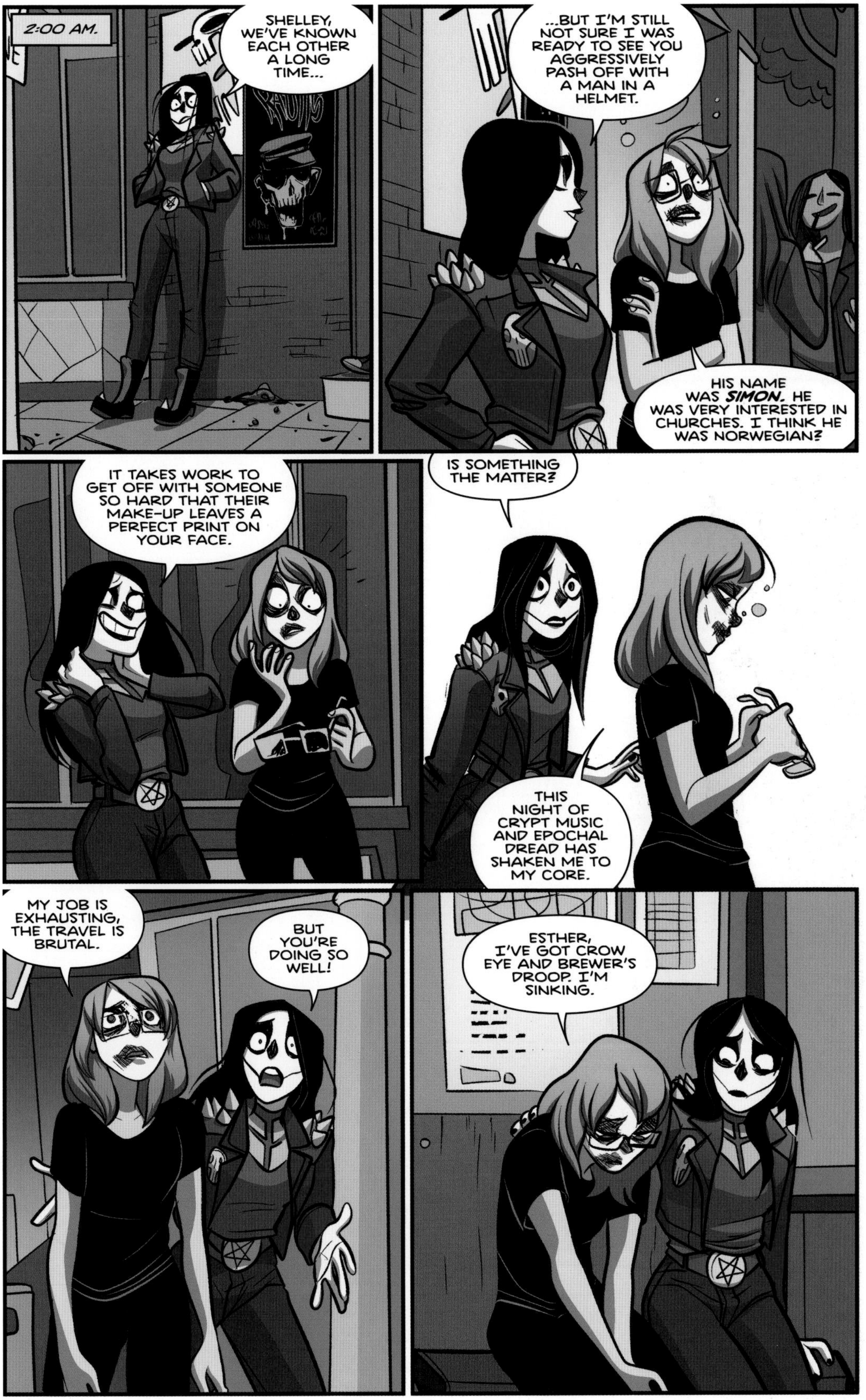

2:00 AM.
SHELLEY, WE'VE KNOWN EACH OTHER A LONG TIME...
...BUT I'M STILL NOT SURE I WAS READY TO SEE YOU AGGRESSIVELY PASH OFF WITH A MAN IN A HELMET.
HIS NAME WAS SIMON. HE WAS VERY INTERESTED IN CHURCHES. I THINK HE WAS NORWEGIAN?
IT TAKES WORK TO GET OFF WITH SOMEONE SO HARD THAT THEIR MAKE-UP LEAVES A PERFECT PRINT ON YOUR FACE.
IS SOMETHING THE MATTER?
THIS NIGHT OF CRYPT MUSIC AND EPOCHAL DREAD HAS SHAKEN ME TO MY CORE.
MY JOB IS EXHAUSTING, THE TRAVEL IS BRUTAL.
BUT YOU'RE DOING SO WELL!
ESTHER, I'VE GOT CROW EYE AND BREWER'S DROOP. I'M SINKING.

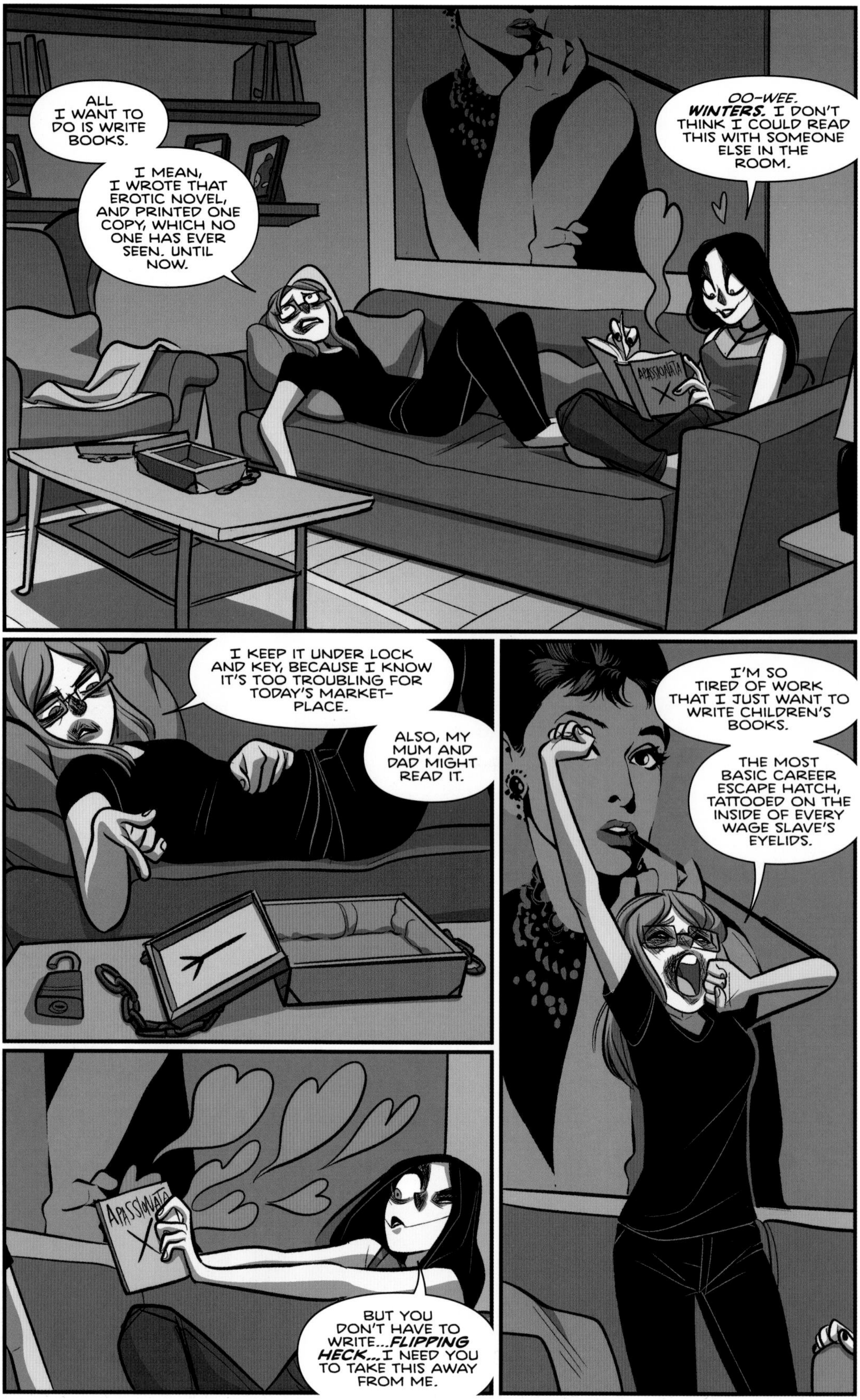
ALL I WANT TO DO IS WRITE BOOKS.
I MEAN, I WROTE THAT EROTIC NOVEL, AND PRINTED ONE COPY, WHICH NO ONE HAS EVER SEEN. UNTIL NOW.
OO-WEE. **WINTERS.** I DON'T THINK I COULD READ THIS WITH SOMEONE ELSE IN THE ROOM.
APASSIONATA X
I KEEP IT UNDER LOCK AND KEY, BECAUSE I KNOW IT'S TOO TROUBLING FOR TODAY'S MARKET-PLACE.
ALSO, MY MUM AND DAD MIGHT READ IT.
APASSIONATA X
BUT YOU DON'T HAVE TO WRITE...**FLIPPING HECK...** I NEED YOU TO TAKE THIS AWAY FROM ME.
I'M SO TIRED OF WORK THAT I JUST WANT TO WRITE CHILDREN'S BOOKS.
THE MOST BASIC CAREER ESCAPE HATCH, TATTOOED ON THE INSIDE OF EVERY WAGE SLAVE'S EYELIDS.

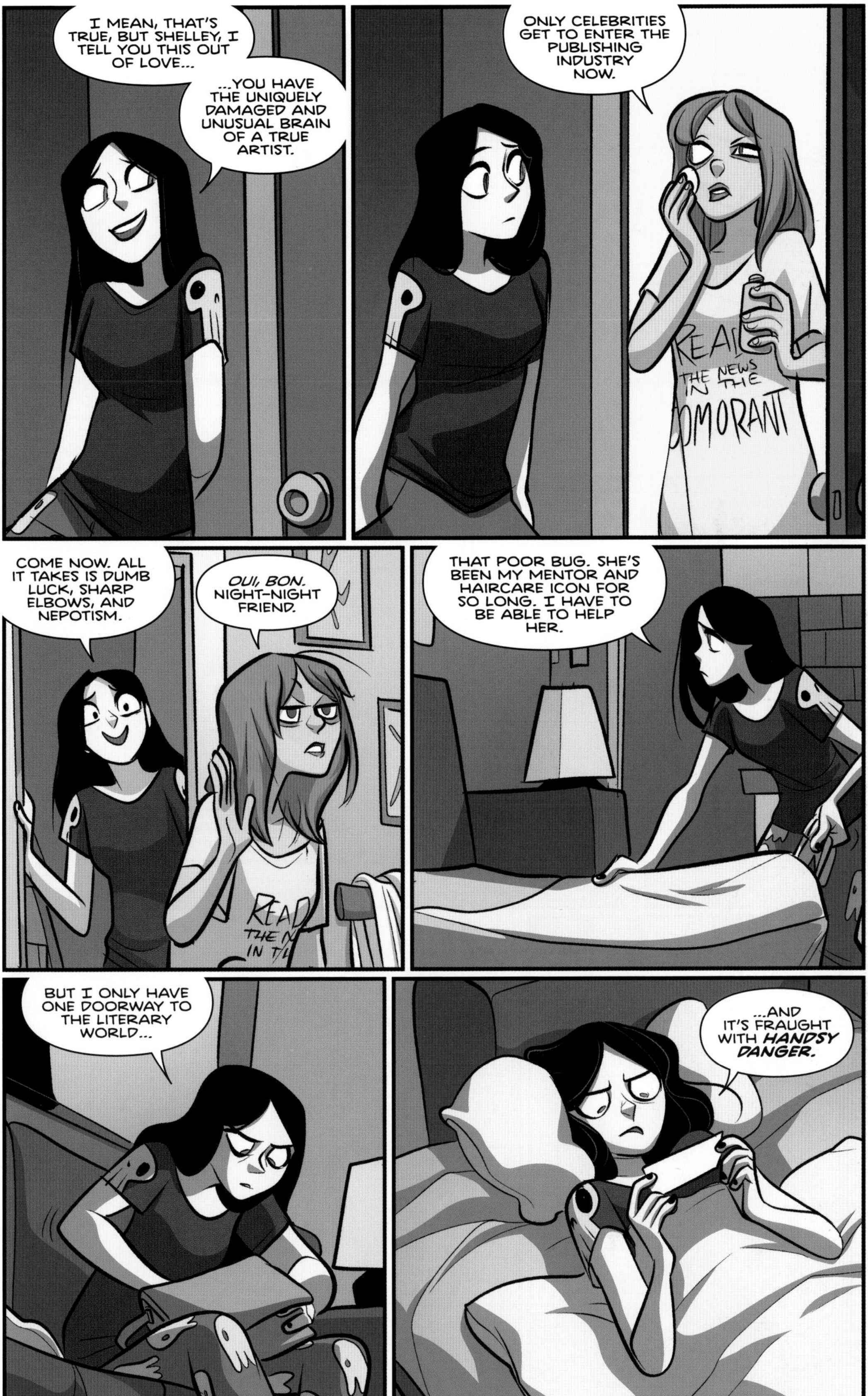
I MEAN, THAT'S TRUE, BUT SHELLEY, I TELL YOU THIS OUT OF LOVE...
...YOU HAVE THE UNIQUELY DAMAGED AND UNUSUAL BRAIN OF A TRUE ARTIST.
ONLY CELEBRITIES GET TO ENTER THE PUBLISHING INDUSTRY NOW.
READ THE NEWS IN THE OMORANT
COME NOW. ALL IT TAKES IS DUMB LUCK, SHARP ELBOWS, AND NEPOTISM.
OUI, BON. NIGHT-NIGHT FRIEND.
THAT POOR BUG. SHE'S BEEN MY MENTOR AND HAIRCARE ICON FOR SO LONG. I HAVE TO BE ABLE TO HELP HER.
BUT I ONLY HAVE ONE DOORWAY TO THE LITERARY WORLD...
...AND IT'S FRAUGHT WITH ***HANDSY DANGER.***

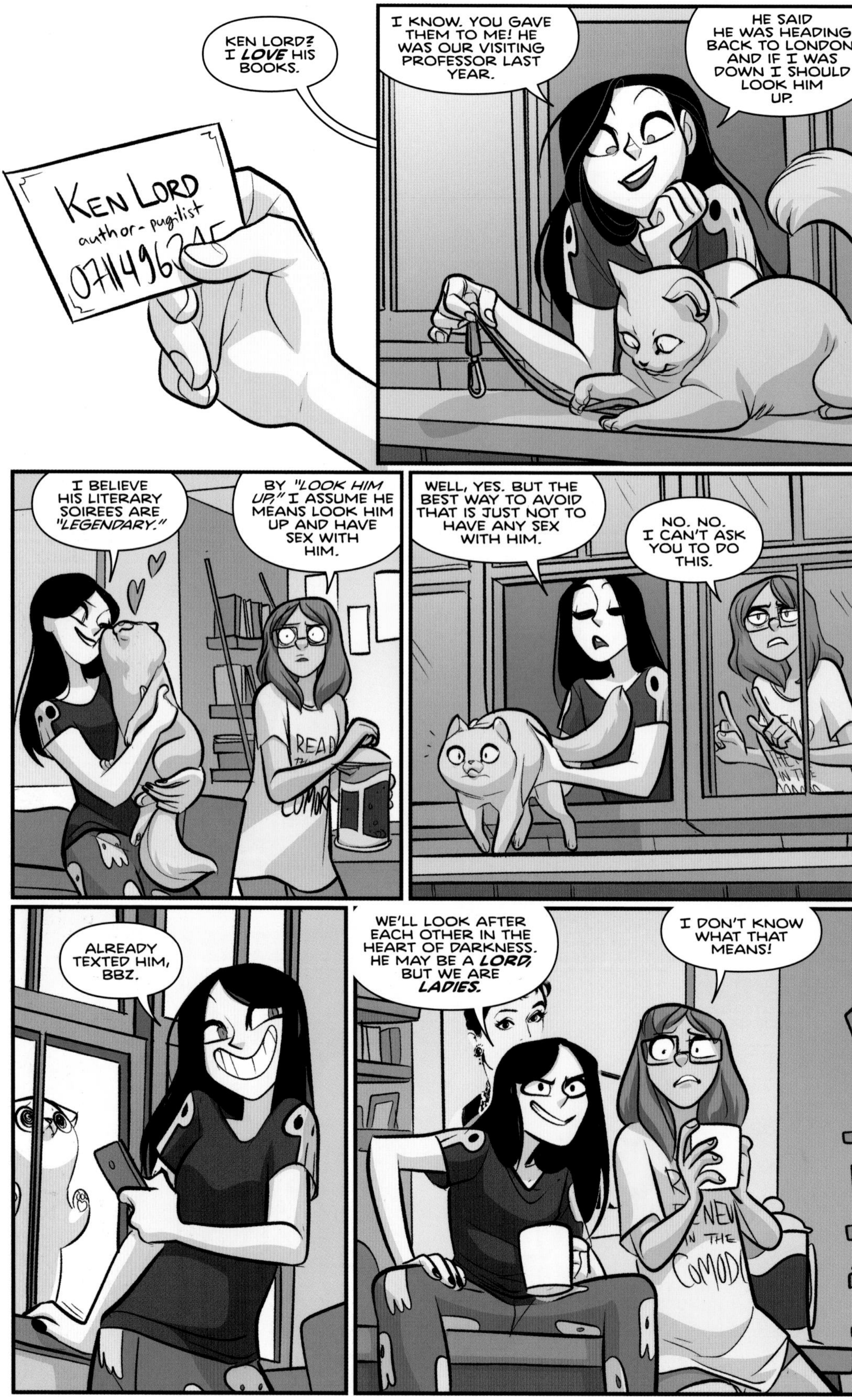

KEN LORD? I LOVE HIS BOOKS.
KEN LORD
author - pugilist
0711496245
I KNOW. YOU GAVE THEM TO ME! HE WAS OUR VISITING PROFESSOR LAST YEAR.
HE SAID HE WAS HEADING BACK TO LONDON, AND IF I WAS DOWN I SHOULD LOOK HIM UP.
I BELIEVE HIS LITERARY SOIREES ARE "LEGENDARY."
BY "LOOK HIM UP," I ASSUME HE MEANS LOOK HIM UP AND HAVE SEX WITH HIM.
WELL, YES. BUT THE BEST WAY TO AVOID THAT IS JUST NOT TO HAVE ANY SEX WITH HIM.
NO. NO. I CAN'T ASK YOU TO DO THIS.
ALREADY TEXTED HIM, BBZ.
WE'LL LOOK AFTER EACH OTHER IN THE HEART OF DARKNESS. HE MAY BE A LORD, BUT WE ARE LADIES.
I DON'T KNOW WHAT THAT MEANS!

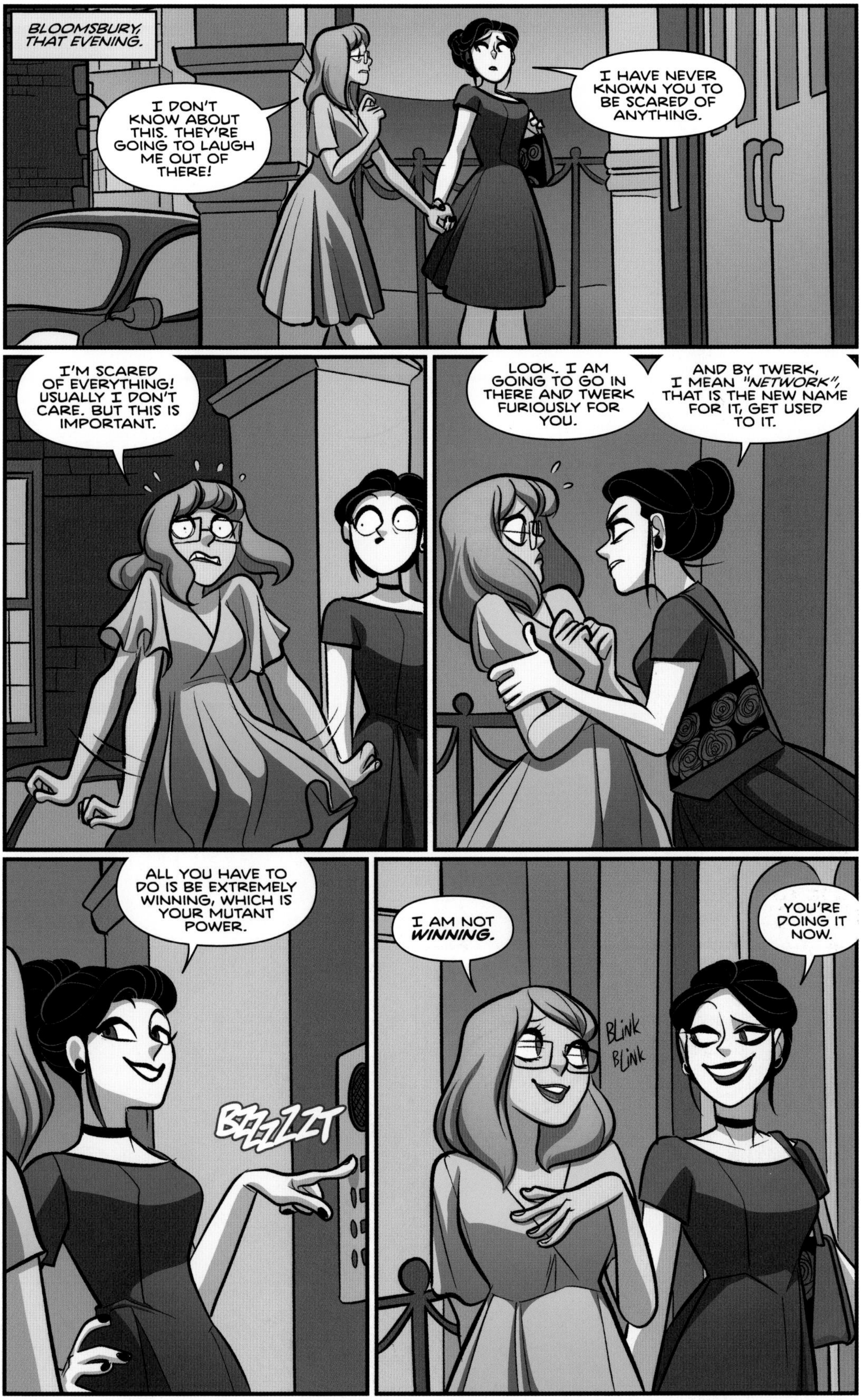
BLOOMSBURY, THAT EVENING.
I DON'T KNOW ABOUT THIS. THEY'RE GOING TO LAUGH ME OUT OF THERE!
I HAVE NEVER KNOWN YOU TO BE SCARED OF ANYTHING.
I'M SCARED OF EVERYTHING! USUALLY I DON'T CARE. BUT THIS IS IMPORTANT.
LOOK. I AM GOING TO GO IN THERE AND TWERK FURIOUSLY FOR YOU.
AND BY TWERK, I MEAN *"NETWORK"*, THAT IS THE NEW NAME FOR IT, GET USED TO IT.
ALL YOU HAVE TO DO IS BE EXTREMELY WINNING, WHICH IS YOUR MUTANT POWER.
BZZZZT
I AM NOT ***WINNING.***
BLINK BLINK
YOU'RE DOING IT NOW.

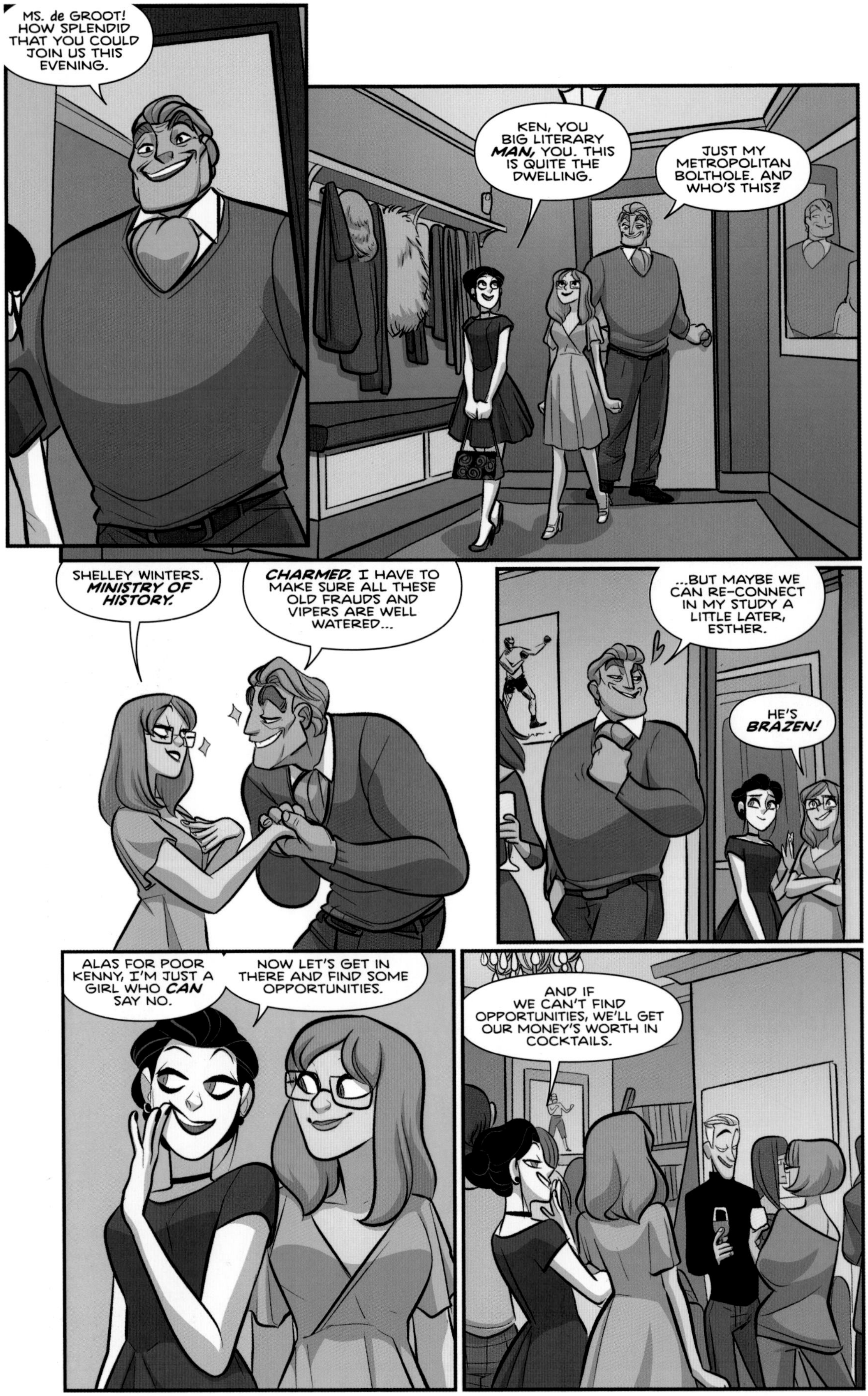
MS. de GROOT! HOW SPLENDID THAT YOU COULD JOIN US THIS EVENING.
KEN, YOU BIG LITERARY MAN, YOU. THIS IS QUITE THE DWELLING.
JUST MY METROPOLITAN BOLTHOLE. AND WHO'S THIS?
SHELLEY WINTERS. MINISTRY OF HISTORY.
CHARMED. I HAVE TO MAKE SURE ALL THESE OLD FRAUDS AND VIPERS ARE WELL WATERED...
...BUT MAYBE WE CAN RE-CONNECT IN MY STUDY A LITTLE LATER, ESTHER.
HE'S BRAZEN!
ALAS FOR POOR KENNY, I'M JUST A GIRL WHO CAN SAY NO.
NOW LET'S GET IN THERE AND FIND SOME OPPORTUNITIES.
AND IF WE CAN'T FIND OPPORTUNITIES, WE'LL GET OUR MONEY'S WORTH IN COCKTAILS.

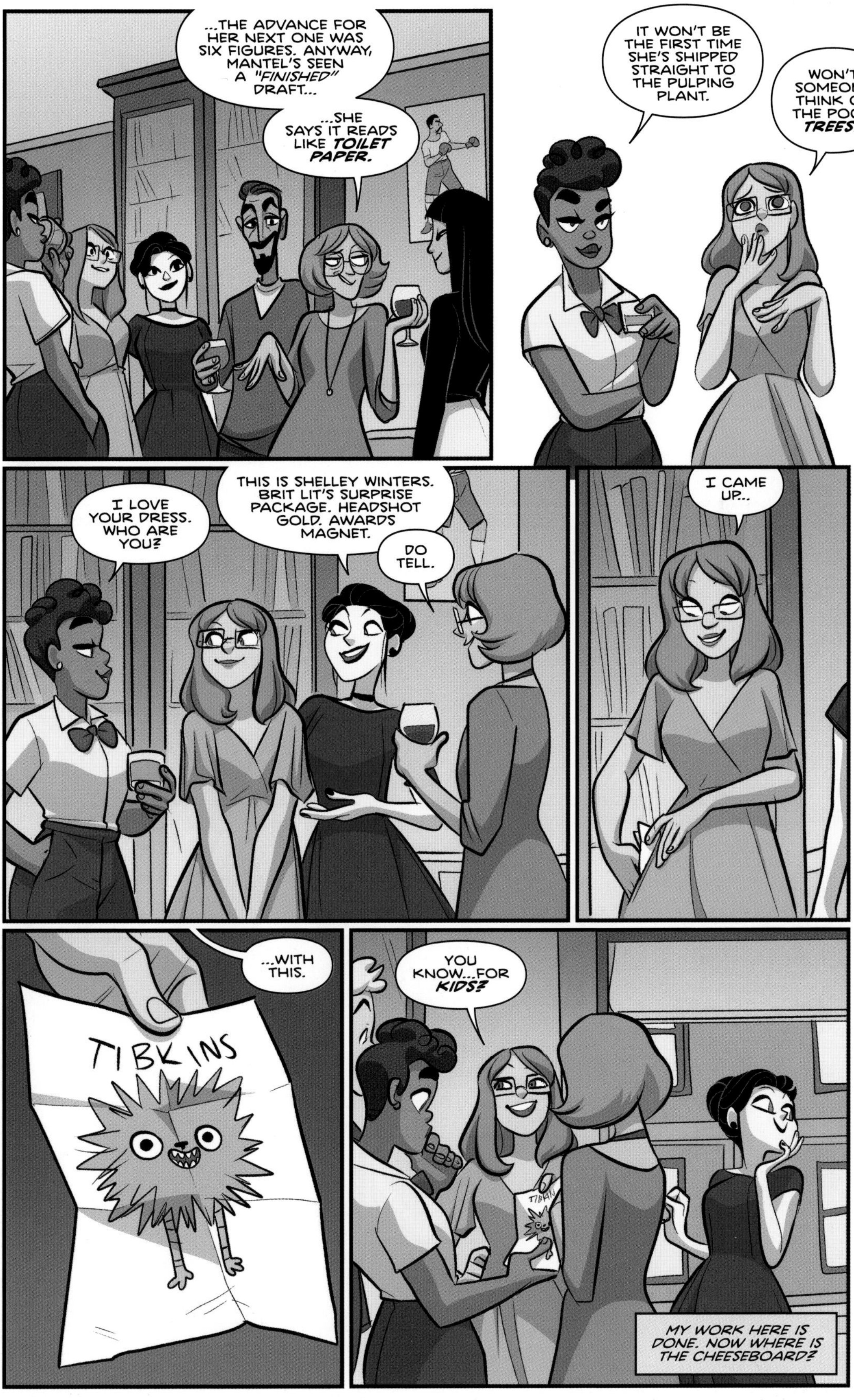
...THE ADVANCE FOR HER NEXT ONE WAS SIX FIGURES. ANYWAY, MANTEL'S SEEN A "FINISHED" DRAFT...
...SHE SAYS IT READS LIKE TOILET PAPER.
IT WON'T BE THE FIRST TIME SHE'S SHIPPED STRAIGHT TO THE PULPING PLANT.
WON'T SOMEONE THINK OF THE POOR TREES?
I LOVE YOUR DRESS. WHO ARE YOU?
THIS IS SHELLEY WINTERS. BRIT LIT'S SURPRISE PACKAGE. HEADSHOT GOLD. AWARDS MAGNET.
DO TELL.
I CAME UP...
...WITH THIS.
TIBKINS
YOU KNOW...FOR KIDS?
MY WORK HERE IS DONE. NOW WHERE IS THE CHEESEBOARD?

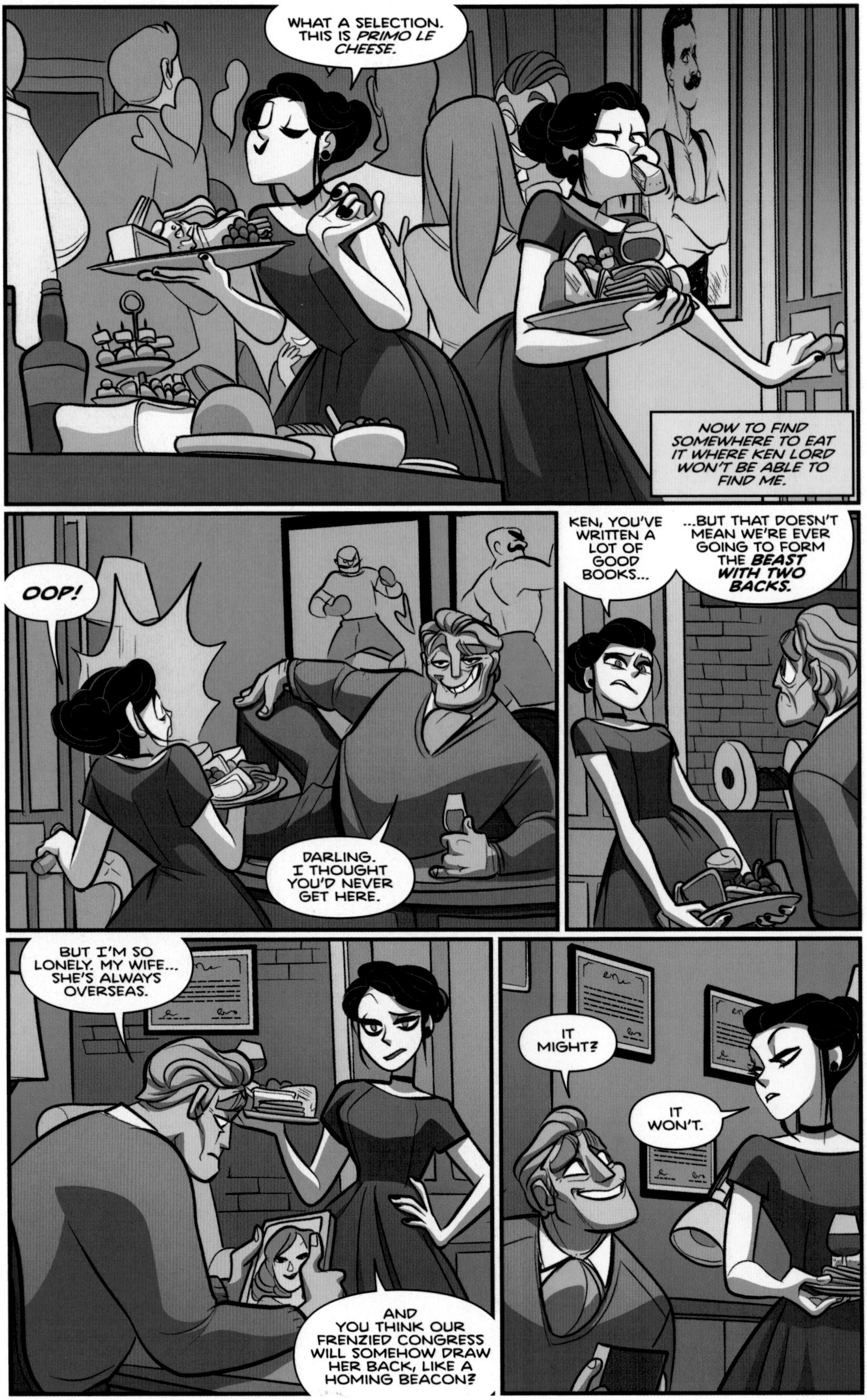
WHAT A SELECTION. THIS IS PRIMO LE CHEESE.
NOW TO FIND SOMEWHERE TO EAT IT WHERE KEN LORD WON'T BE ABLE TO FIND ME.
OOP!
DARLING. I THOUGHT YOU'D NEVER GET HERE.
KEN, YOU'VE WRITTEN A LOT OF GOOD BOOKS...
...BUT THAT DOESN'T MEAN WE'RE EVER GOING TO FORM THE BEAST WITH TWO BACKS.
BUT I'M SO LONELY. MY WIFE... SHE'S ALWAYS OVERSEAS.
AND YOU THINK OUR FRENZIED CONGRESS WILL SOMEHOW DRAW HER BACK, LIKE A HOMING BEACON?
IT MIGHT?
IT WON'T.

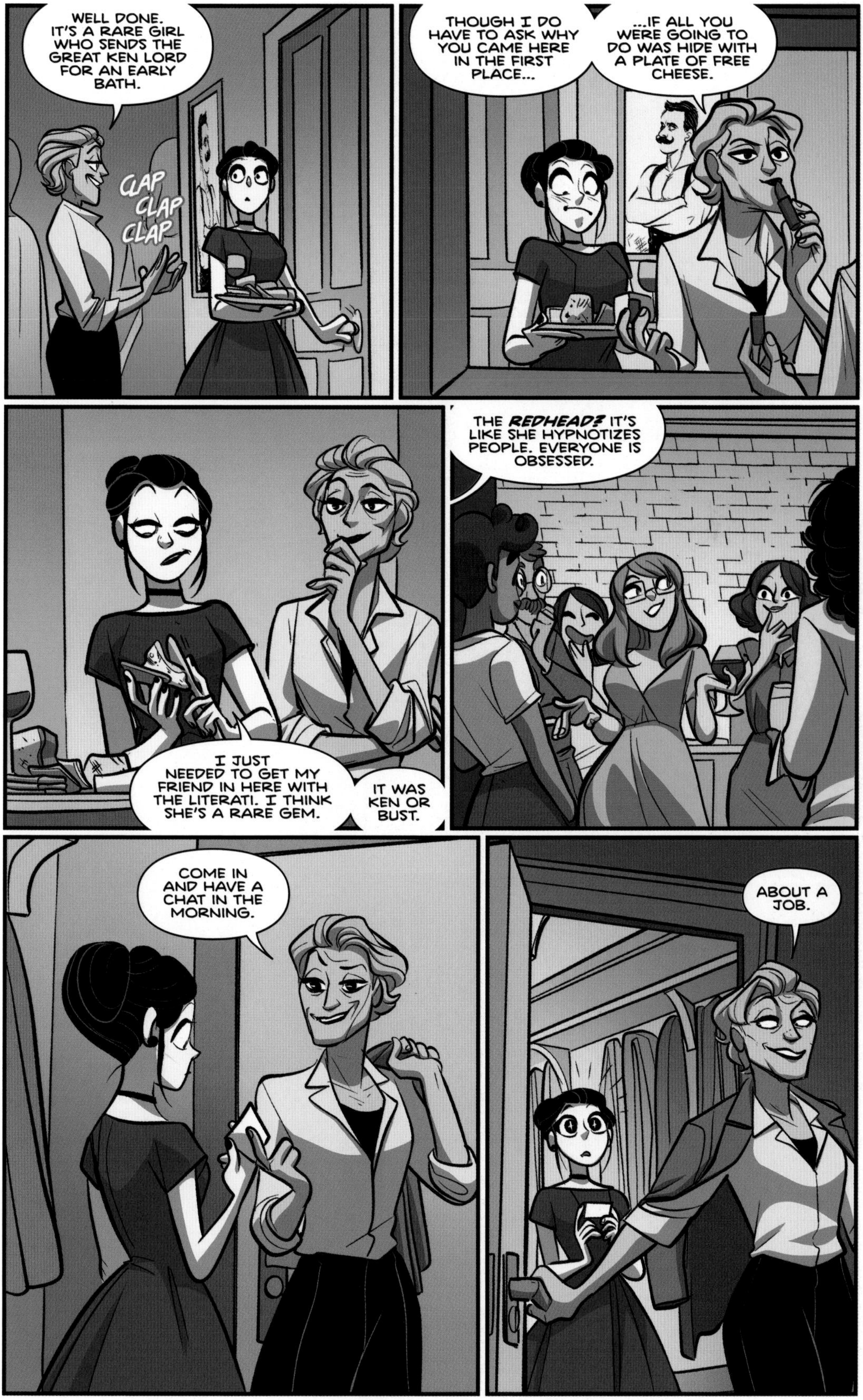
WELL DONE. IT'S A RARE GIRL WHO SENDS THE GREAT KEN LORD FOR AN EARLY BATH.
CLAP CLAP CLAP
THOUGH I DO HAVE TO ASK WHY YOU CAME HERE IN THE FIRST PLACE...
...IF ALL YOU WERE GOING TO DO WAS HIDE WITH A PLATE OF FREE CHEESE.
I JUST NEEDED TO GET MY FRIEND IN HERE WITH THE LITERATI. I THINK SHE'S A RARE GEM.
IT WAS KEN OR BUST.
THE REDHEAD? IT'S LIKE SHE HYPNOTIZES PEOPLE. EVERYONE IS OBSESSED.
COME IN AND HAVE A CHAT IN THE MORNING.
ABOUT A JOB.

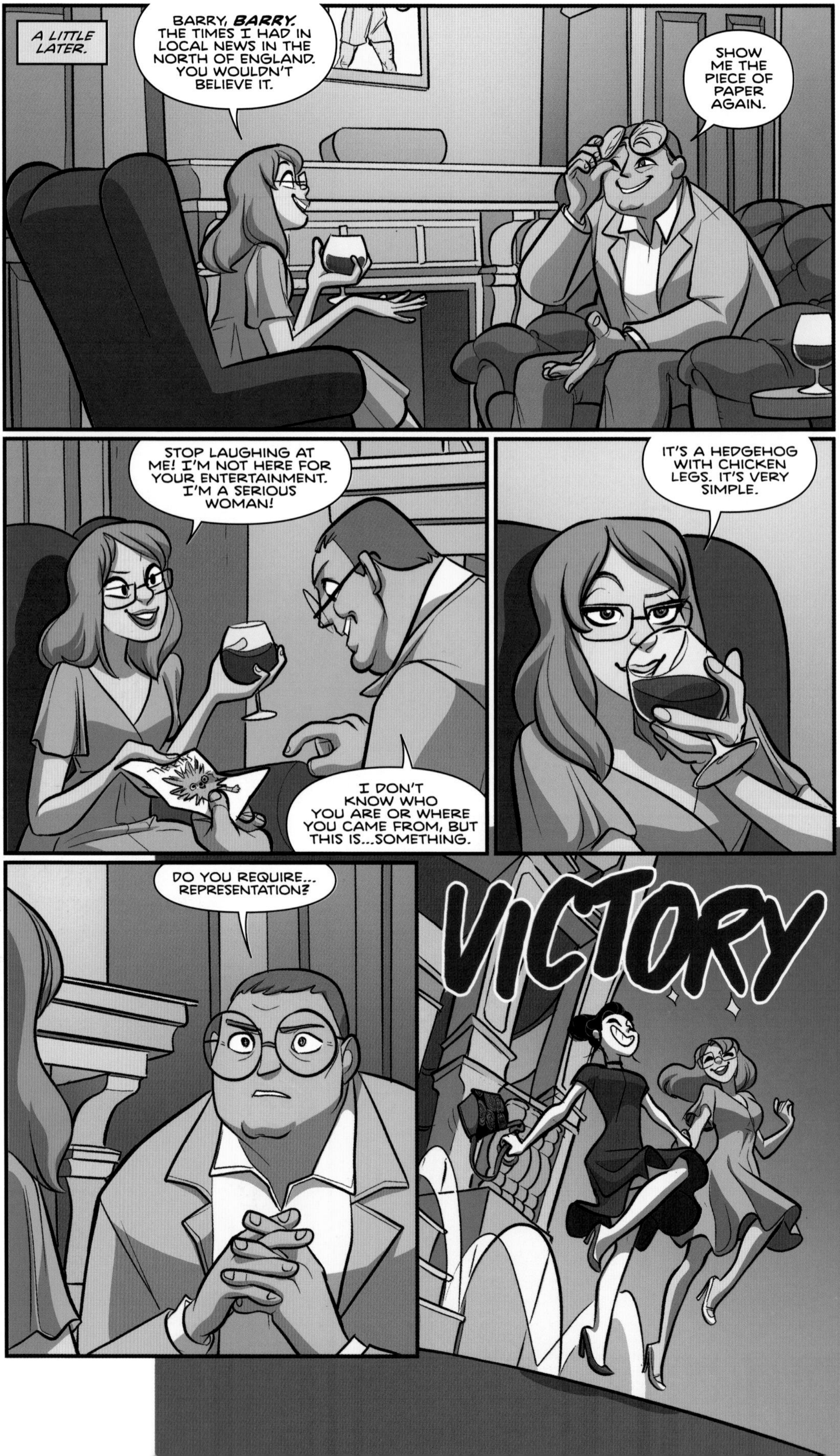
A LITTLE LATER.
BARRY, BARRY. THE TIMES I HAD IN LOCAL NEWS IN THE NORTH OF ENGLAND. YOU WOULDN'T BELIEVE IT.
SHOW ME THE PIECE OF PAPER AGAIN.
STOP LAUGHING AT ME! I'M NOT HERE FOR YOUR ENTERTAINMENT. I'M A SERIOUS WOMAN!
I DON'T KNOW WHO YOU ARE OR WHERE YOU CAME FROM, BUT THIS IS...SOMETHING.
IT'S A HEDGEHOG WITH CHICKEN LEGS. IT'S VERY SIMPLE.
DO YOU REQUIRE... REPRESENTATION?
VICTORY

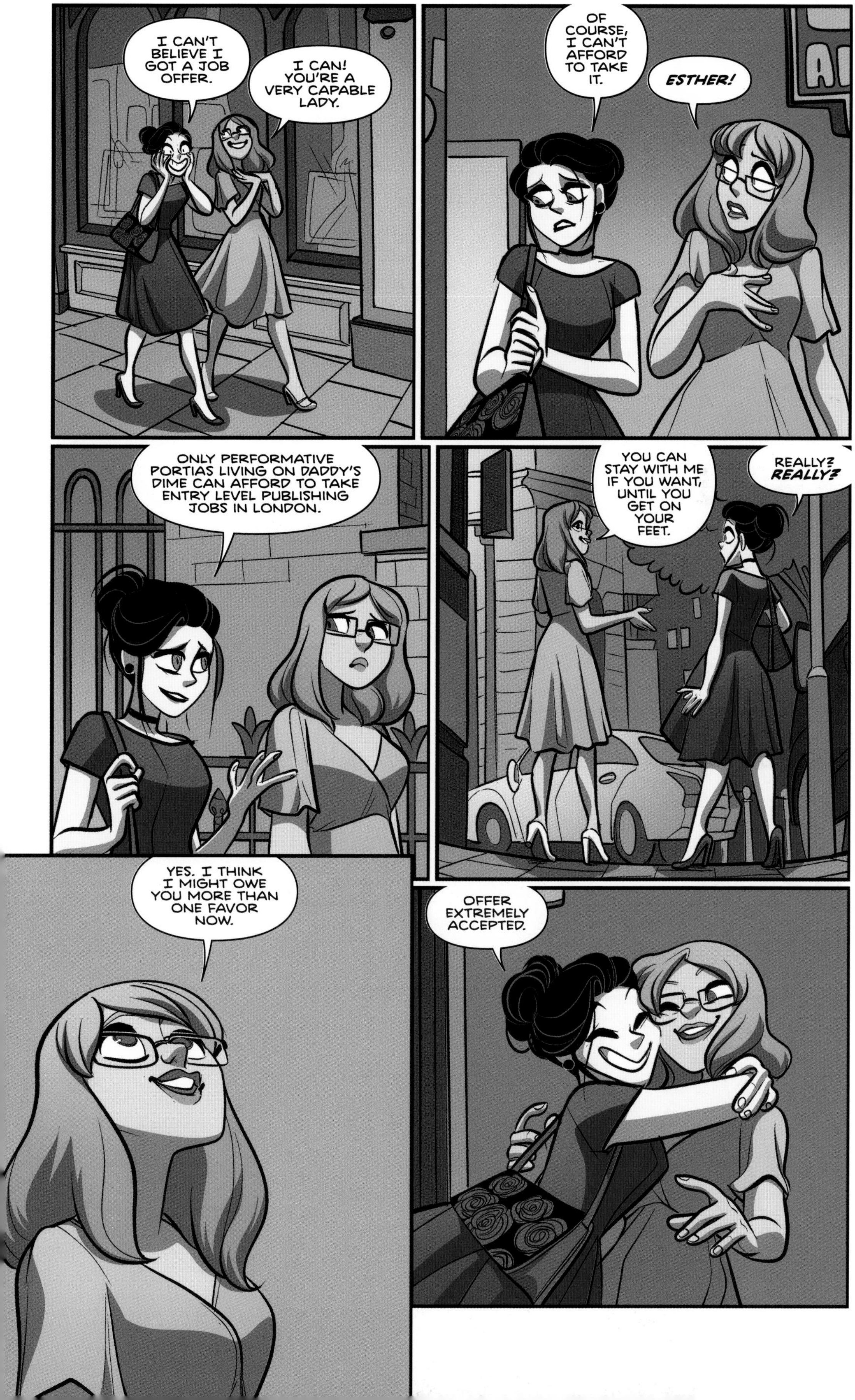
I CAN'T BELIEVE I GOT A JOB OFFER.
I CAN! YOU'RE A VERY CAPABLE LADY.
OF COURSE, I CAN'T AFFORD TO TAKE IT.
ESTHER!
ONLY PERFORMATIVE PORTIAS LIVING ON DADDY'S DIME CAN AFFORD TO TAKE ENTRY LEVEL PUBLISHING JOBS IN LONDON.
YOU CAN STAY WITH ME IF YOU WANT, UNTIL YOU GET ON YOUR FEET.
REALLY? REALLY?
YES. I THINK I MIGHT OWE YOU MORE THAN ONE FAVOR NOW.
OFFER EXTREMELY ACCEPTED.

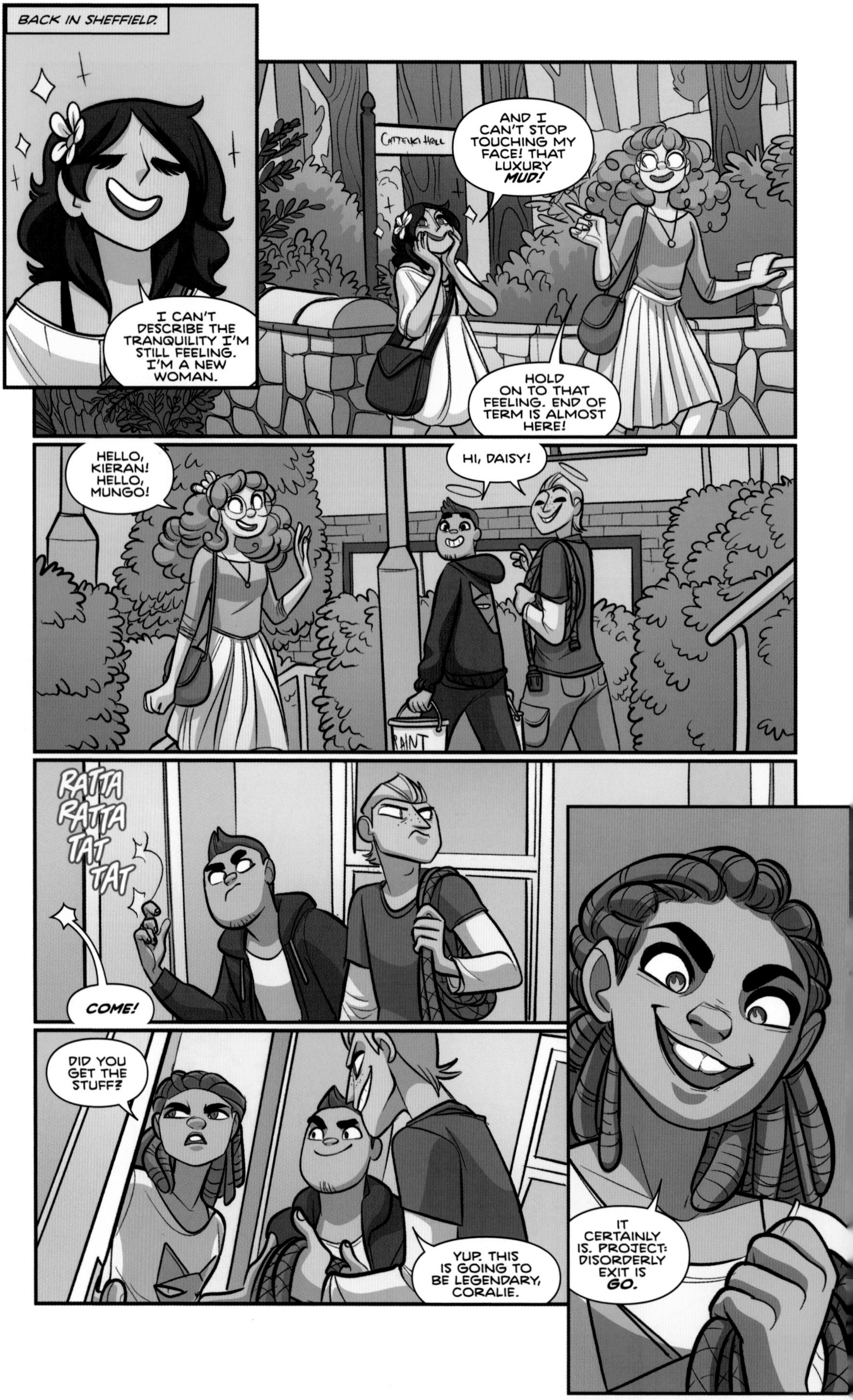
BACK IN SHEFFIELD.
I CAN'T DESCRIBE THE TRANQUILITY I'M STILL FEELING. I'M A NEW WOMAN.
AND I CAN'T STOP TOUCHING MY FACE! THAT LUXURY MUD!
HOLD ON TO THAT FEELING. END OF TERM IS ALMOST HERE!
HELLO, KIERAN! HELLO, MUNGO!
HI, DAISY!
PAINT
RATTA RATTA TAT TAT
COME!
DID YOU GET THE STUFF?
YUP. THIS IS GOING TO BE LEGENDARY, CORALIE.
IT CERTAINLY IS. PROJECT: DISORDERLY EXIT IS GO.

COVER GALLERY

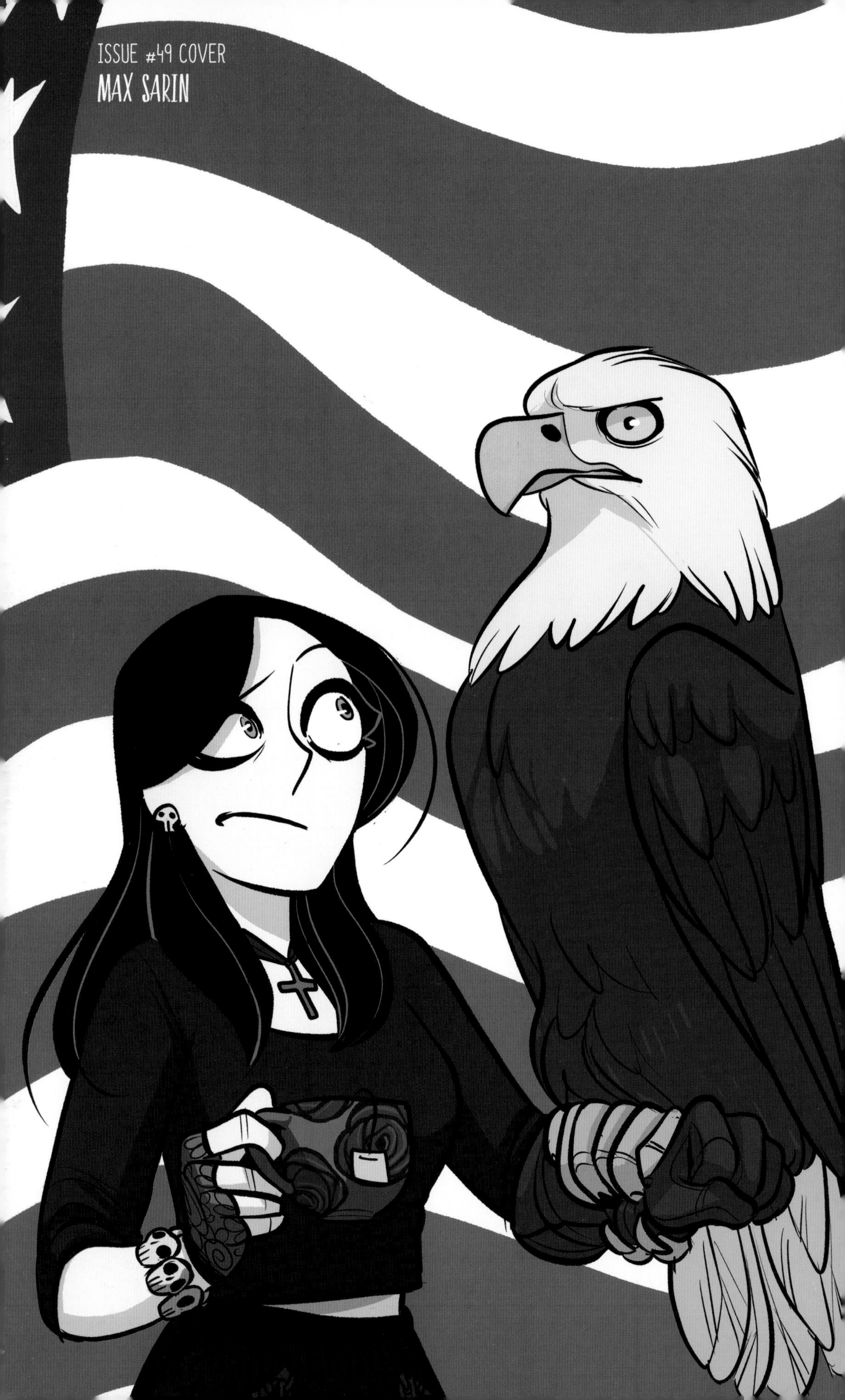

ISSUE #49 COVER
MAX SARIN

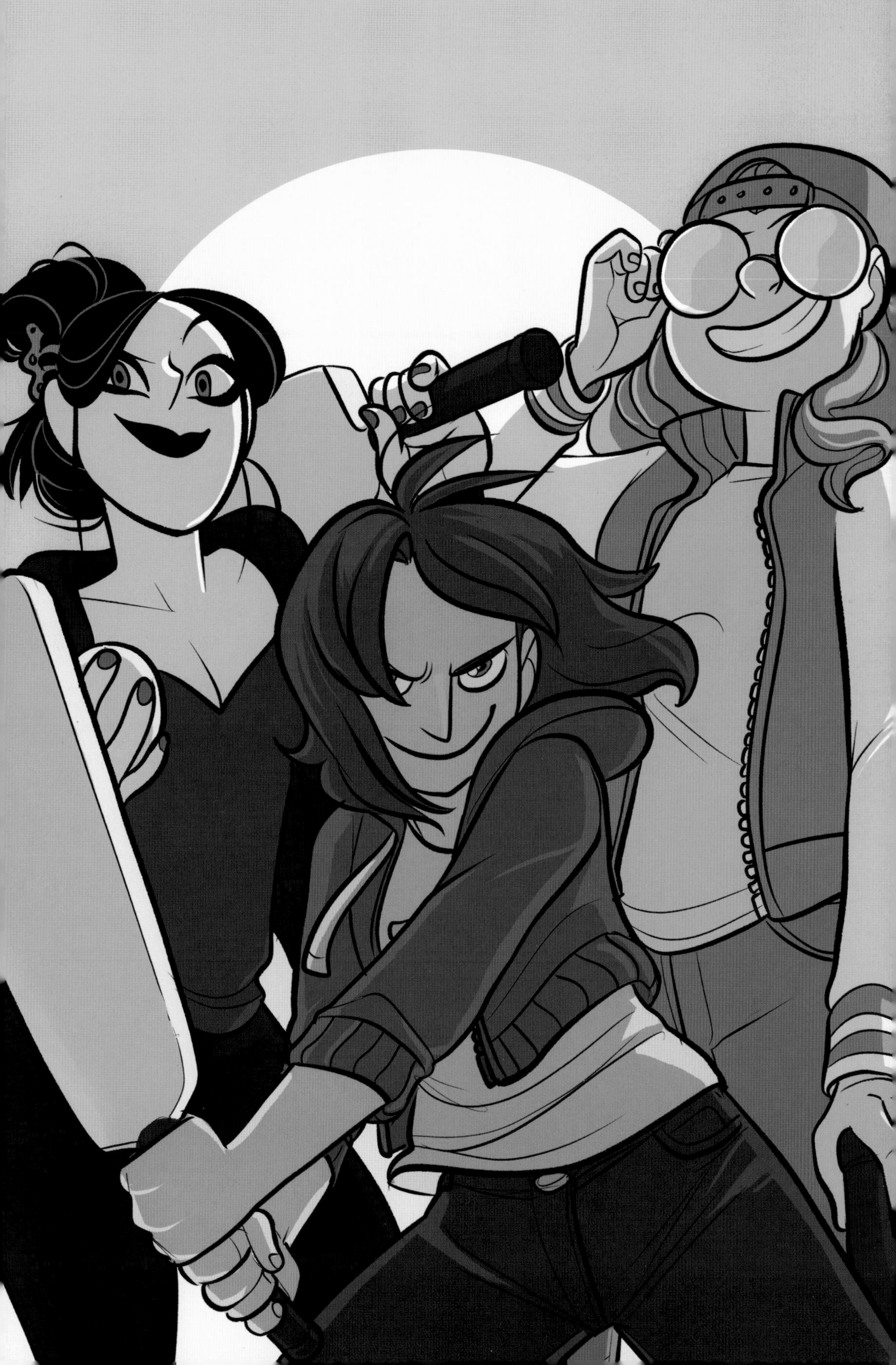

ISSUE #50 COVER
MAX SARIN

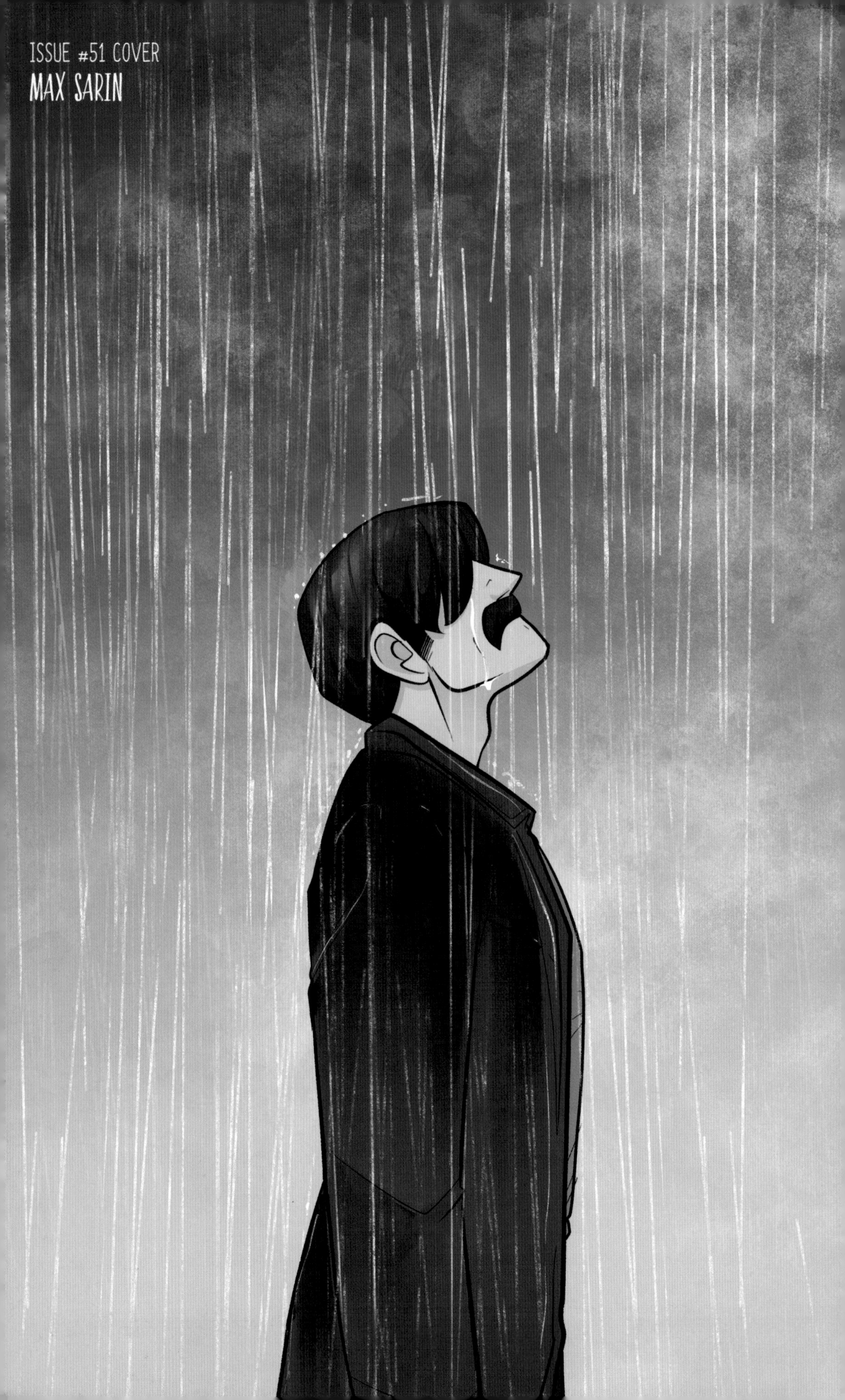

ISSUE #51 COVER
MAX SARIN

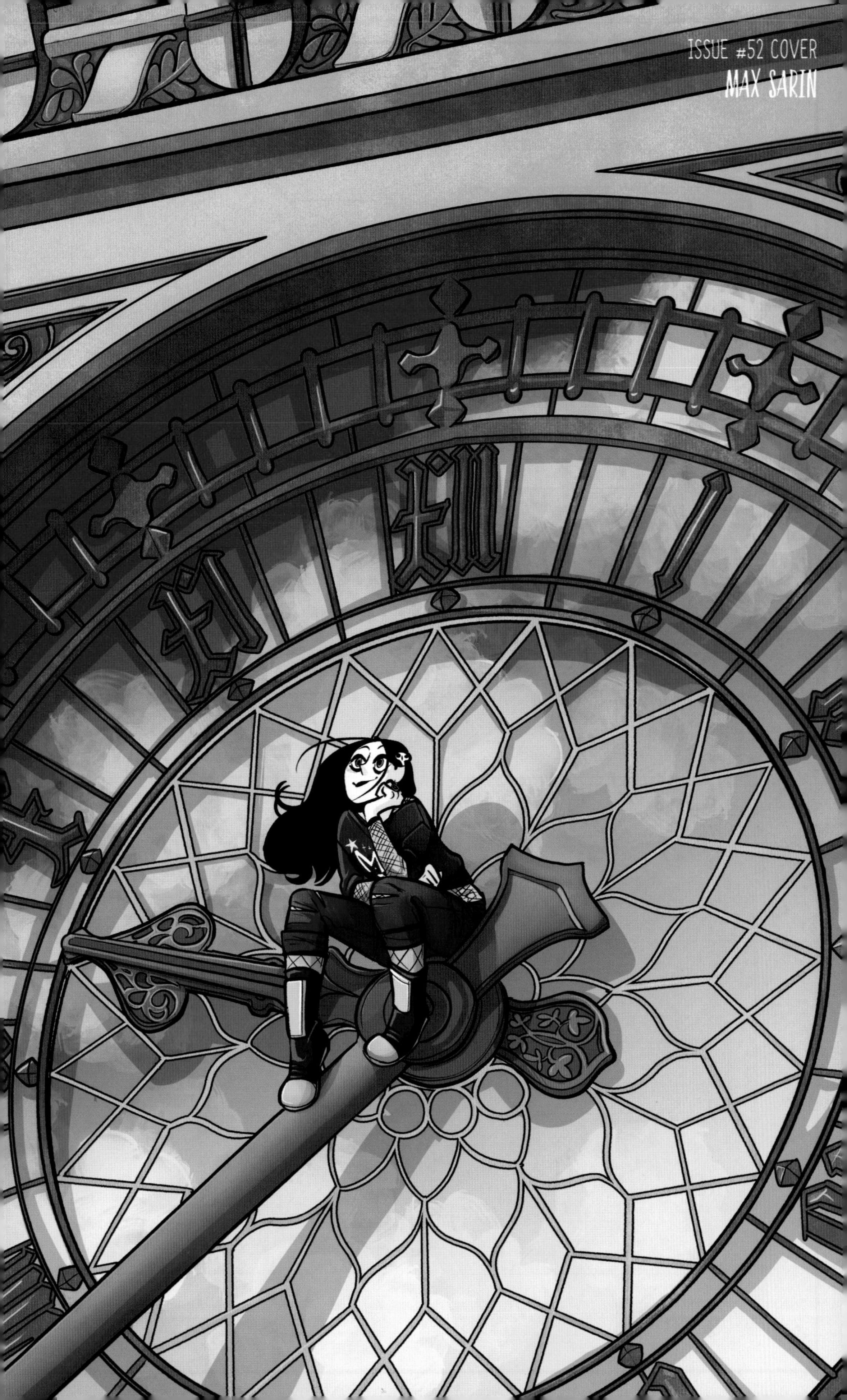

ISSUE #52 COVER
MAX SARIN

PENCILS FOR #49 BY MAX SARIN

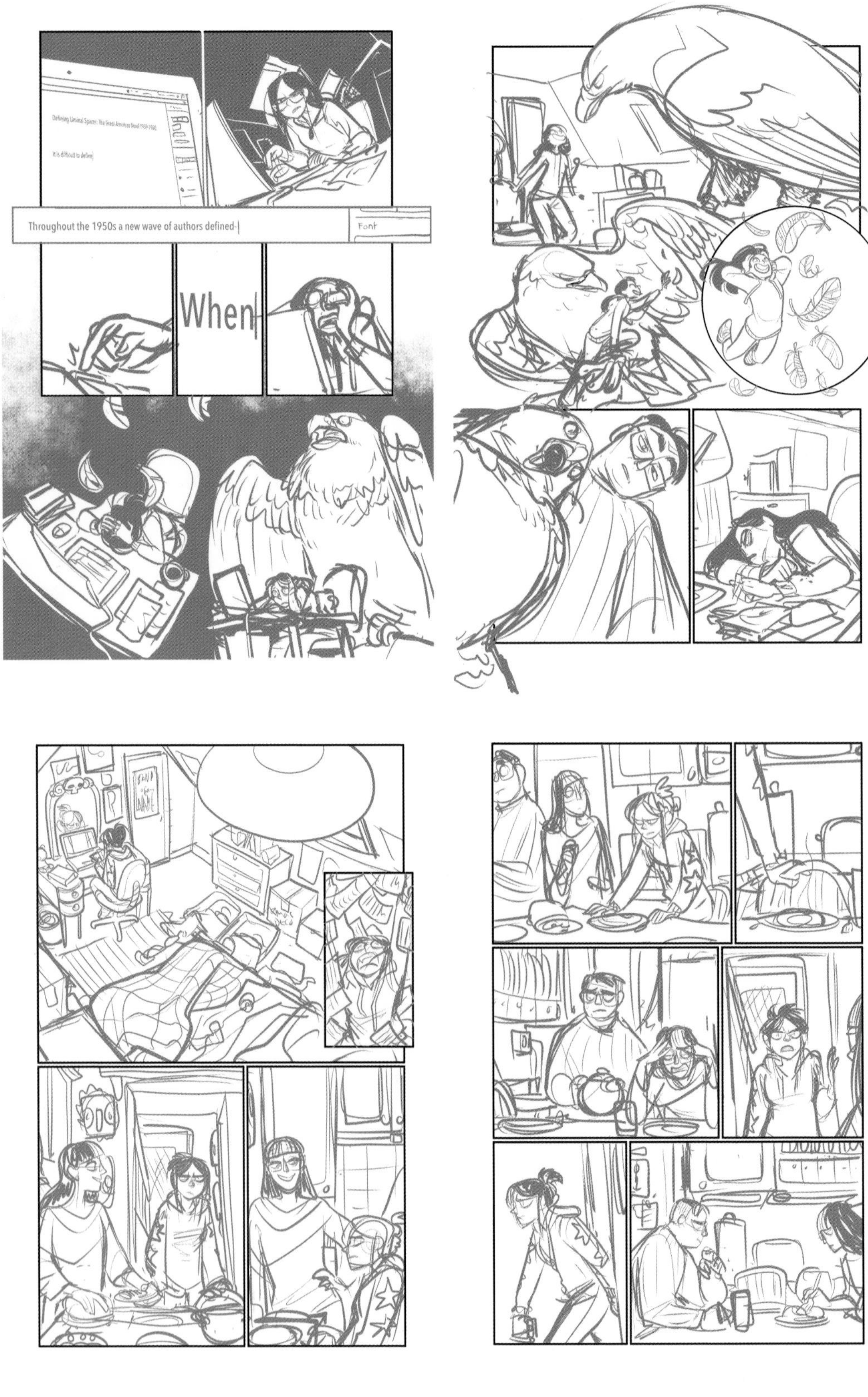
Defining Liminal Spaces: The Great American Novel 1959-1980
It is difficult to define|
Throughout the 1950s a new wave of authors defined-|
Font
When|

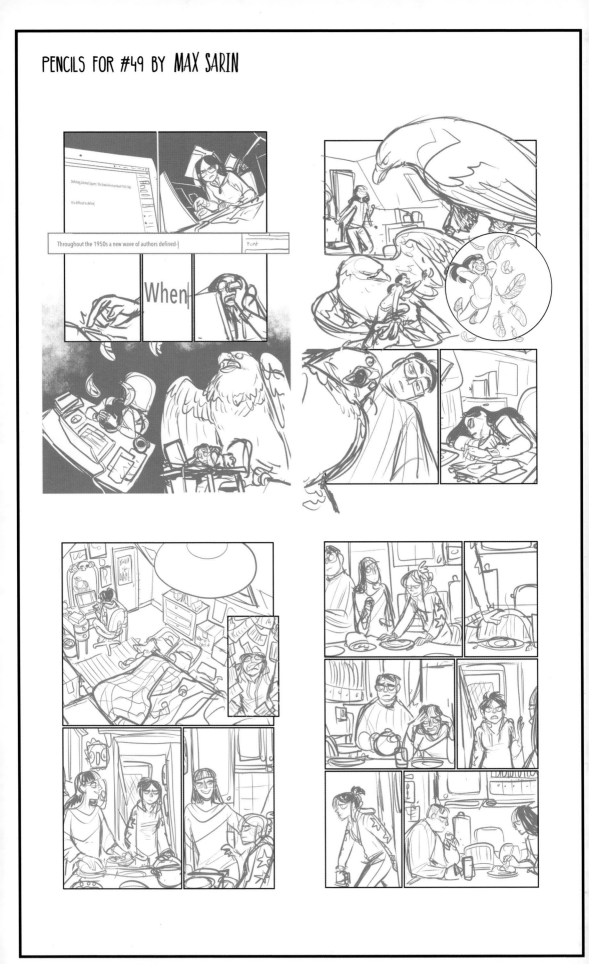

PENCILS FOR #49 BY JOHN ALLISON

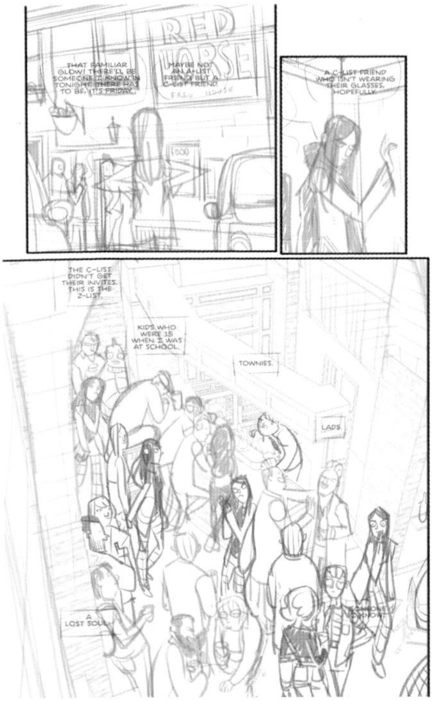
RED HORSE
THAT FAMILIAR GLOW! THERE'LL BE SOMEONE I KNOW IN TONIGHT. THERE HAS TO BE. IT'S FRIDAY.
MAYBE NOT AN A-LIST FRIEND BUT A C-LIST FRIEND.
A C-LIST FRIEND WHO ISN'T WEARING THEIR GLASSES, HOPEFULLY.
THE C-LIST DIDN'T GET THEIR INVITES. THIS IS THE Z-LIST.
KIDS WHO WERE 15 WHEN I WAS AT SCHOOL.
TOWNIES.
LADS.
A LOST SOUL.

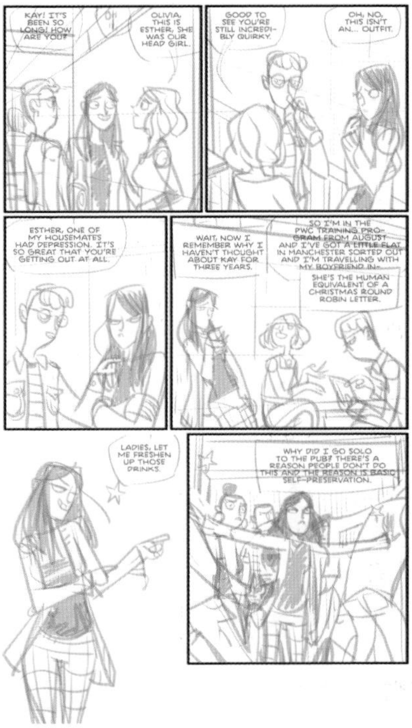
KAY! IT'S BEEN SO LONG! HOW ARE YOU?
OLIVIA, THIS IS ESTHER, SHE WAS OUR HEAD GIRL.
GOOD TO SEE YOU'RE STILL INCREDIBLY QUIRKY.
OH, NO, THIS ISN'T AN... OUTFIT.
ESTHER, ONE OF MY HOUSEMATES HAD DEPRESSION. IT'S SO GREAT THAT YOU'RE GETTING OUT AT ALL.
WAIT, NOW I REMEMBER WHY I HAVEN'T THOUGHT ABOUT KAY FOR THREE YEARS.
SO I'M IN THE PWC TRAINING PROGRAM FROM AUGUST AND I'VE GOT A LITTLE FLAT IN MANCHESTER SORTED OUT AND I'M TRAVELLING WITH MY BOYFRIEND IN–
SHE'S THE HUMAN EQUIVALENT OF A CHRISTMAS ROUND ROBIN LETTER.
LADIES, LET ME FRESHEN UP THOSE DRINKS.
WHY DID I GO SOLO TO THE PUB? THERE'S A REASON PEOPLE DON'T DO THIS AND THE REASON IS BASIC SELF-PRESERVATION.

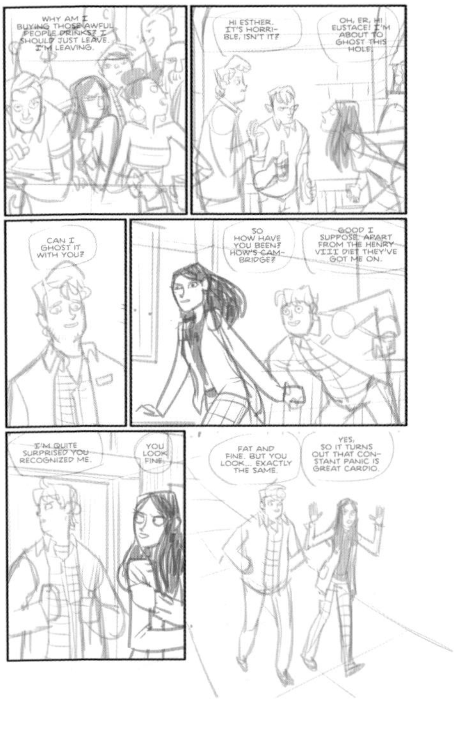
WHY AM I BUYING THOSE AWFUL PEOPLE DRINKS? I SHOULD JUST LEAVE. I'M LEAVING.
HI ESTHER. IT'S HORRIBLE, ISN'T IT?
OH, ER, HI EUSTACE! I'M ABOUT TO GHOST THIS HOLE.
CAN I GHOST IT WITH YOU?
SO HOW HAVE YOU BEEN? HOW'S CAMBRIDGE?
GOOD I SUPPOSE. APART FROM THE HENRY VIII DIET THEY'VE GOT ME ON.
I'M QUITE SURPRISED YOU RECOGNIZED ME.
YOU LOOK FINE.
FAT AND FINE. BUT YOU LOOK... EXACTLY THE SAME.
YES, SO IT TURNS OUT THAT CONSTANT PANIC IS GREAT CARDIO.

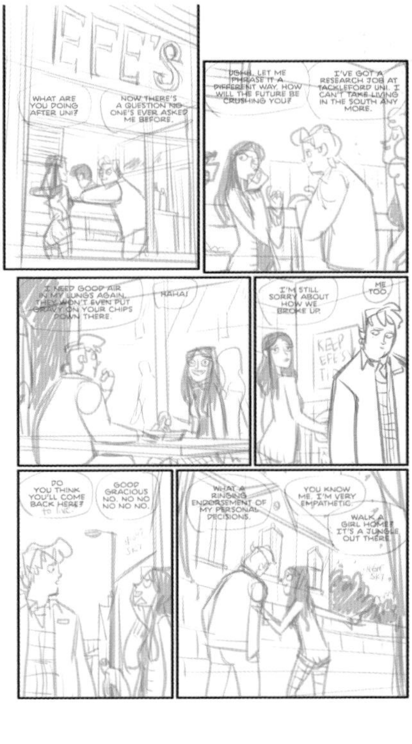
EFE'S
WHAT ARE YOU DOING AFTER UNI?
NOW THERE'S A QUESTION NO ONE'S EVER ASKED ME BEFORE.
UGHH. LET ME PHRASE IT A DIFFERENT WAY. HOW WILL THE FUTURE BE CRUSHING YOU?
I'VE GOT A RESEARCH JOB AT TACKLEFORD UNI. I CAN'T TAKE LIVING IN THE SOUTH ANY MORE.
I NEED GOOD AIR IN MY LUNGS AGAIN. THEY WON'T EVEN PUT GRAVY ON YOUR CHIPS DOWN THERE.
HAHA!
I'M STILL SORRY ABOUT HOW WE BROKE UP.
ME TOO.
DO YOU THINK YOU'LL COME BACK HERE? to live
GOOD GRACIOUS NO. NO NO NO NO NO.
WHAT A RINGING ENDORSEMENT OF MY PERSONAL DECISIONS.
YOU KNOW ME, I'M VERY EMPATHETIC.
WALK A GIRL HOME? IT'S A JUNGLE OUT THERE.

DISCOVER
ALL THE HITS

Lumberjanes
Noelle Stevenson, Shannon Watters, Grace Ellis, Brooklyn Allen, and Others
Volume 1: Beware the Kitten Holy
ISBN: 978-1-60886-687-8 | $14.99 US
Volume 2: Friendship to the Max
ISBN: 978-1-60886-737-0 | $14.99 US
Volume 3: A Terrible Plan
ISBN: 978-1-60886-803-2 | $14.99 US
Volume 4: Out of Time
ISBN: 978-1-60886-860-5 | $14.99 US
Volume 5: Band Together
ISBN: 978-1-60886-919-0 | $14.99 US

Giant Days
John Allison, Lissa Treiman, Max Sarin
Volume 1
ISBN: 978-1-60886-789-9 | $9.99 US
Volume 2
ISBN: 978-1-60886-804-9 | $14.99 US
Volume 3
ISBN: 978-1-60886-851-3 | $14.99 US

Jonesy
Sam Humphries, Caitlin Rose Boyle
Volume 1
ISBN: 978-1-60886-883-4 | $9.99 US
Volume 2
ISBN: 978-1-60886-999-2 | $14.99 US

Slam!
Pamela Ribon, Veronica Fish, Brittany Peer
Volume 1
ISBN: 978-1-68415-004-5 | $14.99 US

Goldie Vance
Hope Larson, Brittney Williams
Volume 1
ISBN: 978-1-60886-898-8 | $9.99 US
Volume 2
ISBN: 978-1-60886-974-9 | $14.99 US

The Backstagers
James Tynion IV, Rian Sygh
Volume 1
ISBN: 978-1-60886-993-0 | $14.99 US

Tyson Hesse's Diesel: Ignition
Tyson Hesse
ISBN: 978-1-60886-907-7 | $14.99 US

Coady & The Creepies
Liz Prince, Amanda Kirk, Hannah Fisher
ISBN: 978-1-68415-029-8 | $14.99 US

AVAILABLE AT YOUR LOCAL COMICS SHOP AND BOOKSTORE
To find a comics shop in your area, visit www.comicshoplocator.com
WWW.**BOOM-STUDIOS**.COM

BOOM! BOX™